C000243938

LAND VALUE TAXATION

LAND VALUE TAXATION

THEORY, EVIDENCE, AND PRACTICE

Edited by
Richard F. Dye and Richard W. England

L LINCOLN INSTITUTE
OF LAND POLICY
CAMBRIDGE, MASSACHUSETTS

© 2009 by the Lincoln Institute of Land Policy

All rights reserved.

Library of Congress Cataloging-in-Publication Data
Land value taxation : theory, evidence, and practice / edited by Richard F. Dye and Richard W. England.
p.   cm.
Includes bibliographical references and index.
ISBN 978-1-55844-185-9
1. Land value taxation.   I. Dye, Richard F.   II. England, Richard W.
III. Lincoln Institute of Land Policy.
HJ4165.L375 2009
336.22'5—dc22   2009007248

Designed and typeset by Technologies 'N Typography in Merrimac, Massachusetts.
Printed and bound by Puritan Press in Hollis, New Hampshire.
♻ The paper is Rolland Enviro100, an acid-free, 100 percent recycled sheet.

MANUFACTURED IN THE UNITED STATES OF AMERICA

CONTENTS

ILLUSTRATIONS

Tables

Figures

FOREWORD

Among economists, a tax on land value is renowned for being an especially efficient tax because it produces few unintended costs while raising revenue. What does this mean? Taxes are normally levied on economic activity or assets to raise financial resources for the government. However, in addition to producing tax revenues, taxes typically raise the market price of the good that is taxed, which makes consumers buy less of it. The resulting reduction in production and consumption of the good is a distortion caused by the tax, and this reduction imposes an additional cost on the local economy. When a tax does not affect the amount of the commodity produced or consumed, there is no additional cost, and such a tax is more efficient (less costly to the local economy) than other taxes that reduce production. Land is one of the special commodities whose amount is fixed and unaffected by a tax on its value, so economists agree that a tax on land value is efficient.

Of course, it is often said that economists agree on a great many things, but tend only to discuss the things about which they disagree. This observation helps inform the contents of this volume. While it spends several pages laying out the aspects of land value taxation on which there is much agreement—such as its efficiency—most of the volume addresses the existing theoretical and empirical evidence in support of other claims made for a tax on land value. For example, some of the additional benefits claimed for a land value tax are that it reduces speculation in land, increases the density of urban development when it replaces a typical property tax, promotes economic development generally, encourages investment in real property, and fosters compact development by stimulating infill development and reducing leapfrog development. In addition, views range widely about how practical it is to implement a land value tax and what legal frameworks are required to support it.

The challenge for the contributors to this volume has been to survey the literature on land value taxation and to synthesize their surveys in a single volume covering global experience that serves as a point of reference for researchers, specialists, and practitioners. This is a special challenge because there is a wide-ranging and sometimes fugitive literature on land value taxation theory and measurement. Moreover, a great deal of implementation experience and empirical work relevant to land value taxation has taken place in countries other than the United States.

The contributors to this volume have done an admirable job of reviewing and assessing the ongoing debates about the theory of land value taxation. They have taken pains to document where theory is well or poorly supported by empirical work, to note the lessons derived from experience with implementation, and to relate current views about the necessary supporting legal framework to relevant legal contexts. This volume provides guidance for additional empirical work by identifying areas where existing studies are weak or contradictory, and informs new attempts to implement land value taxation. It also settles some debates about land value taxation and initiates new ones.

Gregory K. Ingram
President and CEO
Lincoln Institute of Land Policy

INTRODUCTION
AND
PRACTICE

❖ 1 ❖

The Principles and Promises of
Land Value Taxation

RICHARD F. DYE AND RICHARD W. ENGLAND

> The property tax is, economically speaking, a combination of one
> of the worst taxes—the part that is assessed on real estate
> improvements . . . and one of the best taxes—the tax on land or
> site value.
>
> —William Vickrey (1999)

THE LAND VALUE TAX is a variant of the property tax. Taxation of real property is almost as old as civilization itself. Property taxes were levied in Egypt,
Babylonia, China, and other parts of the ancient world to build palaces and
temples and to maintain imperial armies. For nearly five centuries, Romans
paid taxes on the assessed value of land, buildings, livestock, trees, and vines
(Carlson 2005). In contemporary times, the property tax is widely used
around the world. It accounts for nearly half of local government tax revenue
in the United States and generates all local tax receipts in Australia (England
2007; see also chapter 3 of this volume).

Although it is a venerable and important source of government revenue in
various nations, the property tax is controversial because it is widely perceived to be unfair and inequitable (Youngman 2002). Forty-three states in
the United States have enacted some form of legal limitation on property
taxation to mitigate its impact (N. Anderson 2006). In 1994, for example,
Michigan amended its constitution to cap increases in real property assessments and raised its retail sales tax to help pay for public schools.

A strong case can be made for reforming the property tax instead of eliminating it. The loss in revenue following repeal of the property tax would have
to be made up with other taxes, each with its own problems, or with massive
cuts in local government services. Moreover, the loss of this key local revenue
source might mean the loss of local control over politically sensitive government services like public schools and public safety. There are many different
ways that the property tax could be reformed. This book looks in particular
at the reform suggested by the quotation at the opening of this chapter from
the Nobel laureate William Vickrey—keep what is best about the property
tax, *land value taxation,* and eliminate or move away from what is worst, the
tax on the value of buildings and other improvements.[1]

Great claims have been made for the promise of land value taxation,
dating back to the nineteenth-century political economist Henry George
([1879] 1962) and even earlier to the classical economists. George argued
that taxes on land promote fairness because the value of land is determined
by community rather than individual efforts. A tax on land is efficient in that
it does not distort investment choices, whereas a tax on the value of improvements discourages economic development. Given the current heightened interest in property tax reform, we believe that now is a good time to assess the
state of knowledge regarding land value taxation. The authors in this volume
address the following questions:

- What has been the actual experience with land value taxation in various
  nations?
- What predictions about the effects of land value taxation flow from
  modern economic theory?
- Does statistical evidence support these theory-based predictions?
- What can we say about the fairness or equity of land value taxation?
- Supposing that land value taxation is a fair and efficient form of taxa-
  tion, are there constitutional or other legal obstacles to its adoption?
- Do assessors and appraisers of property values have the tools needed to
  measure land values for tax purposes?
- Who are the gainers and losers when a land value tax is implemented,

---

1. The traditional property tax applies the same rate to both improvement values and
land values. A pure land value tax exempts improvement values from taxation altogether and
taxes only land values. A graded, dual-rate, or split-rate property tax applies a lower rate to
improvement values. The term *land value taxation* is used to represent both its pure and partial forms.

and what political coalitions are likely to form in support of and in opposition to this kind of tax?

The historical experience with land value taxation has been quite substantial, dating back to the late nineteenth century in Australia and the early twentieth century in Pennsylvania and South Africa. Modern economic theory suggests that land value taxation might offer various advantages over traditional property taxation by encouraging more efficient resource use, more rapid economic development, and more compact urban development. Unfortunately, research-based evidence in support of these theoretical predictions is a bit scanty, and additional statistical research is needed to buttress the case for land value taxation. As with any change in taxation, adopting a land value tax would pose issues of fairness that are of central importance from ethical and political perspectives. Enacting a land value tax also requires careful attention to both its legal viability and practical issues of assessing land values separately from improvement values.

EXPERIENCE WITH LAND VALUE TAXATION

Steven Bourassa, in chapter 2, reviews the experience with split-rate taxation in U.S. jurisdictions. Except for brief experiments in several other states, the U.S. experience with land value taxation has been in Pennsylvania and Hawaii. Sixteen jurisdictions in Pennsylvania currently have split-rate systems. Land value taxation was adopted but later rescinded in seven other Pennsylvania jurisdictions, most notably in Pittsburgh, which had a split-rate system from 1913 until it was repealed in 2001. The rejection of land value taxation in Pittsburgh was not based on the merits, or demerits, of the tax; rather, an increase in the tax rate on land happened to occur at the same time as a long overdue reassessment of property values, which resulted in major shifts in the tax burden and a political backlash. Other Pennsylvania cities have repealed split-rate taxation because it apparently failed to reverse the local economic decline caused by powerful forces acting on the broader region. In Hawaii, the split-rate tax was the scapegoat for bad land use planning that had permitted too much development in Waikiki and other areas of the state.

Riël Franzsen, in chapter 3, reviews the experience with land value taxation in jurisdictions outside the United States. The fact that at least 25 countries currently use some form of land value taxation makes the concept seem practicable and much less utopian. Case studies of five nations at various levels of economic development highlight the importance of statutory and administrative choices regarding the definition of the tax base and the measurement of land values for tax purposes. Land value taxation has to be examined in the context of national legal institutions and practical issues of implementation. There has been a movement away from land value taxation in favor of a more conventional property tax in several countries. In New Zealand over the last 20 years, various local jurisdictions have elected to replace a land-only tax with a land-and-improvement property tax. In South Africa, a recent law will eliminate the local option of a split-rate tax in favor of a single-rate property tax by the middle of 2009.

THEORY AND EVIDENCE

Wallace Oates and Robert Schwab explore the theory of land value taxation in chapter 4. Using basic economic theory and numerical examples, they first consider the impact of increasing the tax on land while keeping the tax on improvements constant. They establish three key results in this case: (1) the burden of a land tax falls entirely on landowners; (2) a land tax does not distort economic decisions, because the supply of land is fixed; and (3) a tax on land has no impact on the timing of development.[2]

Oates and Schwab next look at the impact of simultaneously raising the tax on land and changing the tax on improvements so as to leave total revenue unchanged. This is the more policy-relevant case, but the theory is more complicated because a tax on improvements distorts economic decisions. The results can go either way, and they turn on how responsive the supply of improvements is to the change in the tax on those improvements. Following Brueckner (1986), the authors conclude that for plausible values of this elasticity, the revenue-neutral tax rate on improvements is lower, the intensity of improvements per unit of land will rise, and—surprisingly—the value of land may rise, too (because, even though increasing the tax on land will make land less valuable, decreasing the tax on improvements will make land more valuable). Oates and Schwab then consider how a shift to a land tax will affect urban sprawl. The theory is complicated, with forces pulling in both directions, but the most likely result is that increasing the land tax will

2. Results (2) and (3) hold only if the land appraisal is based on "highest and best use" or is otherwise independent of current use.

decrease sprawl. Finally, they look at the revenue potential of a land tax and conclude that it is much greater than is often supposed.

In chapter 5 Elizabeth Plummer takes a careful look at the fairness and distributional issues surrounding land value taxation. The attractiveness of a land tax depends on its efficiency and neutrality advantages, as well as on how it conforms to the principles of ability-to-pay, horizontal equity, and vertical equity compared with alternative revenue sources. A switch from a traditional property tax to a land value tax could result in substantial shifts in the tax burden, which would affect the political acceptability of such a change. The burden of a shift to land taxation will fall most heavily on owners of properties with a high value of land relative to the improvements that are on it—what is called a *high land intensity*. With awareness of such changes in tax burdens, it might be possible to include transitional rules or targeted tax relief to soften the negative impacts. A major problem is that the data needed for thorough distributional analysis are hard to come by. So, unfortunately, the few studies that explicitly try to compare the pre- and postreform burdens provide mixed results as to whether the land value tax would be more or less progressive than the traditional property tax. Plummer then tries to get at the question implicitly by examining how land ownership varies across the income distribution. In the United States and the United Kingdom, land ownership is concentrated among the wealthiest, but land value as a percentage of net wealth decreases as wealth increases. Regrettably, it is almost impossible to obtain data that measure land value, improvement value, or other wealth value in a comparable way. The nature of the country or jurisdiction considering a land value tax can also affect the distribution of its burden among taxpayers. Plummer compares two studies of U.S. municipalities. One is in a built-up and in-demand area where the value of land relative to improvements is high and a land tax would be more progressive than a property tax. The other is less developed with relatively lower land values, and a land tax would be less progressive.

The evidence on the effects of implementing land value taxation is reviewed by John Anderson in chapter 6. He begins, importantly, with a careful explication of just what constitutes evidence. We never observe the effects of land value taxation per se, only the differential effects of a change in tax regimes in the context of initial conditions and local institutions and along with the effects of any other changes that may have occurred at the same time. The effects of land value taxation must be seen in some measurable variable, such as an increase in the value of building permits, and should be estimated with sufficient controls for the other factors or local conditions that might also cause the outcome variable to change. Anderson carefully reviews a large number of studies using several different approaches—including theoretical models, simulation models, regression models, and comparison studies. The overwhelming majority of studies can be rejected as inconclusive because of some methodological flaw or data limitation. What remains are some credible studies that show no effects and other credible studies that show measurable effects. Anderson considers the two best studies to be Oates and Schwab (1997), which indicates that a move to land value taxation does not hurt building activity, and Plassmann and Tideman (2000), which indicates that land value taxation may actually help building activity. A number of the studies, including Oates and Schwab (1997), do show a positive association between adoption of land value taxation and building activity, but have to be characterized as inconclusive regarding causation because of an inability to rule out the confounding effects of other factors.

IMPLEMENTATION

In chapter 7 Richard Coe addresses the legal framework for land value taxation in the United States. The implementation of a land tax might seem a simple proposition administratively, since virtually all taxing jurisdictions already value land and improvements separately. But differential taxation of the land and improvement components of the same parcel of property could encounter legal obstacles and be challenged as a violation of the uniformity, equality, and proportionality provisions commonly found in state constitutions. In some cases it may be allowable to designate improvements as a separate class of property. Or, it might be possible to designate improvements as exempt from property taxation. Coe carefully analyzes these legal issues and provides a detailed listing of the relevant provisions of all 50 state constitutions. In many cases it might take a constitutional amendment to permit land value or split-rate taxation.

The enactment and implementation of a land value tax require an accurate assessment of the value of land separate from the value of the improvements on that land. Even though most jurisdictions do report separate values for land and improvements, several eminent economists have expressed doubt that existing land assessments satisfy the accuracy requirement (E. Mills 1998; Netzer 1998c). Michael Bell, John Bowman, and Jerome German address the feasibility of accurate land assessment in chapter 8. As the authors point out, assessing the value of undeveloped parcels is relatively straightforward in rural areas because recent sales transactions can be mined for data. However, in urban areas, sales of vacant lots are rare, and alternative assessment techniques must be employed to measure land values. A comparison of the abstraction, allocation, and contribution value methods using data from Virginia, Maryland, and Ohio reveals that assessed land values vary with the choice of assessment technique. This result is somewhat worrisome from the perspective of tax administration, but the authors argue that recent developments in assessment practices have improved our capacity to quantify land values for tax purposes. These developments include the use of sophisticated econometric techniques to decompose parcel values and geographic information systems to analyze the spatial dimensions of land values.

The political acceptability of land value taxation is crucial to its implementation, and this is the topic of chapter 9. Steven Bourassa asks the question, If land value taxation is such a good idea, why haven't more jurisdictions adopted it, and why have some who have tried it later rejected it? He organizes his answers around five issues. First, the property tax is unpopular, in large part because it taxes wealth—which includes unrealized capital gains—rather than current cash flow. Land value taxation can aggravate this concern. Second, land value taxation requires separate assessment of land and improvements, which is harder to do accurately than determine the total value of a parcel. Land values are also more volatile than total values, so, if rates are not sufficiently flexible, absolute and relative shifts in the tax burden will be larger. It was the confounding effect of downwardly inflexible tax rates and the resulting large increase in average tax burdens that led to the rejection of land value taxation in Pittsburgh. Third, changing the incentives for economic development can interfere with economic planning. In Hawaii, land value taxation was rejected because it was seen as contributing to overdevelopment of parts of the islands. Fourth, as with any major tax regime shift, there will be both winners and losers. This affects the fairness and political acceptability of land value taxation, regardless of its other virtues. Finally, and perhaps most importantly, the land value tax and its benefits are not well understood by elected officials and the public.[3]

---

3. Bourassa notes earlier in chapter 2 that after the rejection of land value taxation in Pittsburgh, the city made much greater use of programs to abate a portion of property taxes on improvements. Abatements are an indirect form of land value taxation, but a form that is perhaps more understandable and acceptable politically.

WHAT HAVE WE LEARNED?

Several conclusions follow from this volume's survey of what we know about land value taxation. First, proposing a land value tax is not an unobtainable utopian ideal, since actual experience demonstrates the feasibility of enacting and collecting land value taxes. Second, proposals to enact a land value tax are likely to provoke heated opposition because the distributional effects of tax reform matter a lot politically and a regime switch from a traditional property tax to a land value tax would undoubtedly create losers as well as winners. Third, there may be constitutional, statutory, or administrative problems that would have to be addressed before a land value tax could be successfully implemented. Despite these challenges, we believe that land value taxation deserves serious consideration by state and local officials, especially now, when other reforms to the property tax are being debated. Economic theory and, to a lesser degree, empirical evidence support the claim that taxing land values instead of wages, profits, or capital values would improve economic performance and could improve people's lives.

❖ 2 ❖

The U.S. Experience

STEVEN C. BOURASSA

Henry George, the leading nineteenth-century proponent of the idea of land value taxation, was born in Philadelphia, Pennsylvania. Thus it is perhaps not surprising that much of the experimentation with land value taxation in the United States has taken place in Pennsylvania or that there is an ongoing effort to establish land value taxation in Philadelphia. The U.S. experience with land value taxation is diverse and highlights the various challenges—political, economic, and technical—that must be overcome if a split-rate tax system is to be implemented successfully and achieve the goal of encouraging economic development. This chapter first reviews the adoption of land value taxation in U.S. jurisdictions. Second, it considers the reasons that the tax has been discontinued in several places. Finally, it discusses the ongoing support for land value taxation in other locations and the continuing effort to adopt it in Philadelphia.

THE ADOPTION OF LAND VALUE TAXATION IN U.S. JURISDICTIONS

Nearly all the experience with land value taxation in the United States has been in two states: Pennsylvania and Hawaii.[1] Pennsylvania adopted legisla-

I thank Shireen Deobhakta for helpful assistance with the research for this chapter.

1. The earliest attempt to establish land value taxation in the United States may have been in Hyattsville, Maryland, in the 1890s. That effort was overturned by a court decision that declared land value taxation unconstitutional in Maryland (Ralston 1945).

tion in 1913 allowing the state's two second-class cities—Pittsburgh and Scranton—to have lower tax rates on buildings or other structures and improvements than on land.[2] Subsequent legislation allowed other Pennsylvania cities to adopt land value taxation, starting with Harrisburg in 1975. Hawaii adopted land value taxation statewide in 1963. Outside Pennsylvania and Hawaii, the U.S. experience with land value taxation has been very limited. Amsterdam, a small city in New York, adopted the tax in 1995 but repealed it the following year. Several "single-tax enclaves"—including Arden, Delaware, and Fairhope, Alabama—were established by followers of Henry George in the early twentieth century, but these communities have actually employed public land leasing rather than land value taxation (Gaston 1955; Stephens 1955).[3] In contrast to land value taxation, which is applied mainly to privately owned land, public land leasing involves public ownership of land, which is leased to private parties in exchange for the payment of ground rent (Bourassa and Hong 2003).

Before 1913, Pennsylvania law required land and improvements to be taxed at equal rates. Large increases in land values in Pittsburgh were seen as the result of speculation by wealthy landowners who were keeping large tracts of land out of productive use. Followers of Henry George initiated a movement that culminated with the introduction of a property tax reform bill in the Pennsylvania legislature in 1913. The bill provided for gradual increases in the land tax rate and gradual reductions in the improvement tax rate over a period of 12 years. After 12 years, the land tax rate was to be set at exactly twice the rate applicable to improvements; the bill mandated that this ratio be maintained despite any subsequent changes in either of the tax rates. The measure applied to both of Pennsylvania's second-class cities, although Scranton, the other affected city, had virtually no representation in the reform movement that introduced the bill.[4] The bill did not face any significant opposition and was passed and signed into law without difficulty. City property tax rates in Pittsburgh in 1913 were 0.89 percent on both land

---

2. Municipal governments in Pennsylvania include first-, second-, and third-class cities, boroughs, townships, and one town. Counties, municipal governments, and school districts all levy property taxes.

3. The term *single tax* refers to Henry George's advocacy of a single tax on land.

4. The fact that the reform movement was focused solely on Pittsburgh probably accounts for the fact that Philadelphia, the state's only first-class city, was not included in the legislation.

and improvements. By 1925, the city rates were 1.95 percent on land and 0.98 percent on improvements.

The Pennsylvania Constitution was amended in 1968 to allow counties and municipalities to adopt home-rule charters (Pennsylvania Department of Community and Economic Development 2003). In 1974, Pittsburgh's voters approved a home-rule charter that permitted the city to change the two-to-one ratio of the land to the improvement tax rate. This provision did not apply to the county and school district, which continued to use the same rates for both land and improvements. By this time, the policy objective of shifting the tax burden from land to improvements had changed from encouraging the development of large land holdings to encouraging investment in and the revitalization of the city. In 1976, the city's nominal tax rates on assessed values were 4.95 percent on land and 2.48 percent on improvements—a ratio of 2 to 1. In 1979, the city portion of the land tax was raised to 9.75 percent but the city portion of the improvement tax remained at 2.48 percent—a ratio of 3.9 to 1. Taking into account the school-district and county rates (which were the same for land and improvements), the total land rate in 1979 was 14.59 percent and the improvement rate was 7.31 percent—a ratio of 2 to 1. By 1984, the total land tax rate had climbed to 22.05 percent and the total improvement tax rate had increased to 9.6 percent (for a 2.3 to 1 ratio). At the time, assessed values in Allegheny County (which includes Pittsburgh) were set at 25 percent of market value. Assuming that this target was met for both land and improvements, the effective tax rates in 1984 would have been about 5.5 percent on land and 2.4 percent on improvements. However, to the extent that assessments were not up to date, the effective tax rates would have been lower. Moreover, the ratio of the effective rates on land and improvements would also have been lower, since land values tend to increase more rapidly than improvement values and assessed land values fall behind market values more rapidly.

A 1951 law allowed Pennsylvania's third-class cities to adopt split-rate property taxes. Harrisburg was the first to take advantage of this law, in 1975. As in Pittsburgh, the school district and county continued to levy single-rate taxes. Harrisburg's motivation for adopting land value taxation was the same as Pittsburgh's motivation for subsequently increasing the ratio of the land to the improvement tax rate starting in 1979: a desire to attract investment and encourage revitalization. Harrisburg was ranked the second-most-distressed city in the country in the early 1980s, after East St. Louis, Illinois (see City of Harrisburg). Harrisburg started out by raising the ratio of the land to the improvement tax rate to 1.35 to 1, gradually increasing it to its current ratio of 6 to 1.

A complete list of Pennsylvania (and New York) municipalities that have adopted land value taxation is given in table 2.1.[5] Legislation adopted in Pennsylvania in 1993 allowed school districts that were coterminous with third-class cities to adopt split-rate property taxes, and a 1998 act also allowed boroughs to adopt split-rate systems. Starting with New Castle in 1982, sixteen additional cities in Pennsylvania, along with two school districts (Aliquippa and Clairton) and two boroughs (Ebensburg and Steelton), adopted land value taxation, bringing the total to twenty-three jurisdictions (including Pittsburgh, Scranton, and Harrisburg). The motivation for all the third-class cities, school districts, and boroughs was the same as for Harrisburg: a desire to reverse economic decline by attracting new investment.

Amsterdam, New York, adopted land value taxation in 1995, after the state passed legislation in 1993 allowing the city to apply lower tax rates to improvements than to land (Reeb 1998). Like Harrisburg and the other Pennsylvania jurisdictions that subsequently adopted split-rate systems, Amsterdam sought to encourage new investment.

The motivation for adopting land value taxation in Hawaii was much the same as the original purpose in Pittsburgh: to encourage property owners to make land available for development, particularly to support tourism. The state also shifted the basis for assessment from existing use to highest and best use (Cooper and Daws 1985). Hulten (1970) noted that 12 owners held 52 percent and 60 owners held 80 percent of the private land in the state. When Hawaii adopted land value taxation in 1963, property taxes were administered centrally by the state. The law provided for phasing in the tax starting in 1965, when the improvement tax rate would be set at 90 percent of the land tax rate; this percentage was scheduled to decrease to a minimum of 40 percent over at least a 10-year period.[6] According to Hulten (1970), by 1969 the tax rate applied to improvements was 80 percent of the rate applied to land (a land-to-improvement ratio of 1.25 to 1).

---

5. The wide range of millage rates listed in table 2.1 reflects the fact that assessed values are not up to date in some jurisdictions and that in some assessed values are intended to be a fraction of market value. For example, Altoona, which has the highest land tax rate, has not had a reassessment since the 1950s.

6. Technically, the law provided for reducing the percentage of assessed improvement value that was subject to tax.

Table 2.1 Status of land value taxes in Pennsylvania and New York

Place	Year established	Year rescinded	Current land rate	Current improvements rate	Ratio
Pennsylvania					
Aliquippa	1988	—	80.60	11.40	7.07
Aliquippa School District	1993	—	177.00	28.00	6.32
Allentown	1997	—	50.38	10.72	4.70
Altoona	2002	—	230.32	14.57	15.81
Clairton	1989	—	28.00	2.22	12.61
Clairton School District	2006	—	75.00	31.00	2.42
Coatesville	1991	2006	—	—	—
Connellsville	1992	2003	—	—	—
DuBois	1991	—	89.00	3.00	29.67
Duquesne	1985	—	19.00	11.47	1.66
Ebensburg	2000	—	27.50	7.50	3.67
Harrisburg	1975	—	28.67	4.78	6.00
Hazleton	1991	1992	—	—	—
Lock Haven	1991	—	96.79	16.97	5.70
McKeesport	1980	—	16.50	4.26	3.87
New Castle	1982	—	24.51	6.92	3.54
Oil City	1989	2003	—	—	—
Pittsburgh	1913	2001	—	—	—
Scranton	1913	—	103.15	22.43	4.60
Steelton	2000	2008	—	—	—
Titusville	1990	—	59.16	19.00	3.11
Uniontown	1992	1992	—	—	—
Washington	1985	—	82.63	3.50	23.61
New York					
Amsterdam	1995	1996	—	—	—

Sources: Telephone interviews with municipal officials; personal correspondence with Joshua Vincent, executive director, Center for the Study of Economics; Hughes (2005); and Reeb (1998).

Note: Tax rates are nominal and are expressed in dollars per thousand dollars of assessed value (mills). Rates are shown only for municipalities that currently have different rates for land and improvements. The rates are current as of late 2007 or early 2008. Rates and ratios are rounded to two decimal places.

RECONSIDERING LAND VALUE TAXATION

The two most important experiments with land value taxation in the United States—Pittsburgh and Hawaii—have for all practical purposes come to an end. The Pittsburgh land value tax, often hailed as a successful example of the use of split-rate taxes to encourage development, suffered a particularly ignominious demise. One of the ironies of the Pittsburgh experience was that the enterprising use of land value taxation was unfortunately combined with substandard assessment practices. An overdue reassessment of property in Allegheny County in 2000–2001 led to substantial increases in assessed land values and tax bills. This in turn led to an outcry from taxpayers, a large percentage of whom filed appeals. The problem was compounded by a perception that downtown property owners with large buildings had been taking advantage of the system by successfully challenging high land assessments, thereby shifting assessed value from land to improvements, which were taxed at a lower rate, and shifting more of the tax burden to residential neighborhoods.

In the end, land value taxation in Pittsburgh was the scapegoat for infrequent and inaccurate assessments and clumsy rate-setting procedures that did not adequately adjust taxes in response to large increases in value. The mayor, Tom Murphy, who initially supported the land value tax, was opposed by the city council president, Bob O'Connor, who argued that the land value tax was confusing and was causing residential neighborhoods to lose out at the expense of downtown interests. Because O'Connor was challenging the mayor in the upcoming election and had the political upper hand on this high-profile issue, the mayor quickly revised his position on land value taxation (and beat O'Connor in the mayoral primary by a small margin). A tax system that was the result of careful study and that had been implemented gradually nearly a century earlier was summarily abolished in the heat of the political crossfire that erupted once the implications of the reassessment became apparent.[7]

Despite the abolition of land value taxation as a source of general revenue in Pittsburgh, the city continues to use a land-based tax to finance the Downtown Pittsburgh Business Improvement District. This district was established in 1996 to provide various services to downtown businesses, and a

---

7. See Hughes (2006) for a more detailed account of the demise of Pittsburgh's land value tax.

resolution to continue it through the end of 2011 was approved in 2006 (Resolution no. 687 [approved 6 November 2006]). Even more important, however, are the property tax abatements available for new construction and renovations. Abatements reduce the effective tax rates on improvements rel-ative to land and thus achieve a similar result as land value taxation. As shown in table 2.2, virtually every kind of new construction or renovation is eligible for some form of property tax abatement. These abatements, which can be quite valuable—particularly if the value of the improvements is close to the maximum that can be abated[8]—have been enhanced in recent years, primarily to encourage residential development. Municipal officials in Pitts-burgh generally seem to believe that tax abatements are the most effective way to encourage new development.[9]

Whereas in Pittsburgh the demise of land value taxation was the result of poor assessment practice and lack of political support, in Hawaii the tax was the victim of its perceived success. A hotel building boom in Waikiki in the late 1960s and early 1970s was widely seen to have been excessive and to have destroyed or at least damaged the character of the place. Hawaiians began to jokingly refer to the construction crane as the state bird, and Joni Mitchell penned her famous lyric "they paved paradise and put up a parking lot" dur-ing a visit to Waikiki in 1972.[10] The high density and unattractive character of new construction in Waikiki apparently led to a backlash against develop-ment and the land value tax that was designed to encourage development. By

---

8. For example, under the Act 42 Enhanced Residential Abatement Program, up to $250,000 of assessed value for new construction or renovations can be abated each year. If a new building worth $250,000 is built on a lot worth $50,000, this program results in savings of about 14.5 percent of the total cost of the project (about $43,400, which is equivalent to $6,180 in annual tax savings over 10 years, using a discount rate of 7 percent). Note that these savings result from the abatement of both city and school-district property taxes. If, in-stead, the city reverted to land value taxation and neither the city nor the school district had abatements, the annual tax savings for this hypothetical property would be worth about 1.5 percent of the total cost of the project (about $4,450, which is equivalent to about $310 in annual savings in perpetuity).

9. Personal interview with William Urbanic, budget director, and Douglas Shields, Pitts-burgh city council president, 7 December 2007. When asked about the cost of the abate-ments, Mary Lou Tenenbaum, the manager of real estate taxation for the city, expressed the view that there was no cost, because development would not take place without the abate-ments (personal interview, 7 December 2007).

10. We thank Paul Brewbaker, chief economist of the Bank of Hawaii, for these details (personal correspondence dated 1 April 2008).

Table 2.2 Pittsburgh property tax abatement programs, 2008

Program	Participating taxing body	Type of abatement	Abatement limit	Abatement period	Future use	Current use	Eligible area
Act 42 Residential	City, county, and school district	Assessment reduction	$86,570/year for new construction $36,900/year for renovations	3 years	Residential (for sale or rent)	Residential or vacant	Citywide
Act 42 Enhanced Residential	City and school district	Assessment reduction	$250,000/year for new construction or renovations	10 years	Residential (for sale or rent)	Residential or vacant	28 defined areas
LERTA Commercial	City	Tax credit	$50,000/year	5 years	Commercial or industrial (for sale or rent)	Commercial, industrial, or vacant	Citywide
LERTA Residential	City, county, and school district	Tax credit	$150,000/year (city) $100,000/year (county) $250,000/year (school district)	10 years	Residential (rental apartments or hotels)	Commercial or industrial	4 defined areas

	Jurisdiction	Type	Amount	Term	Residential	Commercial	Area
LERTA Enhanced Residential	City and school district	Tax credit	$2,700/year (city) $3,480/year (school district)	10 years	Residential (separately assessed units)	Commercial or industrial	4 defined areas
Visitability Residential	City and county	Tax credit	$2,500 maximum over 5 years	5 years	Residential (single-family, duplexes, triplexes, and adaptive reuse)	Residential, commercial, industrial, or vacant	Citywide

Source: Real Estate Tax Abatement Programs Comparison, http://www.city.pittsburgh.pa.us/finance/assets/forms/2008/2008_abatement_table.pdf.
Notes: The assessment reduction or tax credit is applicable to up to 100 percent of the increase in assessment or taxes due to the improvements. LERTA refers to Pennsylvania's Local Economic Revitalization Tax Assistance Act.

the mid-1970s, the legislature rescinded the 1963 act that established the split-rate tax. At the same time, the county governments were pushing for a greater degree of home rule that would give them their own taxing powers.[11]

In 1978 an amendment to the Hawaii Constitution devolved control over property taxation to the counties.[12] Legislation to implement the constitutional amendment was adopted in 1980, but full devolution of responsibility for the assessment process did not take place until 1989 (*Hawaii Revised Statutes* § 246A). In 1981 each county taxed land and improvements at the same rate, except the County of Honolulu, which taxed several classes of property—improved and unimproved residential, hotel, and apartment—at different rates, but with higher rates on improvements than on land. Starting in 1982, the County of Hawaii reverted to land value taxation for all classes of property, and Kauai reverted to it for some property classes. Maui continued to apply a single rate to both land and improvements for all classes of property. For the fiscal year starting in 1983, Honolulu abolished differential taxation, whereas Kauai adopted higher rates on land than on improvements for all property classes and Hawaii retained higher rates on land for all classes except improved residential. Except for some minor changes, this pattern continued until 2002, when the County of Hawaii abolished land value taxation in favor of uniform rates for land and improvements within each class. In 2005, Kauai shifted to *lower* taxes on land than on improvements for most classes of properties, retaining higher land taxes only for agricultural, conservation, and homestead properties. In effect, land value taxation now plays only a minor residual role in the state of Hawaii.[13]

We see from table 2.1 that, in addition to Pittsburgh, six jurisdictions in Pennsylvania, as well as Amsterdam, New York, have reverted from land value taxation to single-rate systems.[14] Hazleton, Uniontown, and Amsterdam all rescinded the tax within one year of adoption, whereas Coatesville, Connellsville, Oil City, and Steelton switched to uniform rates after eight to fifteen years of experience. Of these seven jurisdictions, the Amsterdam case

---

11. Telephone interview with Lowell Kalapa, director of the Tax Foundation of Hawaii, 6 March 2008.

12. This did not apply to Kalawao, which does not have its own government. The other four counties are Hawaii, Honolulu, Kauai, and Maui.

13. Tax rate information for 1981 through the present for all counties is available from the Real Property Assessment Division, City and County of Honolulu (http://www. hono lulu.gov).

14. Steelton claims to have a split-rate system, but the rates on land and improvements are the same.

is the best documented (Reeb 1998). Implementation of the split-rate tax in Amsterdam was complicated by the need to consider how it would interact with nearly 200 property tax exemptions allowed by New York law. Assessment practice in Amsterdam was even worse than in Pittsburgh—as of 1995, when land value taxation was adopted, there had been no reassessments for 36 years. Coincidentally with the adoption of land value taxation, the state mandated that Amsterdam undertake reassessment, which took place mainly in 1995 and 1996. The resulting assessments and tax bills led to a perception that land values were not assessed accurately and thus to a large number of appeals. As in Pittsburgh, the land value tax was blamed for problems associated with the reassessment.

Reeb (1998) also provides some information about the short-lived land value taxes in Hazleton and Uniontown. In Hazleton the tax apparently never had broad support. After the tax was unsuccessfully challenged in court, an influential city council member—who may have been responding to the concerns of a major property owner—urged that the tax be repealed, and upon reconsideration, the city council repealed the split-rate tax. In Uniontown, as in Amsterdam, tax reassessment was long overdue. In Uniontown's case, however, no reassessment took place, and the chamber of commerce argued that the outdated assessments were causing the burden of the split-rate tax to fall excessively on downtown properties. In effect, the chamber argued that the tax would harm, rather than help, the downtown area. This opposition led the city council to repeal the tax in the same year it was introduced.

The Connellsville story was similar, although it took about a decade for the opposition to succeed in having the tax repealed.[15] Outdated assessments contributed to high tax bills for vacant and underutilized properties, as well as establishments with surface parking lots. Some owners of homes on large lots were also actively opposed to the split-rate tax.

The abolition of the split-rate tax in Coatesville was in direct response to the same Allegheny County reassessment that led to the demise of the split-rate tax in Pittsburgh. The reassessment shifted the tax burden from commercial and industrial property to residential property, which led to the shift back to a single-rate system.[16] In Oil City, a long overdue reassessment did

15. Telephone interviews with Paula Childs and Judy Keller, Connellsville Tax Office, 28 February 2008.

16. Personal correspondence from Joshua Vincent, executive director, Center for the Study of Economics, 15 January 2008.

not accurately break down land and improvement values.[17] And there was no convincing evidence that land value taxation was actually aiding economic development in the city. Consequently, the city government decided to abolish the split-rate system when the reassessments became effective in 2003.

CONTINUING SUPPORT FOR LAND VALUE TAXATION

Of the sixteen jurisdictions in Pennsylvania that currently use split-rate systems, eight have increased the ratio of the land to the improvement tax rate since 2000.[18] Of the remaining jurisdictions, seven have decreased the land-to-improvement ratio, and one has not changed the ratio.[19] These statistics suggest that at least some municipalities continue to believe that land value taxation is a useful economic development tool. However, officials in jurisdictions that retain split-rate taxes report quite different perceptions of their impact on economic development.

In Harrisburg, land value taxation has been credited with helping to bring back the city after the devastation and disinvestment that resulted from a major flood in 1972 (Hughes 2006). The population of Harrisburg had been declining since the 1950s, and the flood accelerated that trend. Since adopting land value taxation in 1975 and electing, in 1981, an energetic mayor, Stephen Reed—who has become the city's longest-serving mayor—the city has witnessed substantial increases in building permits and construction activity, in the value of taxable real estate, and in employment, and a substantial decrease in building vacancy.

Even in Aliquippa, which has gradually decreased the ratio of the land to the improvement tax rate over time, there is a perception that the split-rate tax is helping to spur redevelopment of the site of an abandoned steel mill.[20] The closing of the mill, which stretched seven miles along the Ohio River, had helped motivate the adoption of land value taxation in the late 1980s.

---

17. Telephone interview with Tom Rockovich, city manager, Oil City, 28 February 2008.

18. Allentown, Altoona, Clairton, DuBois, Ebensburg, Harrisburg, Lock Haven, and Washington have increased the ratio of the land to the improvement tax rate.

19. Aliquippa, the Aliquippa School District, Duquesne, McKeesport, New Castle, Scranton, and Titusville have decreased the ratio of the land to the improvement tax rate. The ratio has not changed in the Clairton School District.

20. Telephone interview with William O'Neal, treasurer, City of Aliquippa, 28 February 2008.

However, in Clairton, there is a perception that the split-rate tax cannot encourage development, because there is little demand for new improvements in the area. But the tax is nonetheless attractive because it does not penalize property owners who make improvements and it shifts the tax burden from homeowners to businesses. In addition, land value is viewed as a more stable tax base because land values decreased less than improvement values in the most recent assessment in 2005. That is the reason that the Clairton School District shifted to land value taxation in 2006.[21] In Ebensburg, there is a similar perception that the split-rate tax does not encourage development but that it is fairer in the sense that it does not impose a penalty for making improvements.[22] Officials in Scranton and Washington reported that the split-rate tax may have had a positive effect on development initially but that this was no longer the case.[23] Officials in Lock Haven believe that the split-rate tax has been beneficial, whereas McKeesport officials doubt that it ever had a positive effect there.[24]

Proponents of land value taxation continue to be active in numerous jurisdictions in the United States.[25] Of those, Philadelphia is probably the most interesting case. It is the birthplace of Henry George, as well as the home of the Henry George Foundation of America and the Center for the Study of Economics, sister organizations that are among the main proponents of land value taxation in the United States. Efforts to establish land value taxation have been ongoing for a long time in Philadelphia, one of the largest cities in the country and one facing considerable economic and fiscal challenges. Land value taxation was proposed by a city councilman in 1982 and by Mayor Wilson Goode in 1988 (Eisner 1982; Williams 1988). Neither effort was successful, and both proposals appeared to raise more questions than could be answered in the time available for considering the proposals.

---

21. Telephone interview with Scott Andrejack, finance director, City of Clairton, 27 March 2008.

22. Telephone interview with Dan Penatazer, borough manager, Ebensburg Borough, 2 April 2008.

23. Telephone interviews with Nancy Crake, tax clerk, City of Scranton, 2 April 2008, and Sandy Borkowski, tax clerk, City of Washington, 26 March 2008.

24. Telephone interviews with Richard Marcinkevage, city manager, City of Lock Haven, 26 March 2008, and Ray Dockerty, information systems director, City of McKeesport, 27 March 2008.

25. Common Ground–USA lists current and recent legislative efforts in 17 states on their Web site, at http://www.progress.org/cg/feet5.htm.

Goode's proposal was made in the context of an effort to increase revenue to fill a budget gap, and under his proposal property taxes would have increased for many property owners (even though a revenue-neutral shift would likely have reduced taxes for the majority of owners).

Land value taxation was subsequently proposed in a comprehensive report on the structure of taxation in Philadelphia published by the city's controller in 2001 (Saidel 2001). The report made numerous suggestions, including reducing the city's onerous wage tax and replacing the lost revenue with a land value tax. Subsequently, a referendum established the Philadelphia Tax Reform Commission to review the city's tax system and make recommendations for improving the system. The commission proposed, among other things, shifting to land value taxation (Philadelphia Tax Reform Commission 2003). Although some of the commission's proposals have been implemented, land value taxation is not one of them. Those proposals that have not yet been implemented continue to be promoted by an organization called Philadelphia Forward (Mandel 2004). The current mayor, Michael Nutter, who took office in January 2008, is not a proponent of land value taxation, but several city council members support the idea. As the city considers further reductions to wage and business taxes, attention may shift to the property tax, and the possibility of shifting some of that tax's burden from improvements to land will likely be revisited.[26] Meanwhile, Philadelphia is in the process of improving its assessment practices and reassessing property throughout the city. Better systems for determining property values should make it possible to assess land and improvement values more accurately and thus could help pave the way for the introduction of land value taxation in the future.

CONCLUSIONS

Land value taxation has experienced uneven success in the United States for a variety of reasons. In Pittsburgh, the tax became the scapegoat for poor assessment and rate-setting practices, and in Hawaii a perception that there was too much development led to opposition to a tax designed to encourage development. Economic decline has been severe in some jurisdictions, and a lack of demand for new improvements has meant that the tax has been un-

---

26. Telephone interview with Brett Mandel, executive director, Philadelphia Forward, 25 March 2008.

able to achieve its purposes. In some cases, including Pittsburgh, concerns about who benefits or does not benefit from the tax have played a role in its demise.

On the other hand, the economic logic of land value taxation continues to be compelling in some contexts, and 16 jurisdictions in Pennsylvania continue to operate split-rate systems. Efforts to establish land value taxation continue elsewhere, and a longstanding effort to establish land value taxation in Philadelphia is likely to receive renewed attention as that city upgrades its property tax practices and considers alternatives to wage and business taxes that are widely perceived to be impeding economic development.

✧ 3 ✧

International Experience

RIËL C. D. FRANZSEN

LAND VALUE AND SPLIT-RATE taxes have been and are still being used by a number of developed and developing countries. In some countries these taxes date back to the nineteenth century, whereas in others they are of more recent origin. Table 3.1 provides a list of countries where a tax on land value is both permitted under the law and employed in practice.[1]

In some of these countries (e.g., Estonia and Jamaica) the land value taxes are levied and administered by the central government (although the revenue goes to local government), whereas in others (e.g., Kenya and New Zealand) the taxes are levied and administered by the local government. Irrespective of the level of administration, the revenue is generally used to finance subnational government.

Nations or states that have adopted, or are considering adopting, a land value tax have to make a number of statutory and administrative choices regarding how the tax base will be defined and how land values will be determined for tax-assessment purposes. So, before we turn to selected country studies of land value taxation, it will be useful first to introduce some concepts relating to the tax base, the methodology for determining land value, and changes relating to these concepts over time.

A primary distinction must be drawn between property tax systems based on capital value and those based on rental value. In annual rental value systems, the tax is based on the notional or expected rental value of property

---

1. This list is not exhaustive. For additional detail, see Franzsen and McCluskey (2008), Bird and Slack (2004), Dos Santos and Bain (2004), Bahl (1998), and Youngman and Malme (1994).

Table 3.1 Countries using some form of land value tax or split-rate tax

Africa	Kenya, Namibia,[a] South Africa,[b] Swaziland, Zimbabwe
Asia	Japan, South Korea, Taiwan, Thailand[c]
Australasia & the South Pacific[d]	Australia, Fiji, New Zealand, Papua New Guinea, Solomon Islands, Vanuatu
Caribbean & Latin America	Bahamas, Barbados, Belize, Grenada, Jamaica, Mexico
Europe	Denmark, Estonia, France
North America	Canada, United States

Sources: Franzsen and McCluskey (2008); Bird and Slack (2004); Dos Santos and Bain (2004); Bahl (1998); and Youngman and Malme (1994).

Notes:

[a] To accelerate land reform, Namibia introduced a specific tax on unimproved land values for commercial farms in 2004 (Franzsen and McCluskey 2008).

[b] New property tax legislation in South Africa will eliminate land value and split-rate taxation by 1 July 2009, after which date market value (i.e., the total value of the property) will be the only tax base.

[c] The land development tax in Thailand is assessed only on the land value of the property, with no account taken of any improvements thereon or of any crops (Bird and Slack 2004).

[d] Given that Fiji, Papua New Guinea, the Solomon Islands, and Vanuatu are to a large degree within the sphere of influence of either Australia or New Zealand, it is not surprising that these countries introduced land value taxation. For a detailed discussion of the land value tax as levied in Fiji, see Hassan (2005).

(i.e., land and improvements). A further distinction can be drawn between systems in which rental value is determined with reference to the property's current use and systems in which rental value is determined on the basis of a property's highest and best use. Some jurisdictions use net rents (i.e., rent net of expenses such as insurance and maintenance costs) as a tax base, whereas others use *gross rents*.[2] Lastly, in some instances a rental value system is a tax on occupancy rather than a tax on ownership.[3]

---

2. In theory, at least, the tax bases under a rental value system and capital value system are equivalent because a discounted stream of net rent payments for a property should be equivalent to the property's capital value. Problems often encountered with rental value systems are the treatment of vacant land and the impact of rent-control legislation. For a more detailed discussion of annual rental value systems, see Youngman and Malme (1994, 4), Bahl (1998, 145–146), or McCluskey and Williams (1999, 14–15).

3. Under a system in which occupancy is taxed, vacant properties are usually exempt, although it is possible to then tax the owner as a notional occupier.

In capital value systems the tax base is defined with reference to the market value of real property (i.e., what a willing buyer would be prepared to pay a willing seller for the relevant property if the property were sold unencumbered in an open market).[4] In the majority of jurisdictions where a capital value system is used, the tax base is defined as the assessed value of land and improvements—in other words, the total value of the subject property. In some jurisdictions this is referred to as *capital improved value*. In a few jurisdictions, however, land and improvements are treated as discrete taxable objects and valued and taxed separately. Such a system is generally referred to as a *split-rate tax system*.

Some countries or jurisdictions use a capital value system in which only the value of land is taxed and define land value by specifying which improvements to land are excluded from the tax base. For example, taxable land value might include or exclude so-called merged improvements, that is, the value added by clearing, leveling, or draining. Depending on the specified exclusions, this type of land tax is known variously as an *unimproved value tax*, an *unimproved land value tax*, a *land value tax*, a *land tax*, or a *site value tax*.[5]

In the discussion that follows, *unimproved value* or *unimproved land value* is used to describe a tax base that excludes merged improvements, and *land value* or *site value* refers to a tax base in which these merged improvements are deemed part of the land.

COUNTRY STUDIES

I review five countries employing some form of land value taxation: two developed countries, Australia and New Zealand; two developing countries, Jamaica and South Africa; and one transition country, Estonia. I selected these five countries on the following basis:

· Land value taxes have been levied in Australia and New Zealand since the nineteenth century. Although land value taxes are still used exten-

---

4. In some countries other types of property (e.g., personal property) may also be included in the tax base. For purposes of this chapter, however, property tax refers only to a recurring tax on the ownership of real property (i.e., land and improvements).

5. Since different jurisdictions often define the concepts of unimproved value, land value, and site value differently, any comparison across jurisdictions must be undertaken with careful attention to the exact local usage. For a more detailed discussion of capital value systems (including land value tax systems), see Bahl (1998, 142–145) or McCluskey and Williams (1999, 15–17).

sively in both these countries, there is a marked move toward implementing improved capital value (i.e., total market value) and annual value (i.e., rental value) systems.

· South Africa has used a land value system rather extensively since the early twentieth century, but is in the process of phasing it out. By 1 July 2009 only a total market value system will be in operation.

· Jamaica introduced a land value tax in the middle of the twentieth century, and, although various reviews have been undertaken regarding changing the system, it has generally been recommended that the system be retained for administrative reasons.

· Despite an almost nonexistent capital market at the time, Estonia introduced a land value tax in 1993. Although it was introduced as a transitional measure, to be replaced by a system that would tax total value (i.e., a capital improved value system) in due course, there is now some resistance to replacing it.

Australia

In Australia land value taxation with unimproved value as a base has been used extensively and continuously since the nineteenth century.[6] According to Hornby (1999, 313–314), the reason Australia embraced the concept of land value taxation can be traced back to Henry George.

As evidenced by table 3.2, the property tax is an important source of own-source tax revenue at the state level and the only source of own-source tax revenue for local governments in Australia.[7]

The Establishment of Land Value Taxation in Australia

When the Commonwealth of Australia was established in 1901, some of the constituent states were already levying land value taxes—for example, South

---

6. Although land value taxes were already levied in some of the Australian colonies at the time that Henry George visited in 1890, various commentators say that Henry George's views regarding a tax on the unearned income from land were enthusiastically embraced in both Australia and New Zealand (Hornby 1999; Pullen 2003). George's influential presence during his three-month public lecture tour of Australia, as well as the popularity of *Progress and Poverty* throughout the English-speaking world, could indeed have contributed to the growing popularity of land value taxation in the 1890s and first decades of the twentieth century.

7. The property tax is called *rates* or the *rating system* in Australian parlance.

Table 3.2 Importance of taxes on real property in Australia, 2006–2007

Level of government	Percentage of total taxes
Commonwealth of Australia	0.0
State and territory governments	8.9
Local governments	100.0
All levels of government	4.6

Source: Australian Bureau of Statistics (2008).

Australia (since 1884) and New South Wales (since 1895).[8] The introduction of a federal tax on the value of land followed in 1910. It was a wealth tax, introduced with the aim of financing a nationwide old-age pension plan (S. Smith 2005) and as a means to break up large tracts of underutilized land (Reinhardt and Steel 2007). Although the combined burden of federal, state, and local land taxes was significant, at its highest level it was still below 100 percent of the economic rental value (J. Smith 2000).

The federal land tax was abolished in 1952.[9] S. Smith (2005) and Reinhardt and Steel (2007) provide the following reasons for its abolition:

· The land tax was not achieving its stated objective of breaking up large estates, presumably because the tax rates were not high enough and the base became eroded by exemptions to land used for primary production.
· The tax was one on a "capital base," which, particularly in relation to farmers, was a tax on their major income-producing assets. No similar taxes were levied on other forms of wealth. In addition, the land tax was not levied on the net asset value—it did not take into account, for example, mortgage debts.

8. According to Hornby (1999), Tasmania was the first colony to introduce a land value tax in 1857.
9. J. Smith (2000, 6) comments as follows: "In 1952 the Menzies government abolished the federal land tax, so states could replace lost income tax revenues. The states did no such thing. By the 1950s states' land taxes were already substantially eroded. Reflecting the political power of the farm lobby, and in response to political pressures from homeowners, land used for primary production had generally been exempted, as had land used for the principal place of residence."

· The significant growth of other revenue sources, such as the income tax, rendered the federal land tax less important.
· The high administrative costs of the land tax made it less efficient. (Collection costs amounted to 3.9 percent of revenue in the 1951–1952 fiscal year, as opposed to less than 1 percent for the income tax and a general average of less than 1 percent for all revenue sources.)

State and territory land taxes have, however, remained in force. Since the abolition of income taxes at the state level, property taxes (i.e., the land tax), gambling levies, stamp duties, payroll taxes, and motor-vehicle taxes have been the main sources of tax revenue for the states and territories. Since federation, however, the major part of the financing for state and territory budgets has come from commonwealth grants. Table 3.2 suggests that state land taxes are still important—despite the significant erosion of the tax base through exemptions of land used for primary production (J. Smith 2000; Reinhardt and Steel 2007). Property taxes collected at the state and local level accounted for 25.3 percent of state and local government tax revenue in 2006–2007 (Australian Bureau of Statistics 2008).

The Role of Land Value Taxation in Australia

Land taxes are levied at the state level in all six Australian states as well as in the Australian Capital Territory. Table 3.3 provides an overview of land taxation at the state (and territory) level. Except in Queensland, the tax base is the land value (i.e., including merged improvements). In Queensland the tax base is unimproved value. Only the Northern Territory does not levy a jurisdiction-wide land tax.

As shown in table 3.2, the 723 local authorities throughout Australia rely exclusively on property taxes for own-source tax revenue. Table 3.4 provides an overview of the current status of tax bases provided for by legislation and tax bases used in practice at the local level. Given a choice of tax bases, local councils in South Australia and Victoria favor total value, which includes the value of improvements and is thus not a land-only tax. Only a few local councils in these two states still use land value.[10] In Tasmania all the local councils choose rental value as a tax base. Queensland is the only state that still uses unimproved land value as a tax base.

As noted above, states or nations considering a land value tax need to de-

---

10. By 1996, 61 of the 78 local councils in Victoria had already adopted capital improved value as the tax base, with only 17 retaining land value. In 2001 only 3 retained land value as the tax base, and in 2008 only 1 local council still used land value.

Table 3.3 Land value taxation at the state level in Australia

| Australian states and territories | State land tax | |
	First introduced	Tax base
Australian Capital Territory	1987	Land value[a]
New South Wales	1895	Land value
Northern Territory		None
Queensland	1915[b]	Unimproved value[c]
South Australia	1884	Land value
Tasmania	1910[d]	Land value
Victoria	1910	Land value
Western Australia	1907	Land value

Sources: S. Smith (2005) and Franzsen and McCluskey (2005).

Notes:

[a] For the Australian Capital Territory, the term *land value* includes the value attributable to those improvements that have merged with the land (e.g., leveling, draining).

[b] Hornby (1999) says that a land tax was first introduced in Queensland in 1887.

[c] Queensland is the only state that still exclusively uses unimproved value, defined as the value of the land in its original condition (i.e., ignoring so-called merged improvements), as its tax base.

[d] Hornby (1999) puts the date at 1857, stating that Tasmania was the first state to introduce a tax on land values.

Table 3.4 Land value taxation at the local government level in Australia

Australian states and territories	Tax base options (and local practice)
Australian Capital Territory	Land value
New South Wales	Land value
Northern Territory	Total value; land value; rental value
Queensland[a]	Unimproved land value
South Australia	Total value (64 councils); land value (4 councils)
Tasmania	Total value (0 councils); land value (0 councils); rental value (all councils)
Victoria	Total value (72 councils); land value (1 council); net rental value (6 councils)
Western Australia	Land value (rural properties); gross rental value (urban properties)

Sources: Franzsen and McCluskey (2005); Australian Local Government Association (2006).

Note:

[a] Queensland is the only state that still exclusively uses unimproved land value (i.e., the value of the land in its original condition) as its tax base.

cide how to define the tax base and how to determine the value of land. This point is illustrated by issues currently facing three Australian states.

NEW SOUTH WALES.   The land values assigned for property tax purposes in New South Wales are supplied by the valuer general. Even though the valuer general regularly (every two to four years) provides new land values, a recent study (S. Smith 2005) suggests that the state land tax (and the local property tax system, which relies on the same land values) in New South Wales is under some pressure. Rapid increases in land values, especially along the coast, have resulted in higher levels of land-related taxation, which has in turn raised the political visibility of both the state land tax and local property tax.

QUEENSLAND.   Values for land tax and local property tax purposes are determined at the state level by the Department of Natural Resources and Water. Since the turn of the nineteenth century, the local property tax in Queensland has been levied on the unimproved value of land. Although it may have been a workable concept at a time when much of the state was still undeveloped, the concept of unimproved value is no longer well understood by politicians, taxpayers, or even appraisers. The value to be determined is the price at which one could expect to sell a parcel of land without improvements such as houses, fences, piping, or leveling. A parcel's proximity to roads, railways, schools, and shopping centers will, however, affect that property's value. McCluskey (2005c) argues forcefully that the determination of the unimproved land value of improved land is basically an impossible task under the existing definition. For example, improvements such as leveling, clearing, and filling carried out many years earlier are becoming virtually impossible to identify. How can an appraiser ascertain the original state and condition of the land when any evidence as to that state and condition long ago disappeared?

The retention of this archaic and artificial tax base introduces unnecessary uncertainty and complexity in the valuation process. Over time and with continuing urban development, the difficulties and anomalies associated with the definition of land are increasing. Not surprisingly, recent reviews of the system in Queensland have supported the adoption of the concepts of land value or site value used extensively in other states (Hornby 1999; McCluskey 2005c).[11]

---

11. It is noteworthy that Victoria adopted land value as its tax base in 1958, New South Wales adopted it in 1970, and South Australia adopted it in 1971. Indeed, except for Queensland, all the states and territories in Australia now use land value (although Western Australia does not use land value for certain rural properties).

The rapid development occurring all along the coast further bedevils the current unimproved land value system in Queensland. As is the case in New South Wales, land values for coastal properties are extremely volatile. For example, Brisbane City's total taxable value as determined on 1 October 2006 had increased by 21 percent since the last valuation carried out in October 2004.

WESTERN AUSTRALIA.   The statutory base for local government property tax is unimproved value in rural areas and gross rental value in urban areas. Unimproved value is the tax base for the state land tax in both urban and rural areas. In rural areas, unimproved value indeed excludes merged improvements. Over time, however, it became impractical to use pure unimproved value in respect of land situated within a so-called townsite (i.e., all land within the metropolitan area or in a city or town outside the metropolitan area) because of the nature of merged improvements (Franzsen 2005a). Therefore, the tax base for land within a townsite is site value (i.e., land value).[12]

The systems seem to function very well, primarily because of a long history of land taxation in the state as well as regular, statewide valuations. Where land is used predominantly for nonrural (i.e., urban) purposes, the statutory basis for the local rate is the gross rental value of the land. Gross rental values are determined every three years for the 30 local governments in the Perth metropolitan area and on a four- to six-year cycle for town councils and shires.

For purposes of Western Australia's state land tax, land values are assessed annually by the valuer general for approximately 750,000 taxable properties in the state. Regular revaluations mean that significant shifts in tax incidence are effectively countered and that the tax base is swiftly extended to cover new properties (e.g., those resulting from subdivisions or the establishment of new townships).

New Zealand

New Zealand provides another interesting case study of land value taxation. As Hargreaves (1991) points out, land value taxation was already used in

---

12. In the Valuation of Land Act 1978, the site value of land is defined as "the capital amount that an estate of fee simple in the land might reasonably be expected to realize upon sale assuming that any improvements to the land, other than merged improvements, had not been made."

Table 3.5 New Zealand local government revenue sources (percentage of total
revenue)

Revenue source	1993–1994	2005–2006
Property tax	57.3	56.1
User charges and all other income	20.3	19.7
Grants and subsidies	10.3	12.7
Total investment income	7.0	5.7
Regulatory income and petrol tax	5.1	5.8
Total	100.0	100.0

Source: Local Government Rates Inquiry Panel (2007).

New Zealand when Henry George was only 16 years old. Since the early days
of colonial settlement, local authorities have been granted the choice of three
tax bases, namely,

- annual rental value;
- capital improved value (i.e., the total value of property); and
- land value.

As is evident from table 3.5, property taxation constitutes an important
source of own-source revenue for New Zealand local authorities.

The Establishment of Land Value Taxation in New Zealand

As far back as 1844, local authorities were authorized to raise revenue
through the taxation of property. During the early years of the colony, the
principal system was a rental value system, which was in effect a form of the
English property tax system.[13] Because this system was inconsistent with
the predominant pattern of land tenure, it was not successful (Dowse and
Hargreaves 1999). In this new and developing colony where land was sold in
freehold, capital value taxation was favored. However, as both rental value
and capital value systems increased the tax burden on industrious settlers
who improved their properties, the system of land value taxation became
increasingly popular. Proponents of land value taxation argued that such a
system would also raise the cost of holding vacant land and thus discourage speculation and absenteeism. Wellington was the first region to introduce the concept of unimproved land value taxation in 1849 (Dowse and

---

13. As is the case in Australia, the local property tax system in New Zealand is also referred to as the rating system.

Hargreaves 1999). Especially after the statutory consolidation of property tax legislation in 1912, there was a steady move away from rental value and capital value taxation in favor of land value taxation.

The Role of Land Value Taxation in New Zealand over Time

As happened in the Australian states, land value effectively replaced unimproved land value as the basis for valuation for local property tax purposes in 1970. Until 1976, local authorities could switch from a capital value to a rental value tax system without taxpayer approval (McCluskey 2005b), but the adoption or abandonment of a land value tax required the approval of a majority of taxpayers. Local authorities can now change the property tax system without conducting a taxpayer poll; however, public consultations normally take place.

All three property tax systems are used by the five largest cities in New Zealand. Auckland, the largest city, is one of only two jurisdictions using rental value. Christchurch, Dunedin, and Wellington all use total value. Only Hamilton still uses a land value system (McCluskey et al. 2006).

Recent Trends in New Zealand

Local property taxation in New Zealand has been undergoing a significant process of evolution, particularly since new legislation was enacted in 2002. As explained by McCluskey and Franzsen (2004, 3), the main goals of the new legislation were to provide local authorities with flexible powers to set, assess, and collect property tax and to ensure that tax-related decisions were made in a transparent and consultative manner.

By 1985 the use of land value as the preferred tax base for the property tax in New Zealand was at an all-time high. However, since then, there has been a significant reversion to the use of total value as the preferred tax base (Dowse and Hargreaves 1999; McCluskey and Franzsen 2004; Local Government Rates Inquiry Panel 2007, par. 9.16), as evidenced by table 3.6. By 2007 capital value had indeed become the valuation basis for the majority of local authorities. In the 2006–2007 fiscal year, forty-four local authorities used capital value for their general property tax, thirty-six used land value, and only two used rental value. Three local authorities had no general property tax (Local Government Rates Inquiry Panel 2007, par. 9.17). This trend is especially evident in, but is not limited to, larger urban local authorities (McCluskey et al. 2006; Franzsen and McCluskey 2008). As jurisdictions are built out, there is less and less evidence from sales of undeveloped

Table 3.6 New Zealand local government utilization of property tax base measures (percentage of all jurisdictions using each)

Year	Land value	Total value	Rental value	Land and total value	Total
1942	55	37	8		100
1955	66	27	7		100
1972	80	16	4		100
1985	80	10	5	5	100
1995	64	30	2	4	100
2007	44	54	2		100

Sources: Dowse and Hargreaves (1999); McCluskey et al. (2006); and Local Government Rates Inquiry Panel (2007).

land. Therefore, appraisers must extrapolate sales data over much wider geographic areas to assess values for tax purposes (McCluskey and Franzsen 2004; see also chapter 8 of this volume).

According to the recent report of the Local Government Rates Inquiry Panel (2007, par. 9.11), "valuation problems are greater under land value rating systems. Use of a single system is likely to lead to enhanced public understanding of the rating system. The Panel supports capital value as the preferred basis for rating valuations. Capital value also has the advantage of being a somewhat more progressive system, especially for rural properties." The report concludes that since the Local Government (Rating) Act of 2002 (LGRA) was enacted, property tax systems in New Zealand have become generally more regressive as tax systems have shifted away from taxes based on the value of property to those with a higher proportion of tax from a uniform annual general charge and a targeted fixed rate (i.e., a flat tax). Since 2002, uniform charges have become increasingly popular, whereas the use of general property taxes has decreased (Local Government Rates Inquiry Panel 2007, par. 9.15).

South Africa

Property taxation[14] has been a source of revenue for urban municipalities in South Africa since 1836. Since 1997 it has been a constitutionally guaranteed

14. As in Australia and New Zealand, property taxes are also referred to as rates in South Africa.

Table 3.7 Property tax base and revenue share for the six metropolitan municipalities in South Africa, 2005–2006

Metropolitan municipality	Property tax base	Property tax share (percentage of total revenue)
Tshwane (Pretoria)	Land value	21.3
Johannesburg	Land value	18.3
Ekurhuleni	Land value	18.0
Ethekwini (Durban)	Land and improvement values— separately	30.9
Nelson Mandela Bay	Land and improvement values— separately	17.0
Cape Town	Total value	20.8

Source: South Africa National Treasury (2007).

source of revenue for municipalities. In the context of the far-reaching local government reforms currently under way, it is a primary source of revenue for metropolitan and local municipalities.

Before the new property tax law became operational, municipalities had a choice among the following three tax bases:

- land value (referred to as *site rating*)
- total value (referred to as *flat rating*)
- the value of both land and improvements (i.e., a split-rate system, referred to as *composite rating*)

In 1994 use of these three different property tax systems was spread almost evenly among South African municipalities: site rating was used by 34 percent of South African municipalities, flat rating by 27 percent, and composite rating by 39 percent (Bell and Bowman 2002a).

Table 3.7 shows that comparable revenue shares were realized by all three property tax systems in South Africa's six metropolitan municipalities. In short, site rating and composite rating can generate the same level of revenue as flat rating (i.e., a tax on total value).

Although the sample of local municipalities[15] referred to in table 3.8 was randomly selected and not large enough to be statistically meaningful, it is noteworthy that a higher percentage of total revenue was generated in

15. Local municipalities in South Africa typically consist of urban areas (e.g., a small city or a few towns) and rural properties (e.g., commercial farms, tribal land, or nature reserves).

Table 3.8 Property tax base and revenue share for seven South African municipalities, 2005–2006

Local municipality (province)	Property tax base	Property tax share (percentage of total revenue)
Greater Tubatse (Limpopo)	Land value	16.0
Polokwane (Limpopo)	Land value	14.9
Seme (Mpumalanga)	Land value	10.1
Mamusa (North West)	Land value	10.3
Msunduzi (KwaZulu-Natal)	Land and improvement values—separately	22.7
Hessequa (Western Cape)	Land and improvement values—separately	23.2
Swartland (Western Cape)	Total value	19.7

Source: South Africa National Treasury (2007).

the three municipalities that also taxed improvements. However, it must be noted that in 2005–2006, the Greater Tubatse and Mamusa local municipalities had not yet extended their tax bases to include rural properties, whereas both the Hessequa and Swartland local municipalities already taxed rural properties.

Thus, irrespective of the tax base used, the property tax constitutes an important source of own-source tax revenue for municipalities, and the percentage generated by the property tax (regardless of the base used) is comparable. Since the 2001–2002 fiscal year, property tax revenues constituted approximately 20 percent of total operating income for all municipalities.

The Establishment of Land Value Taxation in South Africa

As early as 1903, legislation in two former provinces required that site values and the value of improvements be reflected separately in municipal valuation rolls (i.e., the list of assessed values for all taxable properties). This separation was a precursor to the introduction of land value taxation in the Transvaal province in 1916, with other provinces following suit (McCluskey and Franzsen 2004)—as indicated in table 3.9.

Land value taxation was introduced in South Africa because it did not inhibit the development of undeveloped property. One of the further arguments in favor of a land value tax is its assessment advantage (Bahl 1998). Valuation rolls can be prepared and maintained more uniformly and at

Table 3.9 Dates for land value taxation in South Africa

Province	Year of enabling legislation for determining land values	Year of enabling legislation allowing a land value tax system
Cape	1912	1917
Natal	1911	1924
Orange Free State	1903 and 1904	1920
Transvaal	1903	1916

Sources: McCluskey and Franzsen (2004) and Franzsen (2005b).

reduced administrative cost if improvements are not included in the tax base. However, this advantage did not apply in practice in South Africa (McCluskey and Franzsen 2004), because the former provincial laws required that valuation rolls reflect at least two (i.e., land value and improvement value) or three values (i.e., land value, improvement value, and total value) irrespective of the tax base used in practice. The administrative burden of these multiple assessments was given as one of the reasons for adopting a uniform system throughout the country.

The Role and Demise of Land Value Taxation in South Africa over Time

In 2001, as part of the property tax reform, a uniform system based on market value (i.e., the total value of taxable property) was mandated across all of South Africa. Municipalities that use a land value tax or split-rate tax system must replace these systems with one based on market value by 1 July 2009—ending almost a century of land value taxation in South Africa.

As indicated by a number of studies, the recent migration to total value as the only tax base has resulted in significant shifts in tax burdens in many municipalities that previously used a land value or split-rate tax system (Franzsen and McCluskey 2007; Van Ryneveld et al. 2006). As noted in chapter 5, the distribution of ratios of land value to improvement value for taxable properties is a primary determinant of the incidence of a shift to or from land value taxation. Any country contemplating changes in its property tax system must take cognizance of possible shifts in tax burdens, perform appropriate modeling, and manage these changes carefully, points discussed in chapter 8 of this volume.

Jamaica

Despite political, administrative, and technical problems (McCluskey 2005a; Sjoquist 2004; Lyons and McCluskey 1999), a national land value tax has been an important and integral source of revenue for the local parish councils in Jamaica for over 50 years. Taxes relating to property date back to the early years of British administration (Lyons and McCluskey 1999).

The Establishment of Land Value Taxation in Jamaica

The adoption of a land value tax in Jamaica was recommended in 1943 (Copes and Rybeck 2001), but the proposed reforms only gained momentum in 1955 after the government employed the services of J. F. N. Murray, "a qualified advisor practiced in the 'unimproved value system'" (Lyons and McCluskey 1999, 389). Murray prepared a comprehensive report in 1956, which served as the blueprint for the development of the system of land taxation based on unimproved values. His report addressed, among other key issues, country-specific valuation problems and the legislative amendments necessary to give legal effect to his recommendations (McCluskey 2005a). By providing the legislative and practical framework for the implementation of a land value tax, Murray laid the important foundation for its adoption.

It took Jamaica another 18 years to complete the first comprehensive revaluation of the island's properties. Although legislation in Jamaica provides for general revaluations every five years, this standard has not yet been achieved in practice. McCluskey (2005a) points out that the Land Valuation Department has the professional and technical skills to undertake regular revaluations. The infrequency of revaluations is due to a lack of political will and a lack of understanding of the equity and cost implications of irregular revaluations.

The Future of the Land Tax in Jamaica

The government of Jamaica has on a number of occasions considered the possibility of replacing the current land value system with a capital value system based on the total value of property (McCluskey 2005a; Sjoquist 2004). The argument that the tax base under a land value tax is too narrow has appeared in a number of the reports following reviews of the current tax system. Aside from the obvious political and economic considerations of such a policy shift, there are major administrative hurdles involved in gathering all the prerequisite data on buildings and other improvements (Franzsen and McCluskey 2008). To date, these hurdles relating to data have resulted in the retention of the land tax in Jamaica (Sjoquist 2004).

Estonia

A land value tax was introduced in Estonia in 1993, shortly after independence from Russia was achieved in August 1991. Land value taxation was adopted even before the property market was sufficiently mature to produce credible land price information. As Tiits (2008) points out, revenue from the land tax represented 7.2 percent of all local revenue in 2005, a significant increase from approximately 2 percent in 1997 (Tiits and Tomson 1999). However, the importance of the land tax varies significantly among municipalities: the tax represents only 3 percent of revenue in Tartu and 4.8 percent in Tallinn (the two largest cities in Estonia), but approximately 30 percent in some rural municipalities—despite the much lower values generally encountered in rural jurisdictions. Some commentators argue that, given the values determined in the last revaluation in 2001, the revenue from the land tax could be substantially higher (Tiits 2008).

The Establishment of Land Value Taxation in Estonia

The introduction of the land tax in Estonia had more to do with land reform (i.e., privatization generally and restitution of land to owners from the pre-Communist era more specifically) and general tax reforms (Mikesell and Zorn 2008; Tiits 2008; Youngman 2008; Tiits and Tomson 1999). The following direct and indirect reasons for its introduction are provided by Tiits (2008, 398):

- Increasing revenues and strengthening the tax base for local government
- Redistributing the tax burden from indirect to direct taxes
- Using a tax that could be collected effectively
- Accelerating land reform
- Activating real estate markets
- Supporting effective land use
- Raising awareness of the concept of land values
- Providing ancillary support for the revision of land registers

Mikesell and Zorn (2008, 188) point out that the taxation of both private and public land in Estonia indeed provided additional encouragement for privatization as well as the more efficient use of land that was privatized or restored to former owners. Furthermore, the reduction of stamp duties on registrations in the land registry to below 1 percent also had a positive impact on the regularization of the land market, with both sellers and buyers prepared to provide more reliable sales evidence and the market becoming more transparent (Tiits 2008; Mikesell and Zorn 2008).

The land tax in Estonia has as its base the market value of land only. Improvements, crops, and forests are not taxed. In the absence of credible sales data, land values were initially estimated using expert opinions.

The Role of Land Value Taxation in Estonia over Time

At first, the tax base of the land tax in Estonia was shared between central and local governments with tax rates determined centrally. In 1995 municipalities were given the responsibility for determining their own tax rates within the range of 0.3 percent to 0.7 percent on their share of the tax. The central government rate remained at 0.5 percent. In 1996 a decision was made to allocate 100 percent of the land tax revenue to local governments, although the land tax remained a state tax. As a result, beginning in 1997, only locally determined tax rates applied, albeit still within nationally determined ranges. In 2002 these ranges were adjusted to between 0.1 and 2.5 percent for nonagricultural land and between 0.1 and 2.0 percent for agricultural land. Land is divided into twelve zones or types, and local governments are allowed to impose classified rates on the basis of property use across zones. Many municipalities, however, differentiate only between agricultural land and all other land use categories.

Very few exemptions exist, and tax relief is minimal in Estonia (Youngman 2008; Mikesell and Zorn 2008; Tiits and Tomson 1999). In the context of a narrow tax base that excludes buildings and other improvements, this is indeed a good policy. Although revaluations were undertaken in 1996 and 2001, revaluation cycles are not regulated by law (Youngman 2008; Tiits and Tomson 1999). From a policy standpoint, that is not good; it undermines equity and puts added pressure on a tax base that already has limited flexibility because it excludes improvements. Tiits (2008) points out that since 2002 municipal councils have been allowed to use differential tax rates. In some instances, municipalities are using this new regulation to lower the tax rate on properties in high-value zones.

The Future of the Land Tax in Estonia

The land value tax in Estonia has always been viewed as merely an intermediate step toward a capital improved value system: once the property market had developed sufficiently, records were updated, and it was possible to determine capital improved values at regular intervals, the tax base would be changed. However, now that those conditions have been met, there seems to be some political and social resistance to move to a capital improved value system (Youngman 2008; Tiits 2008).

CONCLUDING COMMENTS

Tax Base

In the late nineteenth century and early twentieth century, Australia and New Zealand adopted unimproved value as the base for their land value taxes. Given the largely undeveloped state of those countries at that time, determining the original "unimproved" state of the land did not pose significant problems. The unimproved value was relatively easily established since there were sufficient undeveloped land sales upon which to determine assessed values. As a result of activities such as draining, leveling, clearing, and reclaiming, however, the physical state of land parcels changes over time. Determining what the actual state of the land was decades or even a hundred years ago becomes practically impossible. Difficulties in applying unimproved value therefore led most Australian states, as well as Jamaica, New Zealand, and South Africa, to revise or replace it with a more practical statutorily defined concept.[16] The new basis became known as site value or land value. In essence, the so-called invisible improvements are considered to have merged with the land. Of the jurisdictions reviewed above, Queensland is the only one that still perseveres with the more antiquated unimproved value as its tax base.

Assessment

One of the main perceived advantages of a land value tax is that, with a few exceptions, the physical characteristics of land remain constant, resulting in an administrative advantage that improved value systems simply cannot

---

16. Fiji also adopted land value taxation in 1972 (Hassan 2005).

match. Improvements to land vary in type, quality, and degree, and their value varies with time as a result of deterioration, obsolescence, and depreciation. Managing changes in improvements to property presents significant logistical problems for assessors (Franzsen and McCluskey 2008).

However, the collection, verification, and valuation of improvements has in recent times improved significantly with aerial photography, satellite imagery, and statistical modeling. These advances come at a cost in terms of the technology and skills required. In contrast, changes in land parcels tend to be more manageable since they generally relate to the recording and surveying of subdivisions, consolidations, and ownership changes (Franzsen and McCluskey 2008).

One of the main disadvantages of a land value tax system is the difficulty of determining credible land-only values in heavily built-up urban areas (see chapter 8 in this volume). Determining land value is generally straightforward where evidence of demand is present and good sales data are available. However, as is the case in the highly developed inner cities of New South Wales, New Zealand, and South Africa (Franzsen and McCluskey 2008), the paucity of sales of undeveloped parcels poses a challenge to appraisers who have to rely on sales from adjacent neighborhoods to estimate land values. Extrapolation of meager sales evidence over an entire jurisdiction can create problems with uniformity of assessed values and result in taxpayer challenges. The scarcity of undeveloped parcels may also mean that those few remaining parcels command unrealistically high comparable values. The less credible the data become, the more difficult it becomes for politicians and taxpayers to understand the tax base. These are the primary reasons put forward for the shift toward capital value systems in Victoria (Australia), New Zealand, and South Africa.

On the other hand, developing countries often have limited resources available to perform regular and comprehensive revaluations. From a valuation perspective, a capital improved value tax system is a more complex and resource-intensive system (in terms of staff, skills requirements, and data modeling) than a land value system.

Tax Rates

A disadvantage of a land-only tax base relative to a capital improved value tax base is that a land-only tax base generally requires significantly higher nominal tax rates to generate sufficient revenues (Bahl 1998; Hassan 2005).

This makes it politically highly visible and possibly less acceptable to property owners, depending on taxpayers' perceptions and understanding of the tax system. Taxpayers may be prepared to endure high nominal tax rates if they are satisfied with effective tax rates and if they receive acceptable levels of government services in return. This may explain, for example, the acceptance of a tax rate of 14.4 percent of land value in the Tshwane Metropolitan Municipality in South Africa (in the 2007–2008 fiscal year).

Because property values and expenditure responsibilities and needs differ significantly between jurisdictions, an accurate comparison of nominal and effective tax rates in these jurisdictions is difficult, if not impossible. Suffice it to say that, despite the assessment challenges posed by increased development, at appropriate nominal (and effective) tax rates, a land value tax system can generate adequate revenues in a sustainable manner. This is surely evidenced by its effective use over many years in cities such as Brisbane and Sydney, Australia; Hamilton, New Zealand; Johannesburg and Pretoria, South Africa; and Kingston, Jamaica.

THEORY
AND
EVIDENCE

◈ 4 ◈

The Simple Analytics of
Land Value Taxation

WALLACE E. OATES AND ROBERT M. SCHWAB

I N THIS CHAPTER we lay out the basic conceptual framework that economists use to explore the structure and characteristics of land value taxation. We find that some fairly simple analysis can provide deep insights into the way land value taxation works and its effects on economic decisions and out-comes. Two results of special importance emerge. First, we find that the full burden of a land value tax falls on the owner of the land and on no one else. In addition, we see that a land value tax does not distort economic choices, as do most other taxes. These two findings give land value taxation a very distinctive character and appeal.

Before we turn to the formal analysis, it may be helpful to offer a few observations on the economic approach to problems of this sort. Economists typically work at a fairly high level of abstraction. The basic idea is to strip away the detail and to focus on a simplified conceptual construction (often called a *model*) that captures the essential elements of the problem. This allows a certain clarity and precision in seeing and understanding the basic issue. But this approach has a downside as well. It means that much of the complexity and richness of particular cases or settings is lost. Sometimes important qualifications to certain theoretical results can get swept under the

We thank Richard Dye, Richard England, and especially Richard Arnott for their very helpful comments and suggestions on earlier drafts of this chapter.

rug. In this chapter we try to point out instances in which the real world may deviate in certain respects from the formal analysis. However, it is crucial to grasp the fundamental principles of land value taxation before moving on to the complexity and nuance of actual cases.[1]

SOME PRELIMINARIES

It is useful first to put our discussion in the broader context of land taxation in general. There are, in fact, several different ways to levy a tax on land, although (as we will see) the general form of the tax is of little consequence for the basic economic properties of the tax. We could, for example, simply impose a tax of a fixed sum per unit of land (e.g., a tax of $200 per annum per acre of land). Alternatively, the tax could be levied on land rents. In this second case, the tax would typically take the form of a specified percentage of the rental income (either explicit or implicit) from the land. Or, third (and most common), the tax liability could equal some percentage of the value of the land. Under land value taxation, the value of the land is determined through some type of assessment procedure. The actual tax bill thus equals the assessed value of the land multiplied by the tax rate.

We can formalize the relationship between a tax on land rents and a tax on land values with some simple algebra. As it turns out, this exercise generates some additional insights into the properties of land taxation. Consider a particular plot of land that promises to yield an annual rental income of Y dollars every year for the next n years. In equilibrium, the market price for this piece of land will simply equal the present discounted value of the stream of future income. If the interest rate is r, then the value (and therefore the market price) of the land, V, is given by the following formula:[2]

$$(1) \qquad V = \frac{Y}{(1+r)} + \frac{Y}{(1+r)^2} + \cdots + \frac{Y}{(1+r)^n}$$

1. Nearly all the literature on land taxation focuses just on the consequences of the tax in the land market. It is possible, however, that a land tax could have reverberations in other markets as well. For example, a tax on land would reduce landowners' incomes, and as a result, they would buy less of some goods and services. Economists call these secondary consequences of a tax *general equilibrium effects*; we do not consider the general equilibrium effects of the land tax in this chapter.

2. If prices in general are rising, then we should think of Y as constant in real terms and r as the real rate of interest.

The first term on the right-hand side of equation (1) indicates the present value of the payment of Y dollars one year from now (which must be discounted at the rate r); the next term is the present value of a payment of Y two years hence; and so on to year n. We can express equation (1) more compactly by using the summation sign (sigma):

(2)
$$V = \sum_{s=1}^{n} \frac{Y}{(1+r)^s}$$

In the special case where n is infinity, this expression simplifies to

(3)
$$V = \frac{Y}{r}$$

This makes immediate sense. Suppose, for example, that our plot of land yields a rental income of $1,000 per year in perpetuity and that the existing rate of interest (or discount rate) is 5 percent. What equation (3) tells us is that the market value of the land is $20,000. A buyer will pay $20,000 for the asset and will then receive $1,000 per year forever—a return of 5 percent on the investment.

Suppose next that we levy a tax on land values and set a tax rate t_V. This means that the owner of the land must pay t_V percent of the market value of the land each year in taxes. We thus have an annual tax liability of T, where

(4)
$$T = t_v V$$

For the moment, suppose that the landowner is unable to pass any of the tax along to the tenant and thus the annual rent remains Y (we will have much more to say about this assumption shortly). The annual net income from owning the land is now reduced from Y to $(Y - t_v V)$. If we substitute this expression for Y in equation (3) and solve for V, we find that

(5)
$$V = \frac{Y}{r + t_V}$$

The new market value of our piece of land has been reduced by the tax. For example, suppose the community levies a 3 percent tax rate and thus t_v = 0.03. The denominator has risen from 0.05 to 0.08, resulting in a fall in the value of the land from $20,000 to $12,500. A purchaser of the land in the post-tax regime will pay $12,500 for the land in return for which the buyer will receive gross income of $1,000 per year and will pay $375 (i.e., 3 percent of $12,500) in taxes. The net income will thus be $625 annually, which generates the requisite market return of 5 percent per annum.[3]

Our simple algebraic exercise provides three additional insights into how land taxation works in theory. First, we see that the value (i.e., market price) of the land falls immediately by the full present discounted value of the future stream of tax payments. The purchaser of the land after the tax is levied effectively pays none of the tax; the purchaser is compensated for all future tax payments through a reduced purchase price for the land. The full tax burden (including current and all future tax liabilities) falls on the owner of the property at the time the tax is levied. This outcome—in which the current market value of an asset incorporates the present discounted value of the stream of all future tax liabilities—is called *capitalization*. The future tax liabilities are said to be capitalized into the current market price of the asset.

Second, equation (5) has some interesting implications for the effects of the level of the tax on the market value of the land. For instance, it might seem that a land value tax of 100 percent on land values would capture all the land rents accruing to the owner. Indeed, a tax rate of 100 percent would appear to be fully confiscatory. But this isn't so. Looking at equation (5), we can see that a tax rate of 100 percent (i.e., $t_V = 1.0$) on land values will reduce V dramatically, but not all the way to zero. Equation (5) tells us that if the rate of interest is 0.05, then the value of our piece of land equals $1,000 / 1.05 = $952.38. The value of the land has fallen slightly below its annual rental value. With a tax rate of 100 percent on land values, the purchaser will pay $952.38 for the plot, will have an annual tax liability of $952.38, and will receive net income of $1,000 − $952.38 = $47.62 (which is a 5 percent return on the investment). Tax rates on land values above 100 percent are thus feasible in principle. We learn from equation (5) that as tax rates rise, the value of land falls, and approaches zero as a limit as the tax rate goes to infinity. It is thus impossible to capture land rents in their totality through land value taxation. To do so would require a 100 percent tax rate on land rents (not land value).

Third, this simple example is useful in clarifying the relationship between a tax on land rents and a tax on land values. A tax on land rents at a rate t_R in our example would generate an annual tax revenue of $t_R Y$, whereas a tax on

---

3. Note that, as a result of the tax, the market price of the land has fallen by $7,500, which is precisely the present discounted value of the (infinite) future stream of payments of $375 per annum assuming a discount rate of 5 percent.

land values at a rate of t_V would lead to an annual tax revenue of $t_V V$. If the two taxes generate the same tax revenue, and therefore $t_R Y = t_V V$, then equation (5) implies that

$$(6) \qquad t_R = \frac{t_V}{t_V + r}$$

Equation (6) tells us that with an interest rate of 5 percent, a 3 percent tax on land values is equivalent to a 37.5 percent tax on land rents.

Our formal analysis thus provides us with some basic principles and insights into how land taxation works. We must remind ourselves, however, that all of this assumes full information and perfectly functioning land markets with zero (or low) transaction costs. In particular, our analysis assumes that agents (buyers and sellers) in the land market have unbiased expectations concerning future market conditions. In the real world, various sorts of imperfections may, to a certain extent, complicate matters. Nevertheless, the analysis reveals some fundamental and powerful tendencies in the response of land markets to various forms of land taxation.

THE INCIDENCE OF A TAX ON LAND

One of the fundamental questions that an economist asks about a tax is, Who really pays the tax? This question addresses the *incidence* of the tax— who bears its burden (i.e., whose income or wealth is reduced by the tax). The true burden of the tax need not fall on the individual (or entity) upon whom the tax is levied. For example, an excise tax on the production or sale of a particular commodity, say shoes, will not, in general, fall wholly on the producer of the good. Some of the tax burden will be shifted in the form of higher prices to the consumer of the commodity; in terms of our example, a tax on shoes will result in some increase in the price of shoes with a consequent reduction in the quantity of shoes that consumers will want to buy and that producers will supply. The burden of the tax will be shared by the producers and consumers of the good.

This process of shifting a tax is easily seen in terms of the economist's standard supply and demand diagram. In figure 4.1 we see that prior to the introduction of any tax, the market equilibrium occurs where the quantity demanded and the quantity supplied are equal (point A), with an initial equilibrium price of P_o and equilibrium quantity of Q_o. If a tax equal to the

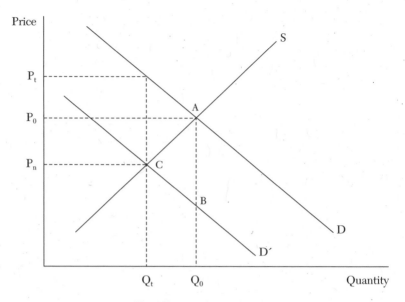

Figure 4.1. Tax effects with upward-sloping supply

distance from A to B (AB) is levied on purchases of the good, the demand curve will shift down by the amount AB to D', indicating that in order to keep consumer purchases at a level of Q_0, the price of the good must fall by AB (the amount of the tax). But this cannot be the new equilibrium, because at a lower price suppliers will see their profits fall and will be unwilling to supply Q_0. The new equilibrium, where quantity demanded equals quantity supplied, occurs at point C. And here we find that the burden of the tax is shared by producers and consumers: the gross price consumers pay for the good (including the tax) rises to P_t, but the net price producers receive falls to P_n.

In the case of land taxation, however, no such shifting takes place. Land cannot be produced like other goods; it is fixed in supply, or to use common economic jargon, the supply of land is perfectly inelastic.[4] As we see in figure

---

4. The notion that the supply of land is fixed is something of an overstatement. There are cases in which land has become so valuable that people have "produced" more land. For example, the Back Bay neighborhood in Boston was created by filling the tidewater flats of the Charles River over a 25-year period beginning in 1857. But thinking of land as fixed in supply is a useful and sensible first approximation.

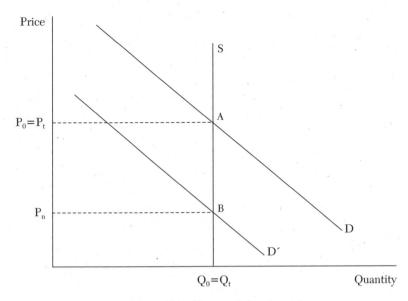

Figure 4.2. Tax effects with fixed supply

4.2, with a fixed supply of land, the net price does indeed fall by the full amount of the tax, AB, to P_n. Any attempt to raise the price (or rents) by landowners would be futile; at a higher price, less land would be demanded, which would result in an excess supply of land and downward pressure on the price of land. One of the principles of the theory of taxation is that a tax on a good that is fixed in supply falls wholly on the owner (supplier) of the good. Thus, basic economic analysis tells us that a tax on land is not shifted at all: it is borne entirely by landowners.

In fact, we already saw this result in the preceding section, where, in our algebraic exercise, we showed that levying a tax on land causes the value of the land to fall immediately by the full amount of the present discounted value of all present and future tax liabilities. Now we can better understand the rationale for this result.

THE NEUTRALITY AND EFFICIENCY OF LAND TAXATION

In addition to the question of who pays a tax, economists are concerned with the effects a tax has on the operation of the economic system. Ideally, what we want is a tax that generates the required level of revenue but has no adverse side effects on economic activities. The problem is that most taxes do have such adverse side effects. A tax on shoes, for example, will drive up the price of shoes and lead to reduced shoe consumption.

To follow our example a bit further, suppose that the initial price of a standard pair of shoes is $50 and that the government levies a $10-per-pair excise tax on shoes. Suppose, moreover, that in the new post-tax equilibrium, the price of shoes to consumers rises to $55 and the net revenue to producers falls to $45 per pair. In this new equilibrium, the quantity of shoes produced and sold will have fallen. The higher price will dissuade some consumers from their original level of shoe purchases. For instance, there may be someone who would have been willing to pay $52 for another pair of shoes but is not willing to pay $55. This represents a loss in economic welfare to society. Since it costs only $50 to produce an additional pair of shoes and someone is willing to pay $52 for another pair, the shoes should, from an economic perspective, be produced and consumed. In our example, there is thus a $2 loss in consumer welfare. That is, the excise tax results in a loss in economic welfare over and above the amount of the tax because it causes a distortion in the composition of output. In our example, too few pairs of shoes are produced and consumed as a result of the excise tax on shoes.

Economists use two different (but synonymous) terms to refer to this loss in economic welfare: the loss is often called the *excess burden* of the tax (i.e., the burden over and above the payment of the tax itself) or the *deadweight loss* resulting from the tax. Note that the excess burden (or deadweight loss) occurs because the tax discourages the production and consumption of the taxed good; output falls below the economically efficient level.

Land taxation is an interesting and important exception to this general rule that taxes cause deadweight loss. If a tax is levied on a good that is in fixed supply (like land), then there will be no reduction in the provision and consumption of the commodity. As we saw in figure 4.2, the tax does not lead to any change in the equilibrium quantity traded. A tax on land induces no change in the quantity of land supplied or demanded, and hence it does not distort the market outcome. The gross price of land (including the tax) remains unchanged; the net price to suppliers (landowners) falls by the full amount of the tax; and the quantity of land remains unchanged.

There is thus an economic argument in favor of land taxation: it generates revenue in an economically efficient way. Unlike most other taxes, it does not have any undesirable side effects on markets. In particular, it doesn't shift the

Two Historical Cases of Excess Burden Associated with Early Forms of Property Taxation

In this chapter we explain that the excess burden of the property tax comes from fewer and smaller buildings and other structures or improvements being built. Two early versions of the property tax created an excess burden by affecting the design of the structures that were built.

In 1696 the taxing authorities in Great Britain, seeking to tax the value of property in a relatively simple manner, introduced a tax on residences based on the number of windows. The "window tax," which lasted (quite amazingly) over 150 years, was the source of much discontent. One response to the tax was to board up windows in order to reduce the taxes on a dwelling. Another was to construct new residences with a minimum of windows. In Edinburgh, builders erected a whole row of houses without a single window in the bedroom story of any house! The loss of welfare (the excess burden of the tax) did not merely take an aesthetic form; the loss of light and fresh air was injurious to "health and vigor" as well.

Across the channel in France, François Mansart introduced a new architectural form (now known as the Mansard roof) in the seventeenth century. Since French houses were taxed according to the number of stories below the roof, Mansart simply extended the eaves downward to convert a three-story house into one with two stories! The excess burden was the choice of one design over others that would have been preferred but for the tax. Interestingly, Mansard roofs became quite popular both in Europe and in North America. For a modern manifestation, look at a McDonald's restaurant.

composition of output away from the taxed good. For this reason, economists refer to it as a *neutral* tax. Most taxes are nonneutral: they change the terms on which producers and consumers choose among goods. But land taxes have no such distorting effect. We have thus found that a tax on land is an efficient form of taxation—it is a neutral tax.

LAND TAXATION, SPECULATION, AND THE TIMING OF DEVELOPMENT

In this section we turn to the question of whether a land tax affects the timing of development. Proponents of land value taxation have long argued that one of its primary virtues is that it discourages speculation in land and encourages relatively early development of land parcels. The basic idea is that a tax on land values makes it more expensive to hold land in an undeveloped state. A land value tax makes speculative activities less profitable by increasing the cost of holding vacant land parcels. For example, in his classic *Progress and Poverty*, Henry George ([1879] 1962, 413) argued that "taxes on the value of land not only do not check production as do most other taxes, but they tend to increase production, by destroying speculative rent. . . . If land were taxed to anything near its rental value, no one could afford to hold land that he was not using, and, consequently, land not in use would be thrown open to those who would use it."

Although this claim seems plausible on first consideration, further thought suggests that it runs counter to one of the principles of land taxation that we have developed in this chapter. We found that land taxation is neutral—it does not directly affect the terms on which people make economic choices. But the antispeculation argument claims the opposite—that the tax is not neutral in a temporal context. The argument is that a land value tax alters decisions as to the timing of development: landowners will not hold land vacant and will develop it earlier than they would have in the absence of the tax.

Thus, we seem to be in an awkward corner: if the tax discourages holding land in a vacant state, it is not a neutral tax. Something has to give here. There was a lively debate on this very issue some years ago in the academic literature. What emerged from the debate very clearly is the following proposition: as long as land is properly assessed for tax purposes according to its "highest and best use," land value taxation is neutral in a temporal setting— that is, the time at which it is most profitable to develop a parcel of vacant land does not depend on whether it is subject to a tax on land value.[5]

---

5. See Bentick (1979), D. Mills (1981a), Wildasin (1982), Tideman (1982), and Oates and Schwab (1997). If land value is assessed for tax purposes at its value in actual use (instead of its highest and best use), then land taxation may induce earlier development. Alternatively, if preferential taxation is associated with the current use, as is the case in many states with respect to agricultural land, use-value assessment might delay development (England and Mohr 2003).

The underlying rationale for the neutrality of land value taxation over time is quite straightforward. As long as the tax on land is based on its highest and best use, and not on its actual use, the tax will be invariant with respect to any decisions made by the landowner.[6] The tax depends on the maximum rental income that the owner of the parcel *could* earn now and in the future, not on what the owner chooses to earn. The tax, at any moment of time, is thus a fixed sum that is independent of the decisions of the landowner. Or, to put it another way, land value taxation places the same penalty on land whether it is developed or not. As we have seen, the present discounted value of the stream of such current and future tax liabilities is immediately capitalized into the current value of the property. Thus, landowners, who suddenly find the value of their land subject to a new (and unforeseen) tax, experience an immediate capital loss equal to the present discounted value of the present and future tax liabilities. This is simply a fixed cost attached to the land. But it has no effect on the land's use. If the most profitable use of the land before the introduction of the tax was to develop it in five years, then its most profitable use after the levying of the tax is still to develop it five years hence. Land value taxation is thus neutral with respect to the timing, as well as the form, of land use.[7]

A simple example helps clarify this point. Consider a landowner who has two options. The owner can develop the parcel now and earn Y per year, every year in perpetuity. Alternatively, the owner can leave the parcel undeveloped this year and develop it the following year. In this case the owner will earn nothing this year and then, starting next year, earn X per year, every year in perpetuity. We would expect the landowner to choose the alternative for which the discounted present value of the rents is higher. The question then is, Under what circumstances will the landowner choose to develop now, and under what circumstances will the landowner choose to postpone development?

---

6. We have simplified things a bit here. As Vickrey (1970) explains, *any* assessment that does not depend on the decisions of the landowner will generate this neutrality result. Vickrey, for example, suggests that freezing land use decisions for assessment purposes at a certain point in time will lead to neutrality. Thus, assessing at highest and best use will lead to neutrality, but there are alternative assessment practices that will lead to the same outcome.

7. A tax on land rents, incidentally, is clearly a neutral tax. It simply reduces the net return on all alternative uses of land by the same proportion. It thus reduces the value of land holdings, but has no allocative effects on land use decisions.

Suppose initially that there is no tax on land. The landowner in this case should wait and develop his property next year if

(7)
$$\frac{0}{(1+r)} + \frac{X}{(1+r)^2} + \frac{X}{(1+r)^3} + \cdots \geq \frac{Y}{(1+r)} + \frac{Y}{(1+r)^2} + \frac{Y}{(1+r)^3} + \cdots$$

Equation (3) tells us that we can rewrite equation (7) as

(7′)
$$\frac{X}{(1+r)r} \geq \frac{Y}{r}$$

or equivalently,

(8)
$$\frac{X-Y}{r} \geq Y$$

Postponing development involves both costs and benefits. If the landowner waits to develop, the owner must forgo the rents that could have been earned in the first year, Y. But in return, starting in the second year, the owner will earn additional rents of $(X - Y)$; the present value of those additional rents is $(X - Y) / r$. The landowner should postpone development if the benefits of waiting are at least as great as the costs.

Now suppose that the government imposes a land tax, the amount of which is completely independent of the way the landowner uses the land. For example, the land could be taxed according to its value in its highest and best use. In this case, when making the decision, the landowner must subtract the present value of the tax payments from both sides of equation (7). But the land tax will be the same regardless of whether the landowner chooses to develop the land now or to wait. As a result, the imposition of this tax will not influence the landowner's decision. It is as if the landowner has a balance scale. The benefits from postponing development are piled on the left arm of the scale and the benefits of developing now on the right side. The land tax removes an equal amount from both arms and thus cannot change the way the scale tips.

There is an important qualification to this proposition. It assumes that the owner of the parcel does not face any liquidity problems. If, for example, the landowner does not have the means to pay the taxes on the land until the time of development (and cannot borrow at existing rates of interest to pay the taxes), then the owner may be induced to develop the land earlier than otherwise. (Of course, a more profitable option, in principle, would be to sell the land to someone who has the wherewithal to hold the land vacant until its profit-maximizing time of development.) But aside from this liquidity issue, the basic neutrality argument holds: land value taxation is neutral in a temporal context, which means that the timing of development that maximizes the return from the use of the land is not affected by whether (or at what rate) land is taxed.

Arnott (2005) presents an intriguing extension of this line of argument. As we explained, the land tax we have described is completely independent of the way landowners choose to use their land. In Arnott's terminology, the land tax that we have described is a tax on raw site value. Arnott argues that it may be difficult to estimate raw site value if there are relatively few sales of undeveloped land in a community. He then asks an important question, namely, Is there an alternative to a tax on raw site value that would also be neutral? The answer turns out to be yes. Arnott shows that a community can achieve neutrality by carefully choosing different tax rates on undeveloped land, the value of buildings and other structures or improvements, and postdevelopment residual site value (i.e., the combined value of the land and improvements minus the value of the improvements). Arnott shows that in the special case where rents grow at a constant rate and vacant land does not generate rent, neutrality can be achieved if (1) undeveloped land is not taxed, (2) postdevelopment residual site value is taxed at a rate chosen to meet the community's revenue requirements, and (3) improvements are subsidized.

Arnott's paper is an important contribution to the land taxation literature. It tells us that neutrality is possible even if communities are unable to develop accurate estimates of the value of undeveloped land. Thus, a trade-off between neutrality and administrative feasibility may not be inevitable.

A NOTE ON PROPERTY TAXATION, LAND TAXATION, AND TAX REFORM

There are two distinct ways in which the taxation of land can be introduced (or increased), and the distinction between the two is crucial to understanding the effects of land taxation in the context of existing proposals for tax reform. In the first instance, the public authority introduces a tax on land (or an increase in the existing rate of land taxation) with no changes in the rates of other existing taxes. In this case, there is an increase in the public revenue that may be employed for increased public spending, to retire outstanding government bonds, or for other purposes. This in fact is the implicit assumption of our analysis to this point; we have looked at the consequences of raising the tax on land while holding all other taxes fixed.

In the second case, the increase in revenues from land taxation is offset by a reduction in rates on other existing taxes. In this case, there is no change in total public revenue (so-called equal-yield tax reform). The increase in revenue from one source (in our case, the taxation of land) is offset by reduced revenue from other taxes.

Why is this distinction important here? We have already seen that the introduction of a tax on land (or an increase in its rate) will not affect the way the land is used. In addition, we have seen that the tax is borne entirely by the landowners when the tax (or its increase) is levied. But suppose that instead of simply introducing land taxation, the government reduces rates on another tax base so that there is no change in total revenue (i.e., our second case above). In the context of property taxation, this type of tax reform typically takes the form of an increase in the rate of taxation of land accompanied by a decrease in the rate of taxation of the improvements on the land. Under the standard or usual form of property taxation, the value of the land and the improvements on the land are taxed at the same rate. The tax base in this case is simply the overall value of land plus improvements. However, this need not be so. The assessor can estimate separately the value of the land and the value of the improvements. (Practical issues of land assessment are addressed in chapter 8.) Land and improvements can then be taxed at different rates. A system of property taxation in which land and improvements are taxed at different rates is usually called a *split-rate system.*

What is important for our purposes here is that the equal-yield type of reform, where an increase in the rate of land taxation is coupled with a reduction in the tax rate on improvements, is not neutral, because, even though the tax on land is neutral, the tax on improvements is not. We might, for example, expect the lower tax on improvements to lead to an increase in the density of land use, since a lower rate on improvements provides an incentive to develop land more intensively. Improvements (unlike land) are not fixed in quantity; thus, a tax on improvements provides a direct incentive to reduce the number of buildings and other improvements per unit of land. Consequently, we get very different answers to our questions concerning the impact of land taxation depending on whether the tax is introduced with no offsetting reductions in other taxes or whether it is part of an equal-yield tax reform package.

Consider, for example, the Pittsburgh experience. In 1979–1980, in response to a severe budget crisis, city officials restructured the existing split-rate tax system by raising the tax rate on land to more than five times the rate on improvements while leaving the tax rate on improvements unchanged. This was clearly a move to increase the revenue from property taxes; it was explicitly not an equal-yield reform. (See chapter 2 for more on the Pittsburgh experience.) The impact of this kind of property tax reform will clearly be very different from that of a reform package that reduces the tax on improvements so as to leave overall revenue from property taxation unchanged. We explore this issue further in the next section.

THE CONSEQUENCES OF SUBSTITUTING A LAND TAX FOR A TAX ON IMPROVEMENTS

In this section of the chapter we consider the consequences of simultaneously raising the tax on land and adjusting the tax on improvements so that total tax revenue remains unchanged. Jan Brueckner's 1986 paper "A Modern Analysis of the Effects of Site Value Taxation" in the *National Tax Journal* is the essential contribution on this question, and we rely heavily on that paper in this section.

Brueckner begins by asking the following question: If a city raises the tax on land, would it need to raise the tax on improvements in order to leave total tax revenue unchanged, or would it need to lower the tax on improvements? At first blush, the answer might seem obvious; the city should lower the tax on improvements. But further reflection suggests that this is not necessarily the case. The intuition is as follows. Suppose that the city lowers the tax on improvements. We would expect developers to substitute improvements for land—for example, they might build four-story buildings instead of three-story buildings (if zoning regulations permit). Suppose that they build so many additional buildings that taxes collected on improvements rise even though the tax rate has fallen. In this situation, the city faces what Haughwout and others (2004) have called a "revenue hill." If we are on the upward-sloping part of that hill, tax revenues will fall when tax rates fall; in contrast, if we are on the downward-sloping part of the hill, tax revenues will rise when tax rates fall. In this case, the city is on the downward-sloping part of the hill and must raise the tax on improvements to offset the increase in tax revenue from the new higher tax on land. As Brueckner shows and this simple example suggests, the key factor is the sensitivity of the supply of improvements to changes in the tax rate on improvements. Brueckner examines the evidence on the magnitude of this elasticity and concludes that for plausible parameter values, the intuitive answer—that the city would need to lower the tax on improvements—is correct. This is what Brueckner calls the normal case.

Brueckner then makes the important point that in the normal case, a revenue-neutral increase in the land tax and decrease in the improvement tax increases the amount of development in the city; that is, the density of development rises. This is not surprising, since if the tax on improvements falls (as it must in the normal case), then the quantity of improvements rises.

Still assuming the normal case, Brueckner next addresses the question of what happens to land values when the land tax rate is increased and the improvement tax rate is decreased. The result depends on whether the shift to a split-rate tax is made by a single community within a larger metropolitan area or by all taxing jurisdictions in the area. In the case of a single jurisdiction cutting its improvement tax—and gaining improvements relative to its neighbors—the value of land will go up. This result is very important, but far from intuitively obvious. How can landowners gain if the city taxes land more heavily? Recall our discussion of the neutrality of the land tax. As we argued above, land taxes are unusual in that the taxation of land does not create a deadweight loss, because the supply of land is perfectly inelastic. So we would expect that lowering the tax on improvements and raising the tax on land would reduce the overall deadweight loss from taxation in this city. We can think of land rent as a residual; that is, land earns everything that remains after the other factors of production (e.g., labor and improvements) earn their normal returns. This means that a reduction in the deadweight loss will be reflected in higher land rents—what was deadweight loss becomes surplus value that is captured by the landowner. Brueckner shows that in the normal case and in the case of a single community making the change, the impact of lower deadweight losses will more than offset the impact of higher land taxes, and as a consequence, land values will rise. Brueckner then looks at the case where all of the communities in a metropolitan area adopt a split-rate tax and shows that, in this case, the value of land will decrease.

Brueckner's single-community result provides a powerful argument in the debate over the political feasibility of a land tax. We might expect landowners to oppose heavier taxes on land. But Brueckner's result tells us that if they understand the economic implications of taxing land, they will realize that their opposition to the land tax may be misguided.

LAND TAXATION AND URBAN SPRAWL

Opponents of land taxation have sometimes argued that a land tax will increase urban sprawl. Their argument is that a land tax gives landowners at the fringe of an urban area (often farmers) an incentive to develop their land. Is this so?

Again, the answer depends in part on what happens to other taxes—in particular, the tax on improvements—when the tax on land is raised. Suppose for the moment that a community raises the tax on land but leaves the tax on improvements unchanged (the Pittsburgh case). It is not difficult to see that this increase in the land tax will have no impact on sprawl. The argument here is a straightforward application of the principle that land taxes are neutral. The land tax will be the same regardless of whether the landowner chooses to develop the land or to continue to leave it in agriculture. As a result, the imposition of this tax will not influence the landowner's decision. Again, we appeal to the analogy of a balance scale we presented above. The landowner piles the benefits from development on the left arm of the scale and the benefits of agriculture on the right side. The land tax removes an equal amount from both arms and thus cannot change the way the balance scale tips.[8]

Now suppose that a community simultaneously raises the tax on land and lowers the tax on improvements so that total tax collections are unchanged. The analysis in this case is less straightforward, but Brueckner and Kim (2003) shed some light on this question. They argue that the traditional single-rate property tax has two effects. First, the property tax reduces density because it encourages developers to use fewer improvements on each acre of land. This is just an application of the principle that, in general, a tax on something discourages its use; the property tax is a tax on improvements (as well as land) and thus discourages the use of improvements. With a fixed population, lower density means that more land will be used for housing, and thus the property tax leads to a larger urban area. So this first effect increases sprawl.

---

8. There is, of course, an implicit assumption that the land tax does not depend on the way the land is actually used (e.g., land is taxed at its highest and best use). If this is not the case, then the land tax could certainly encourage development and sprawl. A tax based on current use, for example, would violate this neutrality result.

Second, the property tax increases the price of housing. People will respond to the higher price by consuming less housing and more of other goods. If each household consumes less housing, then less land is needed to accommodate the city's fixed population. So this second effect decreases sprawl.

Since these two effects go in opposite directions, Brueckner and Kim cannot offer a clear theoretical statement on the impact of the standard property tax. They do, however, show that the net effect of the property tax on sprawl depends on the sensitivity of the supply of housing and other improvements to the tax rate and the sensitivity of the demand for housing to the relative price of land and improvements. In particular, they show that if the demand for housing is fairly insensitive to changes in the price of housing, then the first effect is likely to dominate the second and the property tax will increase sprawl. On the other hand, if the supply of housing is relatively insensitive, then the second effect is likely to dominate the first and the property tax will decrease sprawl. Brueckner and Kim sift through the statistical evidence on these two key variables and conclude that under realistic values of the parameters, the standard property tax leads to a spatial expansion of the city—that is, the first effect is likely to dominate the second effect.

What does the Brueckner and Kim analysis tell us about the impact of substituting a land tax for a traditional property tax, holding revenue constant? Substituting a land tax for a traditional property tax extends the Brueckner and Kim case to the limit. That is, implementing a land tax is equivalent to continually reducing the tax on structures and raising the tax on land until the tax on structures is zero. This implies that a revenue-neutral switch to a land tax will decrease sprawl. Brueckner and Kim's paper will not end the concerns that a land tax will lead to an expansion of cities and the loss of open space. This is clearly a very complicated issue, and undoubtedly more work will be needed to resolve this question. Their paper does, however, suggest that these concerns may not be well founded.[9]

---

9. E. Mills (1998) offers a somewhat different perspective on this issue. His paper focuses on business improvements, as opposed to homes as in Brueckner and Kim's analysis (2003). Mills shows that in this case the impact of a property tax is unambiguous; a traditional property tax must lead to smaller cities than a land tax.

THE REVENUE POTENTIAL OF A LAND TAX

Henry George argued that a tax on land could serve as the "single tax" to finance public expenditure—that we could substitute a tax on land for all other taxes. Although there are probably few people who today would agree with the single-tax proposition, the revenue potential of a land tax remains an interesting and important issue.

There at least two ways to approach this issue. First, we might compare the tax base under a land tax to the tax base under alternative tax policies in order to get some sense of the revenue governments might raise by taxing land. Wolff (1998), for example, estimates that the total value of land held by households in 1995 (in 2007 dollars) was $5.5 trillion, almost exactly the same as total household income. It is tempting to conclude that, since the tax bases are very similar, a 20 percent tax on household income would yield the same tax revenue as a 20 percent tax on land value. This comparison, however, is very misleading. The relevant comparison is between a tax on land rent—not land value—and household income. Household income measures the income households receive in a year. Land value, on the other hand, does not have a time dimension. In order to compare tax rates on income and land, we would need to convert the tax rate on land values into a tax rate on land rents. Equation (6) tells us that a 20 percent tax on land values is equivalent to an 80 percent tax on land rents (assuming an interest rate of 5 percent). We therefore conclude that a very high tax rate on land rents would be required in order to replace the federal individual income tax.

Although it thus seems unlikely that the federal government could raise a substantial share of its revenue by taxing land, it is quite possible that a land tax could generate significant revenue for individual states. Reschovsky (1998), for example, finds that if Wisconsin raised the tax rate on land by roughly one-third, it could reduce income taxes by 10 percent or sales taxes by 15 percent.

Second, we might turn to economic theory to assess the revenue potential of land taxation. The result from theory is striking and provocative: no tax can generate more revenue than a tax on land.[10] The following simple exam-

---

10. There is an implicit assumption here that the other factors of production are always available at the going market price (in economic jargon, the supply of other factors is *perfectly elastic*).

ple illustrates the argument. Consider a firm that produces a good with a fixed amount of land (say 100 acres) and labor. Workers are available at a wage of $10. The first worker that the firm hires can produce goods that can be sold for $13; the second, goods that can be sold for $12; and the third, goods that can be sold for $10.

Suppose initially that there are no taxes in this economy. What will the firm do? At a wage of $10, firms would be willing to hire all three workers, and since, by assumption, all three are willing to work for $10, this must be the equilibrium wage. Together, they will produce goods worth $13 + $12 + $10 = $35, and they will receive $30 in wages. At several points we have argued that we can think of land rents as a residual. That is, land rents are equal to what remains after goods have been sold and other factors of production have been paid their returns (e.g., labor has been paid its wages). Thus, in this simple example, land would earn a rent of $35 − $30 = $5.

Now consider a tax on land rents. A tax on land rents could generate up to $5 in tax revenue. Since the supply of land is perfectly inelastic, landowners can do nothing even if the government taxed away all rents.

Could a tax on wages generate more than $5? The answer, somewhat surprisingly, is no. Suppose, for example, that the government imposes a $2 tax on labor. In this case, the equilibrium wage must rise to $12 so that workers keep $10 after paying the $2 tax. The firm would be willing to hire only two workers at a wage of $12. These workers pay a total of $4 in taxes, less than the taxes collected under the land tax.

Why does a tax on wages in this example generate less tax revenue than the tax on land rents? Consider the economic consequences of the $2 wage tax. The third worker is not hired and therefore pays no tax. But the third worker did not generate land rents before there was a tax on labor (he produced goods that were sold for $10 and he received $10 in wages). The second worker is hired and pays the $2 wage tax. But the second worker generated $12 − $10 in rents when there was no tax on labor. Therefore the second and third workers generate the same tax revenue under both a wage tax and a tax on land rents.

Now consider the first worker. The firm hires this worker when there is a $2 tax on labor, so this worker pays the $2 tax. But in the absence of the wage tax, the first worker generated $13 − $10 = $3 of land rent and all $3 would be captured by a tax on land rents. This result is not an artifact of this particular numerical example. The general result is that a tax on labor can capture only part of the surplus that labor generates, but a tax on land rents captures the entire surplus. Therefore, a tax on land rents can, in principle, generate more tax revenue than a tax on wages. Admittedly, we have provided a highly simplified example in order to make the basic point. Tax policies in the real world obviously introduce a whole raft of complications. But our objective here is simply to show that the revenue potential of land taxation may be much greater than is often supposed.

SUMMARY AND CONCLUSIONS

Our goal in this chapter was to summarize the insights that economic theory can offer on the consequences of land taxation. We initially considered the consequences of raising the tax on land while leaving the tax on improvements constant. Three key results emerge:

- The burden of a land tax falls entirely on landowners.
- A land tax is neutral; it does not distort economic decisions and therefore does not generate an excess burden (deadweight loss).
- A land tax has no impact on the timing of land development.

We then looked at the impact of simultaneously raising the tax on land and changing the tax on improvements so as to leave total tax revenue unchanged. We find that when done by a single community, raising the tax on land and cutting the tax on improvements is, somewhat surprisingly, likely to benefit landowners. We also find some evidence (although this issue is complex) that a shift to a land tax is likely to decrease urban sprawl. Finally, our exercise with some basic economic theory suggests that the revenue potential of land taxation may be much greater than is suggested by simply looking at the share of land rents in national income.

❖ 5 ❖

Fairness and Distributional Issues

ELIZABETH PLUMMER

EVERY TAX CAN and should be evaluated on four basic standards: revenue sufficiency, convenience, efficiency, and equity. Earlier chapters evaluated the land value tax with respect to the first three standards; this chapter focuses on equity—more commonly referred to as fairness.[1] An equitable tax is one that fairly distributes the tax burden. Almost everyone would agree that fairness is an essential feature of a good tax system. It can be difficult, however, to achieve consensus on the relative degree of fairness. When is a tax fair?

Fairness is generally evaluated according to the ability-to-pay principle of taxation—the idea that people should be taxed according to their financial ability to support government activities, regardless of the benefits they receive. In other words, the rich should pay more taxes than the poor. Taxes in most countries are based on some dimension of a taxpayer's ability to pay. For example, income taxes are based on a person's inflow of income during the year, and property taxes are based on a person's accumulation of resources in the form of real property (Jones and Rhoades-Catanach 2008, 32).[2]

---

1. This chapter uses the terms *equity* and *fairness* synonymously.

2. An alternative principle of taxation is the benefit principle, the idea that those who benefit from the government's goods and services should be the ones to pay for them, regardless of their financial ability to pay. The benefit principle suffers from two limitations. First, many government programs provide the greatest benefit to those who can least afford to pay (e.g., welfare). Second, benefits can be difficult to measure (e.g., national defense, educated children, public roads).

VERTICAL AND HORIZONTAL EQUITY

Evaluating the concept of fairness requires consideration of both vertical equity and horizontal equity. *Vertical equity* is the idea that persons with a greater ability to pay (e.g., more income) should owe more tax than persons with a lesser ability to pay. To evaluate the degree of vertical equity, one can examine the amount of taxes paid as a percentage of income and classify the tax system as proportional, progressive, or regressive. In a *proportional* tax system, everyone's tax payment is the same percentage of their income, regardless of income level (e.g., the tax liability for all persons is equal to 10 percent of their income). A *progressive* tax system imposes a relatively larger tax burden on those with a greater ability to pay. Taxes are a larger percentage of income for persons with higher incomes (e.g., persons with $50,000 of income pay 10 percent of that amount as tax, and persons with $90,000 of income pay 12 percent of that as tax). In contrast, a *regressive* tax system imposes a relatively smaller tax burden on those with a greater ability to pay (e.g., persons with $50,000 of income pay 10 percent of that amount as tax, and persons with $90,000 of income only pay 7 percent of that as tax).

Progressive tax systems are generally viewed as more equitable than either proportional or regressive tax systems because the importance of each additional dollar of income declines as a taxpayer's total income increases. In other words, people value income spent on necessities (e.g., food and shelter) more than they value income available for nonnecessities (e.g., a second home, vacations). By imposing a relatively larger tax burden as income increases, a progressive tax system promotes equal sacrifice across taxpayers.

Horizontal equity is concerned with the equal treatment of equals and requires that taxpayers who are equal in all important respects be taxed equally. In other words, persons with the same ability to pay (e.g., the same income level) should pay the same amount of tax. Horizontal equity helps ensure that taxpayers are not taxed arbitrarily. There is little disagreement among economists and policy makers that a tax system should be horizontally equitable (Musgrave 1990; Cordes 1999).

Evaluating a Tax System's Vertical and Horizontal Equity

Vertical and horizontal equity are both desirable features that enhance equity. Actually evaluating a tax system's fairness, however, can be difficult because doing so requires a measure of a taxpayer's economic well-being, which determines the ability to pay taxes. But how should economic well-being be measured? Should it be income or wealth? Over what period of time should it be measured? In an income tax system, for example, a taxpayer's ability to pay is determined by taxable income, which requires adding up income from various sources (e.g., salaries, interest and dividends, business income), and then subtracting allowable expenses. Allowable expenses include business expenses, as well as additional specified amounts that reflect a family's need to provide for basic necessities.[3] Unfortunately, annual income is a twelve-month measure that fails to capture fluctuations in income—for example, taxpayers early in their careers with relatively low salaries but high future earning potential, or business owners having an unusually good or bad year. Therefore, when evaluating tax-system equity, many policy makers and economists favor measuring a taxpayer's ability to pay according to lifetime income as opposed to annual income. Lifetime measures are less subject to temporary fluctuations, and individuals are likely to make consumption decisions on the basis of lifetime income, not annual income (Fullerton and Metcalf 2002).

Consider the simple example, shown in table 5.1, of two taxpayers (A and B) who each live for two years. Their lifetime incomes are the same, but their annual incomes differ. Assume that there is a land value tax in effect with a 2 percent rate and that each taxpayer purchases $10,000 of land at the beginning of year 1. Each taxpayer thus pays taxes of $200 each year.[4]

To evaluate equity, we compute in table 5.1 the relative tax burden for each taxpayer for each year (i.e., $200 of taxes paid, divided by either annual income or lifetime income). If we use annual income to compute the tax burden, the tax burden ranges from 0.8 percent to 4.0 percent, and the land value tax appears to be regressive (i.e., the tax burden is larger for the taxpayer with the smaller income). Alternatively, if we use lifetime income, taxpayer A and taxpayer B are considered equals. The average tax burden is 0.67

---

3. For U.S. federal tax purposes, all taxpayers can deduct a standard deduction amount, which is based on filing status (e.g., single, married filing joint, head of household). In addition, taxpayers are allowed to deduct a specified exemption amount for each household member. These exemption amounts are reduced if a taxpayer's adjusted gross income exceeds a specified threshold. In lieu of the standard deduction amount, taxpayers can itemize and deduct certain personal expenses.

4. Let us assume that A and B were both aware of the obligation to pay a land tax when they purchased their respective parcels. If so, the tax is reflected in, or "capitalized" in, their purchase prices of $10,000. I discuss capitalization further later in the chapter.

Table 5.1 Example of tax burdens with annual versus lifetime income

	Income over time ($)		Tax burden using annual income (%)		Tax burden using lifetime income (%)	
	A	B	A	B	A	B
Year 1	15,000	25,000	1.33	0.80	0.67	0.67
Year 2	15,000	5,000	1.33	4.00	0.67	0.67
Lifetime	30,000	30,000				

percent, and the land value tax appears to be horizontally equitable. In sum, the income measure used to evaluate any tax system—including a land value tax—can greatly affect the inferences about a tax system's vertical and horizontal equity.

Additional Equity Issues to Consider

Proponents of land value taxation often make a very different ethical case for taxing land values. Instead of arguing that some citizens would benefit more from an extra dollar of after-tax income than others, they argue that taxing land more heavily than improvements is fair because land values do not increase through owner efforts. Land values increase over time because of population growth and community improvements made by the government or the private sector (e.g., utility infrastructure, transportation). Taxing land values generates revenue that can benefit the community that provided the individual landowners with their unearned increases in land value. Netzer (1998a, x) describes this as a moral basis for land value taxation. Indeed, Henry George regarded the land value tax as a levy that is "the taking by the community, for the use of the community, of that value which is the creation of the community" (George [1879] 1962, 421).

An additional criterion for evaluating fairness is the wherewithal-to-pay principle, which asserts that taxes should generally be imposed when a transaction occurs and the taxpayer has cash to pay the tax. Although a land value tax violates this principle, a land value tax is no different from the traditional property tax in this respect. Both the traditional property tax and the land value tax are annual taxes based on an asset's value as of the assessment date (e.g., January 1 of each year). A tax payment is required even when there is no corresponding cash flow with which to pay the tax. Regardless, ad valorem taxes are widely used, and their strengths are generally considered to outweigh this downside.

Differential Tax Incidence

The current property tax system of most jurisdictions imposes a uniform tax rate on both land and improvement values. If a jurisdiction were to adopt a land value tax, that tax would most likely replace the traditional property tax. Therefore, most of this chapter's discussion focuses on the differential tax incidence of a land value tax compared with a property tax—that is, how the tax burden would change if a jurisdiction replaced the uniform property tax with a land value tax that generated the same amount of tax revenue. Alternatively, a jurisdiction could adopt a split-rate system and increase the tax rate on land while—most likely—decreasing the tax rate on improvements. Therefore, comparing a land value tax with a traditional property tax still provides an appropriate indication of the direction of tax shifting, although the magnitude of the shifts would be less under a split-rate system.[5]

In the next two sections, I discuss how switching to a land value tax would affect the relative tax burden across taxpayer groups. The relative tax burden depends primarily on land intensity (the ratio of land value to total property value) and on prereform land ownership. I then discuss studies that examine the distributional effects of a land value tax, as well as evidence on how land ownership varies across households of varying income levels. The chapter concludes with a brief discussion of some challenges facing a fair land value tax.

---

5. In chapter 4 of this volume, Wallace E. Oates and Robert M. Schwab discuss the work of Jan Brueckner (1986), who argues that a government might need to increase the tax rate on improvements when it increases the tax rate on land in order to make the tax reform revenue neutral. Whether the tax rate on improvements should be increased or decreased depends on the sensitivity of the supply of improvements to changes in the tax rate on improvements (elasticity of substitution). After examining the evidence, Brueckner (1986) concludes that a government would most likely need to decrease the tax rate on improvements—what Brueckner refers to as the normal case. In chapter 4, Oates and Schwab also discuss differential tax incidence and contrast it with absolute tax incidence.

STATUTORY INCIDENCE VERSUS ECONOMIC INCIDENCE

The evidence and discussion below focus on the statutory incidence of a land value tax—that is, on how a land value tax affects the legal tax liabilities paid by property owners. The discussion does not consider the economic incidence of the land value tax—that is, who bears the ultimate tax burden after we allow for possible tax shifting. In some instances, a tax burden can be shifted from one taxpayer to another so that the tax's statutory incidence differs from its economic incidence. For example, a tax assessed on business property is legally paid by the business, but the tax's real burden can be shifted to customers (higher prices), to employees (lower wages), or to other factors of production (lower payments for materials). If market conditions inhibit tax shifting, then the tax burden will be borne by the business owner in the form of lower earnings or market value.

As with any tax, tax shifting will affect the land value tax's ultimate economic incidence. Shifting opportunities will vary across property types, across industries, and across time. For example, business owners interact with several other parties (customers, employees, and suppliers), which increases their opportunities for tax shifting. Owners of apartments and rental properties can shift some of the tax to their tenants. In contrast, homeowners—in their dual role as owners and occupants—are generally thought to have fewer shifting opportunities and are more likely to bear both the legal and economic incidence of a property or land value tax.

The ultimate economic incidence of a land value tax also depends on how the tax affects property development and land values. A primary reason for advocating a move from a property tax to a land value tax is to change property owners' incentives and encourage them to develop land more intensely. However, whether a land value tax will lead to an increase or decrease in land values is unclear (see Brueckner 1986 and chapters 4 and 6 of this volume). Even if property owners did not change their development plans, land values would change because of capitalization effects, which are discussed below. Any changes in land values will ultimately affect the long-run economic incidence of the land value tax burden.

INCIDENCE OF A LAND VALUE TAX

The statutory tax burden of a land value tax is borne by the landowners. If land ownership is concentrated among high-income individuals, then a land value tax will be more progressive with respect to income than a uniform property tax that taxes both land and improvements. Unfortunately, data on land ownership is poor in most jurisdictions, making it difficult to assess whether a land value tax would be progressive. However, if a land value tax is substituted for a traditional property tax, there are two general observations that hold true regardless of the effects on progressivity. The first observation is that a land value tax increases the tax burden for owners of land-intensive properties. The second observation is that moving from a property tax to a land value tax affects individual landowners very differently, depending on how much they paid for their property. I discuss each of these issues below.

Land Intensity

Land intensity is measured by the ratio of land value to total property value. If a uniform property tax is replaced with a land value tax, owners of property with above-average land intensity will experience a tax increase, and owners with below-average land intensity will experience a tax decrease. Depending on the tax rate, the changes in tax liability could be considerable.

It is important to note that land intensity refers to the ratio of land value, not land size, to total value. Land value depends on both the amount of land and the value per unit (e.g., per acre). Therefore, an owner could own a large parcel of land whose value is not particularly great, because of the property's location or topography. Similarly, the land intensity ratios for identical businesses (e.g., gas stations) may differ significantly depending on whether the business is located in an urban area, with high land values, or a rural area, with relatively lower land values.

Consider the scenario shown in table 5.2. Each of the three property owners has total property valued at $100. Under a uniform 1 percent property tax, each owner's tax liability is $1.00. If the property tax is replaced with a revenue-neutral land value tax, the required tax rate on land is 1.54 percent, and total tax collections remain at $3.00.[6] However, because of differences in

---

6. For simplicity, the example in table 5.2 assumes that land values do not change when a land value tax system is implemented. This is unlikely to be a realistic assumption, at least in the long run, because of the effects of development changes and tax capitalization. However, when transitioning to a land value tax, assessing offices are likely to use the assessed land values that are currently on the rolls. This example should therefore be interpreted as a description of the short-term distribution effects that are likely to occur when replacing the property tax with a land value tax.

Table 5.2 Example of tax burdens with different land intensity

Property owner	Land intensity	Total value ($)	Land value ($)	Improvement value ($)	1% tax on total value ($)	1.54% tax on land value ($)	Change in tax liability
A	0.50	100	50	50	1.00	0.77	23% decrease
B	0.65	100	65	35	1.00	1.00	No change
C	0.80	100	80	20	1.00	1.23	23% increase
Total		300	195	105	3.00	3.00	

land intensity ratios across properties, the land value tax changes the distribution of tax liabilities. Owner A's land intensity ratio is below the average (0.65), which means that A's liability decreases, whereas owner C's ratio is above the average, which means that C's tax liability increases. Owner B's land intensity ratio is exactly equal to the average, so B's tax liability does not change.

Compared with a uniform property tax on both land and improvements, a land value tax shifts a larger tax burden to properties with high land intensity ratios, including vacant land, agricultural land, mineral properties, and land-intensive businesses such as car dealerships. Properties with relatively low land intensity ratios (e.g., condominiums) are likely to see a tax decrease. Because land intensity ratios vary systematically by industry, moving to a land value tax shifts the tax burden across industries. Industries that are more land intensive are likely to see a tax increase, whereas labor- or capital-intensive industries are likely to see a tax decrease.

Whether a land value tax increases progressivity among homeowners depends on whether land intensity ratios increase or decrease as homeowner income increases. If land intensity decreases as income increases—for example, if upper-income individuals buy larger, more luxurious homes, but the lot sizes are not especially large—then a land value tax is less progressive than a property tax.

Prereform Land Ownership

Transitioning from a property tax to a land value tax will also have very different effects on individual landowners depending on how much they paid for their property, because expected future tax costs affect an asset's current

Table 5.3 Example of capitalization of shift from property tax to land value tax

	With property taxes ($)	Taxes increase under a land value tax ($)	Taxes decrease under a land value tax ($)
Expected annual cash flows, before property tax	100	100	100
Annual property taxes	8	10	5
Expected annual cash flows, after property tax	92	90	95
Implied market value at 10% return	920	900	950

market value—an effect referred to as *tax capitalization*. If the tax costs of owning a property increase, there will be less demand for the property and the property's market value will decrease. Conversely, if a property's tax costs decrease, there will be more demand for the property and its market value will increase.

Replacing a property tax with a land value tax will shift wealth among existing property owners because of the effects of tax capitalization. If a land value tax causes a property's future tax payments to increase, then the property's market value will decrease. The decline in property value means that the tax burden is borne by the owner who holds the property at the time the law changes. On the other hand, if a land value tax causes a property's taxes to decrease, the property's market value will increase, creating a windfall gain for the current property owner.

Consider the simplified example shown in table 5.3. Assume that a property generates an annual before-tax cash flow of $100 and that property taxes are $8 annually. Also assume that, because of opportunities to earn an equivalent return in alternative investments, investors require a 10 percent rate of return on this property before they will invest in it. This suggests that the property's market value is $920 ($92/10%). Now assume that the current tax system is replaced by a land value tax and that the property's taxes increase from $8 to $10. This means that the property's market value drops to $900, and the tax burden is borne by the owner who holds the property at the time the law changes. Conversely, if the land value tax caused the property's taxes to decrease from $10 to $5, the property's market value would increase to $950, creating a windfall for the current property owner.

Changing from a property tax system to a land value tax system will redistribute wealth through these capitalization effects, and policy makers might consider ways of compensating taxpayers hurt by the change in tax systems. Significant changes in federal tax policy are often phased in over time or have grandfather clauses to soften the impact. Such features could also be used when transitioning to a land value tax.

EVIDENCE ON THE DISTRIBUTIONAL EFFECTS OF A LAND VALUE TAX

Increased interest in land value taxation has motivated economic researchers to examine the differential tax incidence of a land value tax compared with a traditional property tax. In general, these studies focus on a specific geographic area (e.g., a single city) and estimate the tax burden of a hypothetical land value tax. This hypothetical distribution can be compared with the actual distribution under the current property tax system to determine how a land value tax would redistribute the tax burden across property owners. These studies help identify which taxpayer groups would see a decrease in their actual tax payments (winners) and which taxpayers would see an increase (losers).

Unfortunately, land value data are poor, and data on the income or other socioeconomic characteristics of landowners are generally not available. This limits our ability to assess the land value tax's distributional effects. Moreover, the estimates in the different studies come from different geographic areas with different existing rules for calculating the property tax and from authors who use different assumptions to make up for the problematic data. Regardless of these limitations, the studies discussed below provide useful estimates on a land value tax's redistributive effects.

It is important to keep in mind at least two significant assumptions made in these studies. First, the calculations of differential tax incidence are generally based on the assumption that there is no change in land values after a land value tax is implemented. However, as discussed earlier, property values are likely to change if future tax liabilities change (the tax capitalization effect). Second, these studies generally focus on how a land value tax would affect statutory tax incidence. They generally do not estimate how taxes might be shifted to other groups in the long run—for example, how a business tax might ultimately be shifted to consumers in the form of higher retail prices.

Because of these assumptions, these distribution studies do not provide long-term analysis, which would incorporate the likely market responses such as changes in land values and tax shifting. Although a long-term analysis could provide valuable information about a land value tax's ultimate economic incidence, there are several advantages to examining a land value tax's short-term effects on statutory tax incidence. First, short-term analysis requires far fewer assumptions and estimates, making the results more interpretable and reliable than results from a long-term analysis. Second, a short-term analysis is the first step toward a more complete long-term analysis of the distributive effects of a land value tax. Third, a short-term analysis provides information on how a land value tax would initially shift the tax distribution across property owners. These initial changes in actual tax payments are likely to be a dominant factor in influencing voter attitudes about adopting a land value tax.

Schwab and Harris (1997) examine the distributional effects of a hypothetical switch to a split-rate property tax for the District of Columbia. They argue that a pure land value tax does two things: (1) it taxes land, not improvements; and (2) it taxes all land at the same rate regardless of property class (e.g., residential, commercial, hotel and motel). Schwab and Harris's evidence suggests that a pure land value tax would increase taxes paid by residential homeowners but decrease taxes for owners of residential and nonresidential rental properties.

Schwab and Harris suggest several plausible split-rate tax systems that would not increase the tax burden on Washington, DC, homeowners. However, these alternatives all require some form of property classification, which implies different effective tax rates for different property classes.[7] Unfortunately, tax rates that differ across property classes work against the land value tax's advantage of economic neutrality. Schwab and Harris also examine the effects of the different tax systems on about 70 distinct neighborhoods in Washington, DC, and present evidence that a split-rate tax system could provide low-income homeowners with lower tax payments.[8]

---

7. As discussed in chapter 7 of this volume, property classification would be difficult to achieve in some U.S. states because of constitutional provisions.

8. Schwab and Harris cite two earlier studies that looked at the distributional effects of a land value tax in Washington, DC, but found very different results from one another. The Department of Finance and Revenue's 1994 study concluded that a move to a split-rate tax would "shift property tax burdens generally on to residential property owners and away from other property uses" (p. 1). In contrast, the Pro-Housing Property Tax Coalition's 1991 study found that a split-rate tax would reduce taxes on owner-occupied housing by 12 percent.

England and Zhao (2005) use tax parcel data for Dover, New Hampshire, to provide evidence on how a split-rate tax would redistribute the tax burden across property owners. Dover is a small but growing city north of metropolitan Boston. The authors find that single-family residential properties in Dover would bear a larger percentage of the total property tax under a split-rate approach. Using assessed property value as a rough proxy for household income, the authors find that the tax changes across residential homeowners would be regressive unless some type of tax relief were also implemented.

England and Zhao (2005) also provide summary evidence on the land value tax's likely distributional effects for other property types. The distributional effects on industrial and commercial properties would vary widely—some property owners would pay more and some would pay less. Condominiums generally have a low land-to-value ratio, and most condo owners would enjoy lower taxes under a split-rate tax system. In contrast, all owners of vacant land parcels would pay more. The authors note that a tax credit for these nonresidential properties could be used to affect the distributional effects of a split-rate tax system (see also England 2004).

Bowman and Bell (2008) use residential property data for the city of Roanoke, Virginia, to examine the distributive effects of changing from a traditional property tax to a pure land value tax. They perform an analysis similar to that of England and Zhao (2005), but with very different results. Bowman and Bell find that changing to a pure land value tax would reduce the tax burden on residential properties. The authors then examine the distributional effects across households, using different measures of household income. The first measure of household income is assessed property value, which is the same income proxy used by England and Zhao. Bowman and Bell also link the Roanoke property tax data to income data from the U.S. Census Bureau and use several census tract income measures to measure household income (e.g., per capita money income and median family income). Regardless of the income measure used, the authors find that a land value tax would benefit most those areas with the lowest incomes and the highest poverty rates. In contrast to England and Zhao's study, Bowman and Bell's results suggest that a land value tax would be more progressive than the traditional property tax.

In reconciling their results with those of England and Zhao, Bowman and Bell (2008) suggest that the different results reflect between-city differences in land intensity ratios. The authors suggest that these differences arise because Roanoke has characteristics shared by other mature central cities, whereas Dover is more like a bedroom community of Boston. Residential properties in Roanoke have a much lower land intensity ratio than residential properties in Dover.[9] On average, land value constitutes 14.3 percent of a single-family residence's total property value in Roanoke and 34.7 percent in Dover. In addition, there is more variation in the land intensity ratios for single-family residential properties in Roanoke than in Dover. Together, these two studies suggest that the distributional effects of changing to a land value tax depend on the character of the jurisdiction. Bowman and Bell propose that a land value tax might be more politically feasible in older central cities—like Roanoke—because of the beneficial changes for homeowner-voters.

Bowman and Bell (2004) explore the distributional implications of changing from a traditional property tax to a pure land value tax for two additional Virginia local governments: the counties of Chesterfield (metropolitan, with over 250,000 residents) and Highland (rural, with fewer than 2,500 residents). For both counties, they find that moving from a traditional property tax to a land value tax would decrease the share of taxes paid by residential property owners and increase the share paid by business property owners. This result is consistent with their Roanoke results and suggests that a land value tax would benefit residential property owners. The other consistent finding across all three Virginia jurisdictions is that a land value tax would decrease the property tax liabilities of multifamily residential properties. The likely distributional effects for commercial and industrial properties vary across the jurisdictions, primarily because the relative importance of these properties varies across jurisdictions. The authors find that a land value tax would increase tax liabilities for land-intensive property classes—sometimes significantly so. These property classes include vacant land, mineral properties, trailer parks, and properties with 20 acres or more. The authors also note that, with few exceptions, every property class has individual parcels that would experience a tax increase and others that would experience a tax decrease.

Haveman (2004) examines the distributional effects of a land value tax on commercial and industrial property in Minnesota. In 2001 and again in

---

9. Bowman and Bell (2008, table 3) report the average ratio of building value divided by assessed land value for single-family homes. The average ratio for Dover is 1.88, and the average ratio for Roanoke is 5.99. These values imply average land intensity ratios (land value divided by total property value) of 0.347 and 0.143, respectively.

2003, the Minnesota state legislature considered land value taxation as part of its state property tax reform. The legislation provided that the statewide property tax on commercial and industrial properties be shifted over a 10-year period to a tax on commercial and industrial land values only, where land values would be defined as the "estimated market value of the land value." Under the current Minnesota property tax system, land is classified and valued according to its current use. Under the land value tax proposal, land would be declassified and valued at market value. The land value tax provisions were never adopted, in part because of uncertainties about the tax's distributional effects.

Haveman (2004) uses commercial and industrial property data from Minnesota counties to compare the tax distribution under a pure land value tax with the tax distribution under the existing statewide property tax system. Although some express concerns that a land value tax would shift the tax burden to rural and outstate regions, Haveman finds the opposite to be true. His results suggest that, over time, there would be tax shifting from rural and outstate areas to metropolitan areas, primarily because of the low land values in the outstate areas. Although declassification can adversely impact rural and outstate commercial and industrial properties, this negative effect would be more than offset by implementing a tax system based on land values. Haveman finds that even large stores in the outer suburban and exurban areas would see a lower tax liability with a land value tax because of their relatively low land values. He concludes that commercial and industrial property size is not necessarily a good predictor of tax-shifting impacts, because of the large variation in price per acre depending on location.

Gloudemans's study (2000) also deserves mention. This study's primary purpose is to explore the possibility of using modern mass appraisal techniques to develop separate estimates of land and improvement values for residential properties. The study uses parcel data from the city of Edmonton, Alberta, to develop land values for residential properties. For his sample of residential properties, Gloudemans finds that land intensity is generally higher for smaller, older, and low- or standard-quality homes, whereas it is generally lower for new, large, and higher-quality homes. This suggests that a land value tax would be more regressive than a traditional property tax.[10] Taxes would increase for lower-value homes and decrease for higher-value

---

10. This conclusion assumes, of course, that house values and current income are positively correlated.

homes. Gloudemans notes that he finds similar results when he performs a comparable analysis for Ada County (Boise, Idaho) and Jefferson County (suburban Denver, Colorado).

A few studies have performed tax-shifting analyses for areas outside the United States. De Cesare and others (2003) focus on residential properties in Porto Alegre, Brazil. The authors estimate land values for properties that were recently sold and find that land value accounts for approximately 53 percent of the sales price for houses and only 15 percent of the sales price for individual apartments. The larger proportion of land value for houses means that a land value tax would shift the tax burden from apartments to houses. The magnitude of the shift depends largely on the assumptions made.

Like England and Zhao (2005), De Cesare and others (2003) lack income data and instead use property value as a proxy for household income. The authors examine the distributional impacts across three ranges of property values—low, middle, and high. They find that a land value tax would shift a greater tax burden to low-value properties, which suggests that a land value tax would be more regressive than a traditional property tax. For houses, all three price ranges would see an increased tax liability, but the amount of increase is inversely correlated with sales price. More expensive homes would experience a smaller tax increase. This regressive pattern is also evident in the tax shifting for apartment units. High-priced units would see a tax decrease, whereas low-priced units would see a tax increase. The authors also find regressive effects when they examine properties classified by property attributes. Larger tax reductions would be observed for properties classified as "luxurious" and "high priced," whereas a tax increase would be observed for low-cost houses, including low-quality and small houses.

Sjoquist (2007) examines Jamaica's land value tax system. The country originally implemented a land value tax in 1957, but a major revaluation of property in 2002 led to a restructuring of the tax rate system. Under the 2002 system, the land value tax has a progressive tax rate structure, with four rate brackets and a top marginal rate of 1.75 percent. In addition, there are eleven property-value categories, with tax liability caps for each category. Sjoquist shows how the tax caps create situations where small differences in value result in large differences in tax liability, thereby violating the concept of horizontal equity. He also shows that the tax caps result in higher tax burdens for lower-value property than for higher-value property, making the land value tax less progressive than it otherwise would be. He recommends eliminating the tax caps in order to reduce inequities, increase progressivity, and increase tax revenues. He also recommends introducing a threshold exemption whereby properties under a certain value would be exempt from tax. He argues that such an exemption would increase progressivity and reduce administrative costs.

Studies examining the differential tax incidence of a land value tax and traditional property tax do not provide a clear, consistent prediction of how tax burdens would be redistributed across property owners. For residential property owners, several of the studies suggest that a land value tax would be less progressive than a traditional property tax (England and Zhao 2005; Gloudemans 2000; De Cesare et al. 2003), whereas other studies suggest that a land value tax would be more progressive (Bowman and Bell 2004, 2008). Furthermore, only one study specifically examines the distributional effects of a land value tax on business property (Haveman 2004). Further study is needed to provide more comprehensive and thorough evidence on the distributional effects of moving to a land value or split-rate tax system.

EVIDENCE ON HOUSEHOLD WEALTH, LAND OWNERSHIP, AND THE DEMAND FOR LAND

If we want to estimate the equity effects of a land value tax, it is also useful to consider studies that provide evidence on how land ownership varies across the income and wealth distributions. A household's wealth is composed of financial and nonfinancial assets:

Total Wealth = Financial Assets + Business and Personal Property + Real Estate

and

Real Estate Value = Land Value + Improvement Value.

If land value represents a larger percentage of total wealth as households become wealthier, then a land value tax will tend to be progressive. Furthermore, if land value represents a larger percentage of real estate value as households become wealthier, then a land value tax will be more progressive than a traditional property tax. Conversely, if land value represents a smaller percentage of real estate value as households become wealthier, then a land value tax will be less progressive than a traditional property tax.

Obtaining accurate measures of land ownership and household wealth is difficult, even in the most developed countries. In the United States, there are no ideal data sources on land ownership—other than in the thousands of county courthouses throughout the nation (Gilbert, Wood, and Sharp 2002). Determining land ownership in developing countries is even more difficult. Many developing countries have poor public land registries, making it difficult if not impossible to identify the landowner (MacGee 2006). In addition, substantial percentages of land and real estate in developing countries lack formal title—as much as 25 percent of land in Latin America and the Middle East, to over 40 percent in East Asia and over 50 percent in sub-Saharan Africa (Deininger 2003).[11]

In addition, when evaluating the distributional effects of a land value tax, we are interested in the value of land owned by a household (land wealth), and how land wealth varies across households of different income levels. Unfortunately, much of the data that is available concerns housing wealth or real estate wealth, where both measures include the value of land and improvements. One must be careful when using these other measures as proxies for a household's land wealth.

Nevertheless, what the evidence suggests is consistent in several respects. First, real estate (land and improvements) represents a significant share of household wealth in developed countries, primarily because home ownership is generally the most important component of household wealth—after bank deposit accounts (Jäntti and Sierminska 2007). Data also indicate that real estate represents a significant share of household wealth in developing countries. For example, Davies and Shorrocks (2005) report land value as a percentage of household wealth for several populous developing countries. On average, they find that land value represents 36 percent of household wealth for India and 22 percent for Indonesia. For these same countries, housing value as a percentage of household wealth is 40 percent and 49 percent, respectively.

I discuss two groups of studies below: (1) studies that provide evidence on the relation between land ownership and household wealth; and (2) studies

---

11. For researchers and others to determine land ownership, a country must have a good land administration system that provides accurate information on land ownership. A good system will have a registry that tracks land ownership and transactions, and a database that includes maps, property descriptions, and the owner's identity and legal rights (Deininger 2003). Although most developed countries have a relatively good land administration system, the information is not centralized nationally, but rather collected and archived by state, counties, or other local jurisdictions.

that examine how the demand for land varies across households of different income levels.

Household Wealth and Land Ownership

United States

Evidence suggests that real estate ownership in the United States is concentrated among the wealthy. For example, over 40 percent of privately owned land in the United States is owned by the top 1 percent of the largest landowners (including corporations), and 75 percent is owned by the top 5 percent of landowners. The bottom 78 percent of landowners own about 3 percent of private land. This concentrated ownership is more pronounced in some states than in others. Overall, it is clear that a relatively small percentage of the population owns private land, and this concentrated ownership is increasing (Lewis 1980; Geisler 1993, 1995).[12]

Although land ownership is concentrated among the wealthiest sector of the population, evidence also suggests that real estate value as a percentage of total net worth decreases as net wealth increases. Real estate is typically the largest component of household wealth for the bottom 90 percent of the wealth distribution, primarily because a household's primary residence is its largest asset (Bucks, Kennickell, and Moore 2006, fig. 8B). In contrast, real estate holdings play a much smaller role in the assets of the wealthiest households. Evidence suggests that for the top 10 percent of the wealth distribution, the primary residence represents less than 30 percent of median household wealth. Although these households are more likely to own other

---

12. As of 2002, over 60 percent of the land in the United States was privately owned. The federal government is the next largest landowner, with more than 28 percent. State and local governments own nearly 9 percent, and Indian trust land accounts for over 2 percent (see Lubowski et al. 2006).

Land ownership patterns can differ across states because of differences in the time period and property tax regime when the state was settled. For example, Spanish and Mexican land grants led to very large estates in California, whereas the Homestead Act led to smaller family farms in Kansas. The differences in land ownership patterns increase the difficulty of generalizing across states when considering a land value tax's distributional effects. Geisler (1995) reports that the states with the most concentrated land ownership are Arizona, California, Colorado, Idaho, Louisiana, Maine, Nevada, New Mexico, New York, Oregon, Washington, Wyoming, and Hawaii.

residential and nonresidential properties, these real property holdings account for only about 15 percent to 20 percent of median household wealth (Bucks, Kennickell, and Moore 2006, fig. 8B). For the top 1 percent of the wealth distribution, real estate may represent as little as 9 percent of net household wealth (Geisler 1995).

Although ownership of real property is concentrated among wealthier U.S. households, real estate value represents a smaller percentage of a household's total net worth as wealth increases. If land value represents a relatively smaller percentage of household wealth as income increases, then exemptions or credits for lower-income households may be needed to increase the progressivity of a land value tax. Exemptions and credits are commonly used by taxing jurisdictions to increase the progressivity of the traditional property tax.

United Kingdom

Even more so than in the United States, land ownership in the United Kingdom is concentrated within a small percentage of the population. Land records suggest that about 70 percent of the United Kingdom's 60 million acres is owned by 1 percent of the population (Cahill 2002). As in the United States, housing wealth is the primary component of household wealth (Muellbauer 2007), but housing wealth represents a relatively smaller portion of a household's asset portfolio as overall wealth increases (Banks, Smith, and Wakefield 2002).

The U.K. housing market has seen a long-term upward trend in real house prices and an increasingly inadequate housing supply. In response to concerns over housing affordability and the weak building response to higher home prices, HM Treasury has commissioned several studies addressing these issues. In *The Review of Housing Supply*, Barker (2004, 71) identifies land supply as the major constraint on housing growth and argues that this is due, in part, to the unwillingness of landowners to sell or use their land for residential development. The report argues that a land value tax, relative to a property tax, could be used to provide landowners with incentives for residential development. It discusses how a properly designed land value tax could be used to tax land according to its market value. Higher-value land, such as land appropriate for residential development, would be taxed more heavily, encouraging landowners to free up their land for such use. A land value tax would also be consistent with the country's planning system, which seeks to encourage high-density smaller houses and to discourage large houses that use relatively more land.

Developing Countries

Housing and land are a much more important indicator of wealth in many foreign countries, including the majority of developing countries. Unlike industrialized countries and middle-income developing nations, developing countries are predominantly rural, with agrarian economies. Tangible assets—including land—play a larger role in household wealth, whereas financial assets play a smaller role (Subramanian and Jayaraj 2006).

Even though most of the population of Brazil lives in urban areas, wealth in Brazil is largely associated with land ownership, and Brazil's current distribution of land and income is highly skewed (Assunção 2006). Assunção examines the relation between landholdings (i.e., land area) and several wealth indicators for a large sample of rural households for the period 1992–2002. He finds that the amount of land a rural household owns is highly correlated with per capita income, durable goods, and a house's infrastructure. His evidence suggests that land distribution is closely related to wealth distribution.

Subramanian and Jayaraj (2006) review data on India's wealth distribution for the period 1961–2002, using five decennial surveys commissioned by the Reserve Bank of India. The survey reports the value of asset holdings for eight types of assets, including financial assets, land, buildings, and other categories of tangible assets such as livestock and agricultural machinery. For both rural and urban areas, they find that asset diversification decreases as wealth increases and that wealthier households concentrate more of their wealth in land.[13] They conclude that "land continues to remain the symbol and substance of both wealth and power in rural India" (p. 15). Further analysis shows that wealth inequality among Indian households is driven by un-

---

13. For rural households, land value represents 43 percent of household wealth for the poorest 50 percent of households, but represents 67 percent of household wealth for the richest 50 percent of households. The difference is even more pronounced when they compare the very poorest and richest rural households. Land represents 18 percent of asset value for the poorest 7.5 percent of households, whereas it accounts for about 74 percent of asset value for the richest 14.4 percent of households. A similar pattern holds for urban households: land represents about 2 percent of asset value for the poorest urban households and about 40 percent for the richest urban households.

equal distribution of land in the rural areas and by unequal distribution of both land and improvements in the urban areas.

Li and Zhao (2007) investigate changes in the wealth distribution in mainland China using data from two national household surveys conducted in 1995 and 2002. The survey reports the value of asset holdings for several asset classes, including land.[14] The authors find a significant change in the role of land value as a component of wealth over this period. Land value represented about 32 percent of household wealth in 1995, but only 9 percent in 2002. They also find that land is an important component of household wealth for rural households, but its significance has declined because rural land values have declined. For rural China, land value represented almost 47 percent of household wealth in 1995, but only 30 percent in 2002.[15] Lastly, their evidence implies that land is more important for less wealthy households and that housing and financial assets are relatively more important for wealthier households. Urban households now represent the wealthier households in China, and these households own no land. The ownership pattern of land in mainland China suggests that a land value tax would most likely be more regressive than a uniform property tax on land and improvements.

There is diversity in land ownership patterns in developing countries. Evidence for Brazil and India suggests that wealthier households concentrate more of their wealth in land, whereas the evidence for China suggests that land is less important for wealthier households. For developed countries such as the United States and the United Kingdom, evidence suggests that land ownership is concentrated among the wealthiest sector but that land value as a percentage of net wealth decreases as wealth increases. Even within the United States, there is diversity in land ownership patterns across geographic regions (e.g., Roanoke versus Dover). The differences in land ownership patterns—across countries and within countries—suggest that the

---

14. Note that occupants of land in China frequently possess long-term leases, not fee simple title to the land. Li and Zhao (2007) estimate the value of rural land by capitalizing 25 percent of net agricultural income at 8 percent per year.

15. They attribute this decline to two causes. First, industrialization, urbanization, and construction of the transportation system have used farmland and caused the land size per capita in rural China to decrease. Second, the returns to farmland have decreased because of declining agricultural prices and the leveling off of farming productivity.

distributional effects of a land value tax could vary greatly across taxing jurisdictions.

Household Wealth and the Demand for Land

To increase our understanding of how land ownership varies across income levels, we should also consider studies that examine how expenditures for land change when there is a change in household income. Economists use the term *income elasticity of expenditures* to quantify this relation, where income elasticity is calculated as the ratio of the percentage change in expenditures to the percentage change in income. For example, if household income increases by 10 percent and this causes a 7 percent increase in the household's expenditures on land, the income elasticity would be 0.7 (7 percent/10 percent).

Income elasticity is important because it provides insight into how progressive (or regressive) a tax is likely to be. A land value tax will be progressive if the income elasticity of land expenditures increases as income increases. In that case, higher-income households are more likely than lower-income households to purchase land and are thus more likely to bear the land value tax burden. Whether a land value tax will be more progressive than a traditional property tax depends on several things, including the relative income elasticity of land expenditures versus the income elasticity of expenditures for improvements.

Consider the simple example shown in table 5.4. Household A and household B are lower-income households with $50,000 and $55,000 of annual income, respectively. Households C and D are upper-income households with $200,000 and $220,000 of annual income, respectively. Assume that each household's expenditures on land and improvements can be summarized as shown in table 5.4. In this example, lower-income households prefer to spend additional income on improvements, not land. Specifically, household B's income is 10 percent ($5,000) higher than household A's, and household B spends all of this additional income on improvements. In contrast, upper-income households prefer to spend their additional income on land. Household D's income is 10 percent ($20,000) higher than household C's, and household D spends all of this additional income on land. In this example, a land value tax would be more progressive than a traditional property tax because higher-income households are more likely to spend additional income

Table 5.4 Example of income elasticity and vertical distribution of tax burden

Household	Income	Expenditures on land	Expenditures on improvements	Expenditures on land and improvements
A	$50,000	$20,000	$60,000	$80,000
B	55,000	20,000	65,000	85,000
Percentage increase (A to B)	10.0	0.0	8.3	6.25
Income elasticity of expenditures		*0.00*	*0.83*	*0.625*
C	$200,000	$250,000	$400,000	$650,000
D	220,000	270,000	400,000	670,000
Percentage increase (C to D)	10.0	8.0	0.0	3.08
Income elasticity of expenditures		*0.80*	*0.00*	*0.308*

on land, whereas lower-income households are more likely to spend additional income on improvements.[16]

Unfortunately, there are very few studies that specifically examine the income elasticity of demand for land. Studies more often examine the elasticity of demand for housing, which includes land, improvements, and amenities. Although more research into this area is needed, two studies provide some preliminary insight into how the demand for land changes in response to household income. The first is a study by Cheshire and Sheppard (1998), who specifically examine the income elasticity of demand for land area as well as some distinct housing characteristics. Their sample consists of 305 houses in two cities in England in 1984. The authors find that the demand for land area is more income elastic than the demand for any other housing characteristic and that the elasticity is significantly greater for upper-income households than for lower-income households. This suggests that a household's relative demand for land area increases as income increases and thus

---

16. The effect of additional income on expenditures is summarized by the elasticity measures. Specifically, the income elasticity of land expenditures is 0.8 for upper-income households and 0 for lower-income households, whereas the income elasticity of expenditures on improvements is 0 for upper-income households and 0.83 for lower-income households.

that a land value tax could be progressive, assuming a constant price per acre across households.[17]

Thorsnes (2000) examines the sales prices of building lots within a sample of new residential subdivisions in the Portland, Oregon, metropolitan area for the period 1985–1987. He conjectures that a key concern of home buyers is control over the quality of neighborhood characteristics as a subdivision develops. If this is true, then home buyers should be willing to pay more for lots located in larger subdivisions. Thorsnes's results are consistent with his conjecture. After controlling for lot size and neighborhood characteristics (e.g., distance from a central business district and jurisdiction), he finds that lot prices increase as subdivision size increases. He also finds that higher-income home buyers place greater value on the expected benefits of a larger subdivision and are willing to pay more for those benefits.[18] Thorsnes's results suggest that a land value tax would be progressive, but Thorsnes does not provide evidence on whether a land value tax would be more or less progressive than a traditional property tax.

CHALLENGES FOR A FAIR LAND VALUE TAX

One of the biggest challenges for land value taxation is obtaining accurate, defensible land values. Under a land value tax, it will be important to improve the accuracy of land valuations and consistently assess land according to its highest and best use (Youngman 2006a, 4). Inaccurate land values will cause horizontal inequities if "equal" land parcels are not valued equally. Inaccurate land values will also affect vertical equity, with the direction of the effect—more or less progressive than intended—depending on which land parcels are assigned values that are too low or too high.

Because land values provide a smaller tax base than land and improvements, higher tax rates will be needed to generate the same amount of revenue. Higher tax rates are more likely to generate opposition and are politically more difficult (Bahl 2002). In addition, even if a majority of property

---

17. Cheshire and Sheppard (1998) also examine the price elasticity of demand for land area—how the demand for land area changes in response to changes in land price. They find that the demand for land area becomes more price sensitive (more elastic) as income rises.

18. Specifically, Thorsnes's estimates (2000) indicate that for a 10-acre subdivision, an additional acre adds about 3 percent to each lot's market value. At the median income level for his sample (income of $35,000), an additional acre adds about 1.5 percent to lot price. At a higher income level ($50,000), an additional acre adds almost 4 percent to lot price.

owners are "winners" whose taxes decrease as a result of a switch to land value taxation, the minority of property owners that see a tax increase are likely to be the more vocal group who lobby and report to their legislators (Haveman 2004, 11).

A land value tax system could incorporate tax relief measures to help increase equity. The current property tax systems of most jurisdictions have tax relief measures such as tax credits, exemptions, and assessment limitations. These measures are generally aimed at reducing the tax burden of a selected group of property owners (e.g., the elderly or low-income families), and similar measures could be included in a land value tax system (England and Zhao 2005; Youngman 2006a). It should be noted, however, that tax relief measures can have drawbacks. For example, although relief measures reduce the tax burden of property owners benefiting from the relief, they increase the tax burden of property owners not receiving the benefit (Bowman 2006). Tax relief measures can also result in unintended consequences and can introduce inequities into the overall system (Dye, McMillen, and Merriman 2006; Dye and McMillen 2007a). For example, many relief measures are intended to help low-income taxpayers. However, if relief measures cause too much erosion of a government's tax base, the government may have to cut services or find alternative revenue sources. Low-income taxpayers may be the ones most affected if services are cut or if the government chooses to raise revenue from a tax system that is more regressive than the property tax (e.g., a sales tax).

CONCLUSIONS

Fairness is an essential feature of any good tax system, and progressive tax systems are generally viewed as fairer than proportional or regressive systems. A progressive tax system imposes a relatively larger tax burden on those with a greater ability to pay. Measuring a property owner's ability to pay can be difficult because doing so requires a measure of a household's economic well-being. Possible measures of economic well-being include annual income and lifetime income.

The statutory tax burden of a land value tax is borne by landowners. If a land value tax is substituted for a traditional property tax, the land value tax will increase the tax burden for owners of land-intensive properties. Owners whose properties have above-average land intensity ratios will experience a tax increase, whereas owners whose properties have below-average land intensity ratios will experience a tax decrease. Changing from a property tax to a land value tax also has very different impacts on individual landowners because of the effects of tax capitalization. If a land value tax causes a property's taxes to increase, the property's market value will decrease and cause a loss for the current property owner. Conversely, if a land value tax causes a property's taxes to decrease, the property's market value will increase and create a windfall gain for the current owner.

There are a limited number of studies that specifically examine how replacing a traditional property tax with a land value tax would shift the tax burden across property owners. Unfortunately, the evidence these studies provide is mixed. Several studies suggest that a land value tax would be less progressive than a traditional property tax for residential property owners, whereas other studies suggest that a land value tax would be more progressive. There is little evidence on how a land value tax would affect the tax burden of business property. It is clear that more research is needed on the distributional effects of a land value tax system.

To estimate the equity effects of a land value tax, we should examine evidence on how land ownership varies across the income distribution. If land value as a percentage of net wealth increases as household income increases, then a land value tax will be progressive. For the United States and the United Kingdom, evidence suggests that land ownership is concentrated among the wealthiest sector. However, land value as a percentage of net wealth decreases as wealth increases, which suggests that a land value tax might be somewhat regressive. However, even within the United States, there is diversity in land ownership patterns across geographic regions, so a land value tax might be more progressive than a property tax in some areas (e.g., Roanoke, Virginia) and less progressive in other areas (e.g., Dover, New Hampshire). In developing countries, land is generally a more important indicator of wealth than in the United States. However, this is not true for all developing countries (e.g., China). Differences in land ownership patterns make it difficult to generalize across countries, states, or even cities when considering the distributional effects of a land value tax.

It is important to educate legislators, taxpayers, and administrators on the likely distributional effects of a land value tax. Increased understanding could lead to more support for land value taxation. More evidence is needed on the distributional effects of a land value tax—including whether it will be progressive, whether it will be more or less progressive than a traditional property tax, and which jurisdictional features influence the distributional effects.

❖ 6 ❖

A Review of the Evidence

JOHN E. ANDERSON

FROM THEORY TO EVIDENCE

W̶HAT ARE THE EFFECTS of implementing land value taxation?[1] If a municipality wishes to switch from traditional property taxation to land value taxation—increasing the tax on land to get the benefits from decreasing the tax on improvements—there are a number of potential effects, as outlined by Wallace E. Oates and Robert M. Schwab in chapter 4. But which of the theoretical effects are likely to be realized? What evidence do we have from municipalities that have actually used land value tax systems from which we can draw reasonable inferences about the likely effects? These are the questions to which I turn in this chapter.

Arlo Woolery had it right in 1982 when he wrote in the introduction to Pollakowski's monograph on land value taxation (1982), "The real world is not an ideal laboratory for testing the validity of these theories." Despite the messy nature of the real world for analyzing the effects of land value taxation, there have been a large number of studies over the past 30 years that have attempted to discover the impacts. In this chapter I review the evidence from a number of studies, evaluate the research approaches used, and assess the state of knowledge on the effects of land value taxation implementation.

---

1. For the purposes of this chapter, I will not make a distinction between land value taxation or split-rate variants of property taxation that apply a higher tax rate to land than to buildings and other structures or improvements.

What Constitutes Evidence?

As we consider the evidence on land value taxation effects, it is important to ask at the outset, What constitutes evidence? That is, would we recognize the effect of a switch from a property tax regime to a land value taxation regime if we saw it? Analysts have suggested many observable outcomes. We need to take care, however, in specifying what outcomes we will examine and how we will determine whether the evidence is convincing. We are interested in evaluating evidence on how land value taxation affects land and housing markets, compared with the status quo of traditional property taxation. That is, we are concerned with whether and how a switch to land value taxation affects land prices, housing prices, construction rates, and other features of markets for land and improvements.

First, it is important to keep in mind that any city adopting a split-rate tax or pure land value tax is changing from an existing tax system to a new tax regime. Hence, as we look for effects of the new tax regime, it is essential to keep in mind that any effect we may find is the differential impact of the change in tax regimes. That is, the observed effect involves both the initial and final conditions prescribed by the two tax regimes. The initial tax regime may have as much to do with any observed effect as does the new tax regime. Initial conditions matter. Assessment practices, administrative procedures, and other factors influence the effective rate of taxation on both land and improvements under the conventional property tax that is the usual starting point in an analysis of changes caused by the implementation of an alternative tax system. This point is often ignored in research on the effects of alternative tax systems adopted by cities, and appropriate controls are not included in the analysis. Consequently, any observed effects cannot be fully attributed to the new tax system. Rather, such effects are due to the difference between the new system and the old system.

A related question is that of incidence: Who bears the burden of a tax? In particular, the question is whether the incidence of the land value tax differs from that of a traditional property tax—that is, we are interested in the differential incidence of the land value tax. This is a particularly difficult issue since the incidence of the property tax itself has been and continues to be a contentious issue. There are three competing theories regarding property tax incidence, each with different implications. Zodrow (2001, 2007) provides a good overview of the theories and their implications. The traditional view of the property tax holds that the tax is shifted to consumers in the form of higher housing prices. Since housing expenditures rise with income, but not proportionately, the implication is that the tax is regressive. The benefits view claims that the tax is nondistortionary since it is simply a payment for public goods and services received by the property owner. The capital tax view argues that the tax is a distortionary tax on the use of capital within a local jurisdiction. Since the tax is related to capital ownership, its incidence is progressive by this view. Zodrow (2001) reviews several recent empirical studies that have attempted to test whether the benefits view or the capital tax view can be substantiated. His conclusion—although not yet definitive, because of data limitations—is that these studies lend support to the capital tax view. England and Zhao (2005) simulate the distributive impact of a revenue-neutral shift from a conventional property tax to a split-rate tax regime (with a lower tax rate on improvements than land), recommending that a credit be included with the split-rate tax to reduce the regressivity of the regime change. In the remainder of this chapter, I focus on the effects of land value taxation on markets for land and improvements, although I do not directly address the question of the ultimate tax incidence. (See chapter 5 for a discussion of equity and incidence issues.)

Refutable Hypotheses

The first problem that may arise in studies of a tax regime change is that the basic research hypothesis being tested is ill defined. As in any scientific endeavor, it is essential that the hypothesis being tested be refutable. For example, if we are measuring the effect of a land value tax regime using the value of building permits, a reasonable hypothesis to test is whether adopting a land value tax results in an increase in the value of building permits. When the data are collected and the analysis is conducted, we will see whether the hypothesis is supported or refuted. Hypotheses that are not refutable are not scientifically useful. For example, a hypothesis that says land value taxation may cause the value of building permits to rise or fall (which will happen with certainty) is not refutable and therefore not useful.

DiMassi (1987) has suggested several refutable hypotheses that can be used to investigate the effects of land value taxation. He has suggested checking for the following effects:

· A reduction in land rents
· A reduction in house prices

- An increase in improvements per unit of land in housing
- An increase in population density
- An increase in demand for labor
- An increase in wages
- A reduction in the size of the urban area

These are the key effects researchers may pursue as they seek to find evidence of the effects of land value taxation. Although all of these are potential effects to look for, various strands of literature have emphasized one or another effect. For example, empirical researchers have tended to focus much of their efforts on the increase in improvements per unit of land. As we will see in our review of evidence, measures of increased building activity predominate this literature. On the other hand, we will see that the more general theoretical and simulation studies tend also to include effects on land rents, house prices, population density, and the size of the urban area in their analyses.

Beyond these suggested effects, we might also expect to find that a switch to land value taxation affects the timing of land development. It is important to keep in mind that a pure land value tax, based on assessed values set according to the highest and best use of the land regardless of current use, should be neutral and should not affect the timing of development. If the land value tax replaced a nonneutral property tax with assessments based on current use, however, we might find an impact on timing. I consider this issue further later in the chapter.

I also examine the specific refutable hypotheses used by researchers in the land value taxation literature and evaluate the state of the evidence they report. Not only is it important to clearly identify a refutable hypothesis, but it is then essential that the evidence regarding that hypothesis be interpreted carefully. There are several common pitfalls to avoid in the research design and interpretation of statistical evidence.

Research Design and Issues of Interpretation

It is important to distinguish between association and causation. In logic, a common fallacy is known as *cum hoc ergo propter hoc* (with this, therefore because of this). Just because we observe the number of building permits increase following the adoption of land value taxation in a city, we cannot conclude that the adoption of land value taxation caused the increase in building permits. There may be other factors causing the increase in building permits. Just because we observe that A and B move together does not rule out the possibility that a third factor C could be driving the movement in both A and B. For example, in Pittsburgh the increase in building permits associated with a greater differential in land and improvement tax rates was simultaneously accompanied by a major economic development program that increased the level of economic activity in the region. Unless we can separate the effects of the two events, we cannot conclude that either one was responsible for the increased building activity. Since economic researchers cannot conduct controlled experiments in the classic laboratory sense (implementing land value taxation in one part of town and not in other parts of town, holding all else constant), we must resort to statistical methods of estimating the effects of land value taxation adoption, controlling for other factors. Consequently, we must be careful in examining studies of land value taxation effects to be sure that other factors were held constant.

A common approach used in attempting to analyze the effects of a switch in tax regimes is to compare the situation before the change to that after. These before-and-after studies are particularly susceptible to erroneous conclusions because of *post hoc ergo propter hoc* (after this, therefore because of this) reasoning. It is often tempting to observe the timing of events and simplistically conclude that because event B occurred after event A, A caused B. In the land value taxation context, we must be careful to avoid this potential logical fallacy as we review evidence of certain changes in markets for land and improvements after the adoption or elimination of land value taxation.

A final approach that has been used is a simple comparison of the experience of cities that use different tax regimes. Suppose that city A adopts land value taxation but city B does not. Some researchers look at comparative measures of activity in the two cities, such as building permits, to see whether the adoption of land value taxation makes a difference. The problem with this approach is that only one of many potential factors is taken into account—the presence or absence of land value taxation. There are a wide range of other factors that may affect the number of building permits granted by the cities, factors for which there are no controls in such a research design. More sophisticated studies use statistical regression methods to control for all the known factors that may influence the number of building permits in the two cities.

In some cases, a sample selection problem arises in the research design. For example, the researcher is interested in determining whether land value taxation has an effect on building activity, but the sample data are drawn only from cities that have adopted land value taxation systems, with no representation in the sample of cities that have not adopted land value taxation systems. The problem is that there may be something systematically different about cities that adopt land value taxation compared with nonadopting cities that confounds the analysis. As in the case of Pennsylvania cities in the 1970s and 1980s, which are the focus of a number of land value taxation studies, the problem is that only cities in economic distress adopted land value taxation. Therefore, there is a sample selection bias, which in this case may actually bias the results against finding an effect of land value taxation adoption. For this reason, the research methodology should take care to avoid this type of sample selection problem.

MEASUREMENT OF THE VARIABLES

Once we know what constitutes evidence on the land value taxation adoption issue and what research design problems to avoid, we must consider what measures are available for the dependent variable in research studies.

Although there are a wide variety of effects to consider when a community adopts land value taxation, there are relatively few measures with reliable data. Researchers examining the empirical effects of land value taxation have primarily used measures of changes in structures and improvements. Measures of broader effects on house prices, land values, urban density, and urban size are more problematic and have been used primarily in theoretical modeling and less frequently in empirical research. In what follows, I consider the empirical measures of improvements used in the literature to date.

Some researchers have measured the value of new residential building permits to test whether land value taxation has any measurable effects. Researchers have used the number or the value of permits both before and after a substantial increase in the relative tax rate applied to land and a corresponding decrease in the relative tax rate applied to improvements. The most notable studies in this vein are those by Bourassa (1987, 1990) and Oates and Schwab (1997).

Bourassa (1990) examines the effects of land value taxation on housing development in three distinctly different cities in Pennsylvania: Pittsburgh, a large central city; McKeesport, a suburban city near Pittsburgh; and New Castle, a relatively isolated smaller city on the outskirts of the Pittsburgh metropolitan area. Regression models were developed to explain variations in the dollar value of building permit applications.

Oates and Schwab (1997) assembled time series data on new building activity for a sample of 15 cities in the region surrounding Pittsburgh to conduct their simple before-and-after analysis. They use two measures. First, they use Dun & Bradstreet data on the real value of new building permits for the 15 cities, defined to include just the cities and not the surrounding metropolitan areas. Second, they use census data for the 15 metropolitan areas disaggregated into city-suburb and residential-nonresidential construction.

Plassmann and Tideman (2000) use the number of new building permits in their analysis. They use census data on building permits for Pennsylvania cities over the period 1980–1994. Their data includes both residential and nonresidential building permits for a number of subcategories of construction. The first dependent variable in their analysis is defined as the number of building permits per person per month in each city. Since the dependent variable in this analysis is the number of building permits, Plassmann and Tideman took care to use appropriate statistical methods to estimate their model. Using their estimates of the impact on the number of building permits, they also estimate the impact of differential taxation on the total value of new construction in each city in their sample.

Mathis and Zech (1982, 1983) use the value of per capita construction as the dependent variable in their study of 27 Pennsylvania cities, towns, and boroughs over the period 1976–1978. Their data was obtained from a survey they administered among city officials.

A related measure used in some studies is the number of property transactions, as in Pollakowski's study (1982), which examines the number of property transactions in Pittsburgh over the period 1976–1980.

An important perspective on measurement error must also be noted. There is ample theoretical evidence that a reduction in the tax rate on improvements will increase the intensity of development, with more capital applied per unit of land. Yet attempts to measure the impact of movement to a land value tax are confounded by the reality that the magnitude of the expected change in the ratio of capital to land is approximately equal to the measurement error in the capital to land ratio. Ingram (2008) describes the likely impact on the capital-to-land ratio and the expected range of measurement error in the capital-to-land ratio and shows that the two quantities are likely to be of similar magnitude, which would make it difficult to discern an effect.

REVIEW OF EVIDENCE TO DATE

In this section I examine the land value taxation evidence accumulated to date, organized by research methodology. A brief summary of key land value taxation studies organized by research methodology is also provided in table 6.1 (see page 122). The table is organized by methodology, with purely theoretical models listed first, followed by general equilibrium models, regression models, and other approaches.

Theoretical Models

The theoretical models typically are mathematical summaries of the fundamental relationships believed to be essential for analyzing the effects of land value taxation. These models are, for the most part, partial equilibrium models; unlike general equilibrium models, they focus on a single market (the housing or land market) and do not attempt to model equilibrium in all markets simultaneously.

The first notable theoretical model to consider is Brueckner's (1986). In this benchmark study, Brueckner applies modern economic analysis to the question of the effects of land value taxation à la Henry George. After a review of the existing literature, Brueckner summarizes with a telling assessment: "What is remarkable about this large literature is the almost complete absence of modern analysis. Most studies rely on verbal arguments or simple diagrams, and the few analytical efforts . . . are marred by *ad hoc* assumptions or misplaced emphasis." He finds that some researchers had made correct predictions without the aid of rigorous economic models, but that a lack of precision in the literature had led to substantial confusion on certain points. A correct conclusion established in the literature was that land value taxation increased land intensity. The impact on land value was muddled, however. Using a precise model, Brueckner shows that an improvement tax reduction raises land values whereas the land tax increase decreases values. Only two of the many studies Brueckner reviews recognized the existence of these two opposing effects, although both studies concluded that the net effect is ambiguous whereas Brueckner shows that the land value change is determinate.[2]

Brueckner (1986) distinguishes two cases in his analysis: (1) long-run ef-

---

2. Becker (1969) and Harriss (1970) identify opposing effects.

fects with housing prices taken as given (determined by factors outside the model); and (2) long-run effects with housing prices determined within the model. He finds that the impact of a revenue-neutral shift from a conventional property tax to a split-rate tax system depends crucially on the relative sizes of the tax zone over which the regime change applies and the housing market. If (as explained in chapter 4) the tax zone covers a negligible share of the market area, housing prices remain unchanged, but both improvements per acre and the value of land increase. Brueckner notes that the land value increase is surprising in this case since the direct tax on land is increased. If the tax zone covers the entire housing market area, the price of housing decreases, but improvements per acre increase and the value of land likely decreases. The reduction in land value is due to the depressing effect of lower house prices, which reduce the profitability of housing development.

The value of benchmark theoretical research such as this is that it establishes a set of expectations for what we should look for when we conduct empirical research based on the experience of communities implementing land value taxation or split-rate tax systems. The refutable hypotheses that come out of a model such as Brueckner's are testable with the right empirical data. If we had data, for example, from a city that had introduced land value taxation in the entire urban area, we would look for evidence of lower housing prices, increased improvements per acre of land, and lower land values.

Since Brueckner's seminal theoretical model was published, more recent contributions such as those of J. Anderson (1999), Arnott (2005), and Arnott and Petrova (2006) have advanced the state of the art in theoretical modeling of the effects of taxes on land development and housing. These authors investigate the implications of alternative measures of land value on the neutrality properties of the tax system.

J. Anderson (1999) brings together the results from models of housing development timing and structural density with the results of Brueckner's model of a split-rate property tax in an urban setting. He investigates the effects when a community moves from a conventional property tax with equal tax rates applied to land and improvements to a split-rate tax system where land is taxed at a higher rate. The model indicates that a move to a split-rate tax will speed the timing of development and increase the amount of capital applied to land (the capital intensity) if capital and development time are substitutes (or independent) and if the responsiveness of the capital-land ratio to changes in capital and land prices (the elasticity of substitution) is small, as we would expect to be the case for a declining city. On the other hand, if capital and development time strongly complement one another in the development process, as would be the case for a growing city, the opposite results may occur.

A whole line of papers develops theoretical models of the impact of various forms of property taxation on the timing and capital intensity of land development. Starting in the 1970s with Shoup (1970), Rose (1973), Skouras (1978), Arnott and Lewis (1979), and Bentick (1979) these papers model the impacts of taxation. In the 1980s D. Mills (1981a, 1981b, 1983) and J. Anderson (1986, 1993) made additional contributions to this literature. These papers generally focus on the ways that property taxation may alter development timing and capital intensity of development, showing that the property tax is nonneutral in these regards. Tideman (1982) provides an important clarification to this literature, emphasizing that a true land value tax is neutral in its effects on timing of development. Previous research on this topic had modeled land value in a way that is dependent on how the land is used. Hence, Mills and Anderson find nonneutral effects on timing and capital intensity. Tideman's point is that it is unsurprising to find that a tax on land value affects land use if that tax is related to land use. If land value is defined in a way that is unrelated to current land use commitments, the standard land value taxation neutrality result holds. Whether assessment procedures can be designed so that assessed values are completely independent of current land use is an important practical issue, but one that is beyond the scope of this chapter.

Arnott (2005) begins by making a useful distinction between residual land value (postdevelopment property value minus improvement value) and raw land value (the value of the land without any buildings or other structures and improvements on it) and uses this distinction in his investigation of alternative measures of land value. His model is dynamic, with a focus on the timing and intensity of development. He proves the conventional result that raw land value taxation is neutral and proves that a residual land value tax system is nonneutral. That is, a raw land value tax does not affect the timing and intensity of development, whereas a residual land value tax does. His main contribution is to show that it is possible, however, to configure a property tax system with taxes on predevelopment land value, postdevelopment improvement value, and postdevelopment land value that both uses the residual land value definition of land value and achieves neutrality. In the course of his analysis, he also comments on the assessment process and the administrative feasibility of land value taxation systems. For example, he states that estimating postdevelopment raw land value would be highly complex and would likely result in assessments that are unfair and arbitrary. Furthermore, Arnott and Petrova (2006) analyze the relative efficiency of four property tax systems, including several land value variations. Their model has the advantage of providing estimates of the distortionary effects of alternative tax systems on resource allocation (measured by marginal deadweight loss).

General Equilibrium Models

Beyond the partial equilibrium models that focus on a single market (land or housing), we have a collection of general equilibrium models that have been developed over the past 20 years. These models attempt to describe the equilibrium conditions in all markets simultaneously, including the markets for land, buildings and other improvements, labor, and output. They are often large mathematical models with many equations and assumptions about the responsiveness of economic actors (households, firms, governments, etc.) to changes in prices and other economic variables. The models are often calibrated to replicate an initial description of an economy and then used to compute the changes that would occur in response to a tax policy change. They are often referred to as *computable general equilibrium* models.

Three notable studies of this type were published in the 1980s, two of which were applied to specific locations. Grosskopf (1981) created the earliest general equilibrium model and uses the tax incidence framework of Harberger to analyze the effects of a switch from a property tax to an equal-yield land value tax. Using empirical estimates to calibrate her model, Grosskopf finds that such a switch in tax regime would increase equilibrium land prices (and thereby increase the land value tax base) and generate sufficient revenue to facilitate the switch.[3] DiMasi (1987) developed a model that was calibrated to describe metropolitan Boston in 1980. He examines the effects of switching to a split-rate tax system on land rents, improvements per acre

---

3. Recall from the discussion of Brueckner (1986) earlier in this chapter and in chapter 4 that the tax shift has two opposing effects on land values: the increase in the land tax rate decreases land values, whereas the decrease in the improvement tax rate increases land values. The net result depends on parameter values, in particular on the size, relative to the larger market area, of the jurisdiction making the change. A relatively small jurisdiction cutting improvement taxes will favorably impact the value of its land.

of land, housing prices, population density in the urban area, and wages paid in labor markets. His model indicates that land rents would fall, improvements per acre of land would rise, housing prices would fall, population densities would rise, the spatial area covered by urbanization would retract, and wages would rise. Follain and Miyake (1986) developed a model designed to simulate the effects of a reduction in the Jamaican income tax with an increase in either a land value tax or a capital value tax to replace the revenue. Their model indicates, for example, that using a land value tax to replace 20 percent of the income tax revenue in Jamaica would require effective confiscation of land (equivalent to a tax rate of 100 percent of the land rent).

Since these early studies from the 1980s, there have been relatively few newer models used to simulate a switch to land value taxation. There are just two recent studies of note. Nechyba (1998) examines the effects of a revenue-neutral increase in the land tax rate with a corresponding reduction in the capital tax rate. His paper presents a general equilibrium model of a small economy open to trade. Output is produced using capital and land. The government has a fixed budget requirement, with revenue generated from taxes on capital and land. His model was calibrated to replicate U.S. state and local governments. Results indicate that an increase in the land tax rate with a corresponding decrease in the capital tax rate increases the capital stock and output, but causes land values to fall. The key parameter assumption relates to the responsiveness of the housing production process to changes in the relative prices of capital and land. Nechyba uses a wide range of values for this parameter centered around a reasonable value (where the elasticity of substitution is one-half) based on the evidence from the literature. Nechyba concludes his discussion of the results with the admonition that researchers attempting to more accurately predict the impacts of this type of tax reform must carefully estimate this relationship.

Most recently, Haughwout (2004) developed a general equilibrium model calibrated to replicate the New York City economy. Using that model, he reports results from the experiment of eliminating the city's sales, income, property, and general corporate taxes while retaining the tax on land at its current rate (2.83 percent).[4] Taking technology and preferences as fixed, he sets the current tax on property, including the surcharge on business capital,

---

4. Haughwout (2004) also simulates a revenue-neutral policy change, which requires a land tax rate of 21.7 percent. Aggregate revenues are unchanged in this case, but per capita revenue falls as population rises.

to zero and retains the current land tax. The model indicates that there would be a substantial increase in private output in the economy, increased land values, a larger private capital stock, and a larger population. Indeed, the magnitude of the results is large and invites him to compare his results with those of Nechyba (1998), whose model is similar, and explain why his results are at the upper limit of those reported by Nechyba. The switch in tax regime also reduces the provision of public goods and per capita tax revenue by more than 50 percent.

Regression Models

In an effort to improve on early studies of land value taxation that relied on simple summary statistics, researchers began to use statistical regression methods in the early 1980s. The advantage of using regression models is that they permit researchers to isolate the effect of taxes on the key factor of interest (known as the *dependent variable*), controlling for a number of other factors (known as *independent variables* or *explanatory* or *control variables*) that may also affect the dependent variable.

The earliest published regression models examining the effects of split-rate tax systems in Pennsylvania communities were those of Mathis and Zech (1982, 1983). In their 1982 paper, they test the effect of split-rate tax systems by estimating models of the median and mean value of per capita construction across communities. In their 1983 paper, they estimate models of the value of construction per acre of land across communities. Data on the value of construction was collected from city officials through a survey. Mathis and Zech used both median and mean measures of per capita construction values in their study of 27 Pennsylvania cities, towns, and boroughs over the period 1976–1978. With a cross-section data set of 27 local government units and a single-equation model, they test whether either of two tax variables has an influence on the value of construction.

Their first tax measure is computed as the ratio of the city tax rate on land to the city tax rate on improvements in 1977. Their second measure is the same ratio, but computed for combined city and county tax rates. Defined this way, their key explanatory variables capture the relative tax on land compared with improvements. Hence, they are not using variation in the level of taxation on land or improvements across municipalities in their study. Rather, they are only using variation in the relative land tax rate to explain differences in construction value per capita. Although these measures have been criticized in the literature since we would expect only the tax rate on improvements to potentially have an effect, this study is nonetheless useful to review because it is one of the earliest studies on this topic.[5] It should also be noted that this method of constructing the explanatory variables eliminates problems associated with variation in assessment ratios across municipalities. The authors include an assessment ratio variable in the models to control for variation in assessment practices across municipalities. They estimate two mathematical specifications of the models (linear and double-log models), although the first specification (the linear model) is clearly misspecified.

Mathis and Zech (1982) find no evidence that either tax measure has a significant effect on the median or mean value of construction across Pennsylvania municipalities. Responding to criticism of their ratio tax variable, Mathis and Zech (1983) reestimate the models using the city and county tax rates applied to improvements only, as would be more consistent with the refutable hypothesis developed from economic theory. Again, they find no evidence of a significant tax effect on the value of construction across cities. It should be noted, however, that in their data set, only three cities had land tax rates exceeding improvement tax rates during the time period examined; in the other municipalities, the same tax rates were applied to land and improvements by both the city and the county. Consequently, there was not much variation in the tax measures across the municipalities, which may in part account for the lack of significance.

Following these early regression studies, researchers began to measure the value of new residential building permits in order to test whether land value taxation has measurable effects. Bourassa (1990) examines the effects of land value taxation on housing development in three Pennsylvania cities. Regression models were developed to explain variations in the dollar value of building permit applications. These models were designed to capture both demand- and supply-side determinants of building permit values. The models were estimated using monthly time series data for each city both before and after an increase in the land tax rate and a decrease in the improvement tax rate. Bourassa tests for both (1) liquidity effects of increases in the land tax rate, which he expected to encourage housing development in all three cities by increasing the holding cost of vacant land and reducing the value of

---

5. For critiques of the Mathis and Zech research, see Coffin and Nelson (1983) and Liu (1985).

land and thereby inducing developers to buy and develop land, and (2) incentive effects of decreases in the improvement tax rate, which he expected to encourage housing development in Pittsburgh and possibly in New Castle, but not in McKeesport. The incentive effect is based on the simple notion that a tax on improvements reduces the quantity of improvements produced.

Bourassa's model fits the Pittsburgh data better than the McKeesport and New Castle data. For Pittsburgh, seven of the eleven explanatory variables are statistically significant in explaining the value of building permits. In McKeesport the only factors Bourassa finds to have a significant effect on building permits are the price of other (nonhousing) goods and services and the price of maintenance inputs. In New Castle only the price of other goods and services is significant. On the crucial tax questions, the estimated models indicate a significant incentive effect for Pittsburgh, but no liquidity effect. That is, changes in the improvement tax rate have a significant effect on the value of building permits, but—as theory would predict—changes in the land tax rate have no significant effect. Neither of the tax rate variables has a significant effect in either McKeesport or New Castle. Hence, this study finds a potential effect from land value taxation on residential building permits only for Pittsburgh, a large central city. Bourassa's earlier study (1987) focuses on Pittsburgh alone, using similar methodology, and finds a significant incentive effect, but no significant liquidity effect.

Oates and Schwab (1997) assembled time series data on new building activity for a sample of 15 cities in the multistate region surrounding Pittsburgh to conduct their simple before-and-after analysis. They use two measures. First, they use Dun & Bradstreet data on the real value of new building permits for the 15 cities, defined to include just the cities and not the surrounding metropolitan areas. Second, they use census data for the 15 metropolitan areas disaggregated into city-suburb and residential-nonresidential construction. These basic data indicate that after 1979–1980, when the tax change occurred, something quite dramatic happened to building activity in Pittsburgh compared with other cities in the region.

Oates and Schwab explore several potential causes of the observed change in new building activity, estimating two alternative regression models. Their models of new building activity include explanatory variables for the tax regime change in 1979–1980, a time trend, and a measure of the commercial building occupancy rate. Their results indicate that the increase in the value of building permits was caused by both the tax regime change and the occupancy rate. Yet the tax regime change result is also admittedly confounded by Pittsburgh's economic development program, which included property tax abatements for new construction. Hence, their evidence on the Pittsburgh tax experience is suggestive, perhaps strongly so, yet it is not conclusive regarding causality of land value taxation. In a later reflection on this evidence Schwab and Harris (1997, 7) write, "It appears that a land tax did not cause a building boom in Pittsburgh, but it did allow the city government to avoid policies that might have undercut that boom." They attribute much of the building boom in Pittsburgh to an imbalance between supply and demand for office space in the downtown area, which was generated by important changes in the finance and service sectors of the local economy. In addition, a commitment by several major corporations to downtown Pittsburgh played an important role.

In 2001, in the process of updating assessments, Pittsburgh reverted to a traditional property tax, giving researchers a new opportunity to examine the effects of land value taxation. What remains for future research is to reexamine the effect of land value taxation in reverse, looking carefully at what happens when a city abandons the split-rate tax regime and returns to taxing land and improvements at the same rate.

Pollakowski (1982) examines property transactions in Pittsburgh between 1977 and 1981, analyzing the effect of a change in the land tax rate that occurred between 1978 and 1980. Pittsburgh taxed land at twice the rate of improvements from 1925 through 1978. In 1979 the city raised the land tax rate to four times the rate on improvements, and in 1980 increased it to five times the rate on improvements. The land tax rate increased from 10 percent to 14.6 percent between 1978 and 1979. To test whether such a tax change would alter property holding behavior, he examines the data on parcel transfers. His dependent variable is the probability of a parcel being transferred. Dependent variables include measures of the general economic conditions in the property market, the degree of disequilibrium for a given property in current use, and the land tax payment. He finds a positive and significant effect of the land tax rate. The magnitude of his estimated coefficient indicates that the land tax increase caused the property transfer rate to rise by 0.072 percentage points—less than 1 percent given the initial transfer rate of approximately 8 percent. He estimates that in 1979, of the 6,812 property transactions recorded, about 60 transfers could be attributed to the land tax increase. Pollakowski concludes that although the land tax increase led to a discernable dynamic adjustment effect measured by transfers, the magnitude of the effect was very small.

Plassmann and Tideman (2000) use building permit data for Pennsylvania cities over the period 1980–1994 to examine whether the use of split-rate tax systems in some of those cities had an impact on building activity.[6] Their data includes both residential and nonresidential building permits for a number of subcategories of construction. The first dependent variable in their analysis is defined as the number of building permits per person per month in each city. Their key explanatory variable of interest is an adjusted tax differential. To construct this variable, they first calculated the difference between the city's tax rate on land and its tax rate on improvements. Then they divided that difference by the average ratio of assessed value to sales value in the city to eliminate any potential effect due to differences in the overall assessment ratios across cities. It would have been better to use the separate tax rates on land and improvements in the analysis, as the authors acknowledge, but data limitations forced them to construct this single measure of the tax differential. Since the dependent variable in this analysis is a count of the number of building permits, Plassmann and Tideman took care to use appropriate statistical methods to estimate their model.

Their results indicate that an increase in the tax differential increases the number of building permits significantly. In particular, they estimate that a 0.1 percent increase in the differential increases the number of residential whole units permits by 0.14 percent and the number of permits for residential additions and alterations by 0.14 percent as well. They estimate that the split-rate tax in Pittsburgh over this time period increased the number of residential whole unit permits by 3.41 percent and increased the number of residential additions and alterations permits by 3.55 percent. Finally, they estimate that a switch to a pure land-only tax would increase residential whole units by 6.53 percent and residential additions and alterations by 6.98 percent. Using these results, Plassmann and Tideman also estimate the effect of an increase in the tax differential on a second dependent variable—the total value of construction. Their results indicate that a 0.1 percent increase in the tax differential was responsible for a 1.58 percent increase in the total value of construction.

In an earlier study of Pennsylvania cities, Tideman and Johnson (1995) analyze building permit data over the period 1980–1992 to determine whether a shift of taxes from improvements to land promoted economic

---

6. A precursor to this study is Tideman and Plassmann (1995), in which the authors examine the available building permit data and conjecture about potential methodology that could be used to analyze the data.

growth. They find that the available data are insufficient to identify the effect adequately. Estimates of the effect of a 1 percent differential between the equalized tax rates on improvements and land range from a 0 to 58 percent increase in construction activity.

Lusht (1992) conducts a cross-sectional analysis of communities in the area of Melbourne, Australia, where real property taxes can be based on either a measure of capital value or a measure of land value. His analysis of 53 local government authorities, or communities, in the Melbourne Statistical District finds higher development stocks and a higher flow of new housing in those communities using land value taxation. Further, he finds that in the long run, the land value taxation advantage persists, although it is eroded over time to some extent. His independent variable is the value of the residential stock improvements per acre of land in 1984. Dependent variables include measures of the community's location, age of the housing stock, industrial establishments, and population.

Since this study is based on city-level data, there are important selection bias questions to ask—that is, are the cities that adopt land value taxation regimes systematically different from those that adopt capital taxation regimes? Given the descriptive statistics provided in the study, there is ample reason to think that there may be differences. In general, the land value taxation cities are closer to the Melbourne central business district, are smaller, have less industrial and residential land available, have more industrial establishments and far fewer agricultural establishments, and have far more occupied residential units. Hence, we have reason to believe that the land value taxation communities are systematically different from the capital tax communities. Thus, the adoption of a land value tax regime may reflect the fact that these communities have a fundamentally different economic base. Differences in the economic character of communities may be responsible for the adoption of different tax regimes.

Another question that arises in this analysis has to do with the persistence of the land value taxation effect. Lusht (1992) breaks his land value taxation variable into four separate variables reflecting the time period when the community adopted land value taxation (1920s, 1940s, 1950s, and 1960s). In several of his model specifications, the 1920s site value adoption variable is not significant, but later adoption variables are significant. He interprets this as a land value taxation effect that decays over time. The problem is that in some of those specifications, the 1960s adoption variable is not significant (but the 1940s and 1950s variables are significant). This result is not consistent with a policy regime decay interpretation.

Other Approaches

Skaburskis and Tomalty (1997) study the anticipated effects of land value taxation by interviewing developers, planners, and municipal finance officials in Toronto and Ottawa, Canada. They report the following expectations: faster development, more intense land use, and reduced speculative holding of land. Although very informative of expectations, and thereby insightful, this study provides no evidence on the actual effects of adopting land value taxation.

A number of studies based on comparisons within or across cities have appeared in the literature, among them studies by Cord (1970, 1976, 1985, 1987). Cord (1970) reports on the potential for a split-rate tax regime to stimulate urban redevelopment in the city of Lancaster, Pennsylvania. The study describes how a split-rate tax system would work and claims three advantages of such a system: an increase in housing and new construction, more efficient land use, and a fairer tax system. Cord uses a sample of assessed values for 100 properties in the city to conduct a static analysis of the potential trade-off between higher land tax rates and lower improvement tax rates. He assumes that land and improvement values remain unchanged and that the city budget is unchanged. Starting with an initial property tax rate of 1.2 percent applied to both improvements and land, he uses the existing property values to compute a three-year phased transition to a split-rate tax regime in which 75 percent of improvement value is exempted from taxation. The building tax rate would fall from 1.2 percent to 0.3 percent. With that reduction in the improvement tax rate, he computes the required increase in the land tax rate. According to his computations, the land tax rate would have to rise from 1.2 percent to 7.5 percent. Using these tax rates, Cord then examines the impact of the changed rates on total taxes paid for various types of properties in the city. There is no empirical analysis to substantiate the claims regarding new construction, efficient land use, or fairness of the tax system. There is no model estimating the potential changes in land values, building values, development activity, or other variables.

Similarly, Cord (1976) reports on the potential effects of moving to a split-rate tax system for a sample of rural properties in Indiana County, Pennsylvania. He investigates the effect of a 25 percent reduction in the improvement tax rate and a corresponding revenue-neutral increase in the land tax rate on the tax liabilities of a sample of 60 farms in the county (out of a total of 1,200 farms in the county). The article describes in general terms the type of farms that would experience tax liability increases or decreases. Again, there is no economic model of the market for agricultural land or improvements involved in the analysis. Property values are fixed in the computations of the required tax rates.

Finally, Cord (1987) uses a comparison method to examine the experience of Pennsylvania cities that shifted to split-rate taxes. He compares their experience with that of neighboring cities that did not make the tax shift and finds that cities shifting to split-rate taxes experienced more construction activity. Although suggestive that there may be an effect, such a method does not control for other factors that may affect construction activity. Furthermore, the study does not consider the selection bias question. Caution is necessary when examining such studies, since the research design employed has clear limitations.

ADVANCING OUR KNOWLEDGE

What Do We Know?

The theoretical literature on citywide land value taxation adoption leads us to expect a reduction in housing prices, an increase in improvements per acre, and a reduction in land prices (Brueckner 1986). Computable general equilibrium models generally provide simulations consistent with these expectations, although the precise outcomes vary depending on the parameter assumptions of the model and the urban area for which the model is calibrated (Nechyba 1998; Haughwout 2004). The best empirical models we have to date focus on the effects of land value taxation adoption on building activity, usually measured by residential building permits. Those models indicate that moving toward land value taxation may increase building activity, or at least does not decrease it.

What Is Missing?

Research opportunities are few and far between. Existing experience with split-rate taxes in the United States is confined to about 20 cities in Pennsylvania that began adopting split-rate taxes in 1913. There have been no recent adoptions of split-rate taxes or land value taxation by U.S. cities. The most fruitful case to study at this point may be the experience of Pittsburgh, which recently (2001) eliminated its split-rate tax system (except in the Pittsburgh Improvement District, where a land value tax continues to be used). Researchers may find useful data from this experience to test whether equalizing tax rates on land and capital has the opposite effects of those expected from the adoption of a split-rate tax system. The Pittsburgh experience is confounded, however, by a contentious citywide reassessment that was part of the regime change. Indeed, some say that it was the fundamental need for reassessment, rather than discontent with the split-rate tax system itself, that led Pittsburgh to abandon its split-rate system.

Given the paucity of U.S. data on this issue, researchers should look more seriously at international cases of land value taxation adoption. Riël Franzsen provides an international perspective in chapter 3 of this volume that may prove fruitful for researchers looking for more cases to analyze. The recent experience of cities in transition countries may provide new opportunities for research on this issue.

Where Do We Go from Here?

There are several important issues to consider as we contemplate the future direction of research on land value taxation. Economic theory indicates that land value taxation may lead to a higher equilibrium level of capital per acre of land in an urban area. That requires a higher rate of net investment in buildings until the new steady state level is reached. At that point, we would expect the rate of construction to slow to a replacement rate. Consequently, we should anticipate that land value taxation would at best stimulate a higher rate of construction activity for a period of time, but that increase would be followed by a slow down and eventual return to a more modest rate of activity. Dynamic models of the process are needed to more fully understand the impacts of land value taxation adoption.

Although much of the empirical literature on land value taxation effects has focused on measuring changes in capital applied to land, other effects need to be considered as well. A secondary question of interest is whether a switch to land value taxation affects land and house values. There is a rich literature relevant to this issue, known as property tax capitalization. The capitalization approach views real estate as a long-lived asset that generates an annual rent that can be capitalized to determine the value of the land and the house. Moving from a property tax with equal tax rates applied to land and improvements to land value taxation with a higher tax on land and no tax on improvements will affect both asset prices. Since a land value tax reduces the net annual rent earned by the land, the tax will reduce land prices, and the tax is said to be capitalized into the value of the land. On the other hand, the land value tax reduces the tax on improvements and thus increases their value. (Oates and Schwab provide an overview of the capitalization issue in chapter 4 of this volume.)

Studies of the impacts of land value taxation reviewed here were conducted for cities with explicit split-rate tax systems. As an alternative, researchers may be able to use variations in assessment practices to study the effects of implicit differences in land and improvement tax rates. Since the effective property tax rate is the product of the assessment ratio and the nominal (statutory) tax rate, systematic differences in assessment practices could result in different effective tax rates for land and improvements. Researchers may thus be able to study the effects of split-rate tax systems in cities that have not formally adopted land value taxation.

SUMMARY AND CONCLUSIONS

Attempting to discern the effects of land value taxation and its variants, researchers have tried a number of approaches. They have used theoretical models to predict the impacts. They have simulated computable general equilibrium models. They have estimated a wide range of regression models explaining the number and value of building permits, the value of residential stock per acre of land, the number of occupied residential units per acre of land, population density, and the probability of property transfers. They have built simulation models, interviewed developers, conducted comparison analyses, and generally tried every technique in the book. There are some credible studies showing no effects and other credible studies showing measurable effects. I see no reason to alter Netzer's conclusion (2001, 100): "The persuasive studies have shown mixed results."

The best empirical models we have to date focus on measuring the effects of land value taxation adoption by using measures of building activity—usually residential building permits. Those models indicate that a move to land value taxation does not hurt (Oates and Schwab 1997), or actually may help (Plassmann and Tideman 2000). The evidence supporting that conclusion, however, is limited; the studies were based primarily on just one U.S. city's experience—Pittsburgh. There is clearly a need for more analysis of the effects of land value taxation adoption, but that can only be provided when researchers find more case studies to analyze. Even in the study that found that land value taxation had a significant impact on residential building activity

(Plassmann and Tideman 2000), the magnitude of the effect was modest as a percentage of total building activity—which may help explain why many other studies have failed to find a significant impact.

Theoretical models of citywide land value taxation adoption point to a reduction in housing prices, an increase in improvements per acre of land, and a reduction in land prices. Computable general equilibrium models have provided simulations consistent with these expectations, with precise estimates varying based on the underlying assumptions of the model and the particular urban area for which the model has been developed.

Policy makers considering the adoption of land value taxation should know that the best empirical evidence on its effects is mixed, with some studies showing significant effects on building permits and other measures of construction and other studies showing no effect whatsoever. Although economic theory suggests the prospect for economic improvement from a land value tax regime, in practice our ability to measure discernible effects in the limited cases where land value taxation has been implemented has been hampered. There are measurement difficulties. There are city-specific peculiarities. Ultimately, only a few communities have adopted land value taxes and provide us with very limited evidence to analyze. As it is, testing for the effects of land value taxation adoption is a formidable research task. Casual observation of the effects is often clouded by other factors that we cannot control for and that may confound the picture. We cannot logically conclude that the adoption of a land value tax has caused any of the observed effects merely because we find a correlation between land value taxation adoption and those effects.

With additional research exploiting new and creative ways to test for land value taxation effects, perhaps more definitive results may be obtained. And new research opportunities may arise if more cities choose to adopt land value taxation. In the meantime, we have a limited number of credible empirical studies providing reliable, if mixed, evidence.

Table 6.1 Summary of key studies of land value taxation by type

Study	Measure(s) of economic activity	Research methodology	Findings
		Theoretical models	
J. Anderson (1999)	Timing of development and structural density of development	Theoretical model of developer behavior	The move to a split-rate tax will speed the timing of development and increase its capital intensity if capital and development time are substitutes or independent and the elasticity of substitution is small, as would be expected for a declining city. If capital and development time are strong complements, as would be the case for a growing city, the opposite results may occur.
Arnott (2005)	Timing and capital intensity of development, and deadweight loss	Theoretical model of developer behavior with numerical examples	Develops a property tax system design that is neutral in its effects.
Arnott and Petrova (2006)	Timing and capital intensity of development, and deadweight loss	Theoretical model of developer behavior with numerical examples	Investigates four property tax systems and finds that all are distortionary. Measures the relative inefficiencies of each.
Brueckner (1986)	Improvements (capital per acre of land), value of land, and price of housing	Theoretical models of long-run effects of land value taxation with both exogenous and endogenous housing prices	Effects of land value taxation depend on the size of the tax zone: (1) When the tax zone constitutes a negligible portion of the market, gradation of the tax system leaves the price of housing unchanged but raises both the level of improvements per acre and the value of land. (2) When the tax zone encompasses the entire housing market, gradation of the tax system reduces the price of housing, raises the level of improvements, and lowers the value of land.

Study	Variables	Model type	Results
DiMasi (1987)	Land rents, improvements per acre, housing prices, population density, urbanized area, and wages	General equilibrium computational model, stylized to describe metro Boston in 1980	With a split-rate tax system, land rents fall, improvements per acre increase, housing prices fall, population densities (given distance) rise, the spatial extent of the urban development falls, and wages increase.
Follain and Miyake (1986)	Change in income tax	General equilibrium simulation of replacing the Jamaican income tax with either a land value tax or a capital tax	Simulations provide for a reduction in the Jamaican income tax with increased reliance on either a land value tax or a capital value tax. Using a land value tax to replace 20% of the income tax revenue in Jamaica would require confiscation of land.
Grosskopf (1981)	Land value	General equilibrium model, à la Harberger, of the switch from a property tax to an equal-yield land value tax, with typical values of key parameters taken from the literature	The model shows an increase in equilibrium land prices (and hence the land value tax base), indicating revenue sufficiency for a switch.
Nechyba (1998)	Capital, land values, land rents, and output	Computable general equilibrium model of a small open economy	A revenue-neutral increase in the land tax and a reduction in the capital tax results in higher capital stock, increased output, and generally lower land values.
Haughwout (2004)	Output, land values, capital stock, population, provision of public goods, and tax revenue	Computable general equilibrium model of a small open economy	Simulates eliminating the city's sales, income, property, and general corporate taxes while retaining the tax on land at its current rate (2.83%). Results include a substantial increase in private output, increased land values, larger private capital stock, and larger population. The provision of public goods and per capita tax revenue fall by more than 50%.

(continued)

Table 6.1 continued

Study	Measure(s) of economic activity	Research methodology	Findings
			Regression models
Bourassa (1987)	Value of new building permits	Regression model for Pittsburgh	Finds a significant incentive effect of taxation, but no liquidity effect.
Bourassa (1990)	Value of new building permits	Regression model for three Pennsylvania cities	Finds a significant incentive effect of taxation for Pittsburgh, but not McKeesport or New Castle. Does not find a liquidity effect of taxation in any of the cities.
Lusht (1992)	Value of residential stock per acre of land, number of occupied residential units per acre of land, and population density	Regression model based on city-level data for local government authorities in the Melbourne, Australia, area in 1984	Finds a generally significant positive effect for communities using land value taxation, compared with those using capital taxation, on all three measures of economic activity.
Mathis and Zech (1982, 1983)	Per capita construction (1982) and construction per acre of land (1983)	Regression model for Pennsylvania cities	The ratio of the tax rate on land to the tax rate on improvements is not significant in explaining either variable.
Oates and Schwab (1997)	Average annual value of building permits	Econometric models of time series patterns in average annual value of building permits for Pennsylvania cities	Finds a positive and significant effect of Pittsburgh's 1979 policy change whereby the tax rate on land rose to five times the rate on structures, but no effect in other cities where tax policy did not change in 1979.
Pollakowski (1982)	Probability of property transfer	Regression model for Pittsburgh over the period 1977–1981	Finds a positive and significant effect of Pittsburgh's 1979 policy change on number of property transfers. The size of the estimated effect is very small, however—less than 1% in the typical ward.

Tideman and Johnson (1995)	Construction activity	Regression model of construction activity for Pennsylvania cities	Finds no clear evidence that the differential between land and improvement tax rates leads to higher construction activity.
Other models and approaches			
Plassmann and Tideman (2000)	Building permits per person per month in the municipality (both residential and nonresidential)	Markov chain Monte Carlo analysis of building permits issued by Pennsylvania cities over the period 1980–1994	An increase in the tax differential increases the number of building permits significantly.
Skaburskis and Tomalty (1997)	Timing of development, capital intensity of development, and speculation	Interviews with developers, planners, and municipal finance officials	A switch to land value taxation would (1) speed up development, (2) lead to more intense land use, and (3) reduce speculation.
England (2003)	Total employment, gross state product, residential construction, consumer price index, total exports, total imports, disposable income, total population, and net migrants	Simulation model	Simulation of New Hampshire statewide revenue-neutral shift from a property tax to a land value tax using county-level data and the REMI EDFS forecasting and simulation model. Finds that residential construction would rise by an estimated 1 percent.

(continued)

Table 6.1 continued

Study	Measure(s) of economic activity	Research methodology	Findings
England and Ravichandran (2007)	Building height and footprint ratio	Simulation model	The tax rate on building value influences private investment decisions affecting footprint ratio and building height. The tax rate on land value is largely capitalized into land price paid by the developer and does not have much, if any, influence on the design of development projects.
Cord (1987)	Construction activity	Comparison study	Compares the experiences of Pennsylvania cities that shifted to split-rate taxes with the experiences of neighboring cities that did not make that shift. Cities shifting to graded taxes experienced more construction activity.
Pollock and Shoup (1977)	Capital intensity of land development	Real estate revenue production function model	Elimination of the tax rate on improvements would increase the long-run equilibrium level of improvements by 25%—an upper bound estimate that ignores several general equilibrium effects.

IMPLEMENTATION

◈ 7 ◈

The Legal Framework
in the United States

RICHARD D. COE

IF A GOVERNMENTAL UNIT planned to implement a land tax, what legal issues might it face? This chapter addresses that question.[1] Property taxation is basically a state and local government affair, and thus the legal rules that affect real property taxation are governed primarily by state law, which varies across the 50 states. Given this variation, it is not possible within the context of a single chapter to provide a precise roadmap of the legal issues that any particular state or local government would have to traverse in order to implement a land tax. Rather, the chapter examines some specific legal issues that have been raised with respect to the property tax and hence are presumably relevant to the implementation of a land tax, thus serving as a useful starting point for anyone interested in exploring the legal issues surrounding the adoption of such a tax. The focus is on state constitutional provisions along with accompanying case law.

The first question addressed revolves around enabling provisions. Are

I would like to express my appreciation to the Lincoln Institute of Land Policy for its support for this research. The chapter has benefited immensely from comments by the editors and by Joan Youngman of the Institute.

1. A multinational treatment of legal issues regarding land value taxation is beyond the scope of this book. Chapter 3 covers some of the legal issues and institutions in its five case-study nations.

there state constitutional provisions that explicitly enable a state or local government to levy a land tax, or that explicitly prohibit such a tax? In the absence of any explicit constitutional provisions, are there enabling powers or prohibitions implicit in a state constitution?

The second set of questions, which constitutes the bulk of the chapter, examines possible legal issues that might stem from various state constitutional provisions affecting the legislature's ability to levy taxes. Some common principles governing taxation in general, and property taxation specifically, are found in a number of state constitutions—principles of uniformity, equality, universality, and proportionality. Would a land tax face legal challenges under these general principles? I examine this question within the context of the general administrative framework that characterizes the practice of property taxation in the United States.

ENABLING PROVISIONS

The Federal Government

The position of the federal government is clear. Article I, Section 9, Clause 4 of the U.S. Constitution states: "No Capitation, or other direct, Tax shall be laid, unless in Proportion to the Census or enumeration herein before directed to be taken." There is little question among both legal and economic experts that a property tax, including a land tax, is a "direct" tax within the meaning of the Constitution. This proposition has long been embedded in constitutional law, as illustrated by *Springer v. United States*, 102 U.S. 586 (1880), in which the U.S. Supreme Court stated, "Our conclusions are, that *direct taxes*, within the meaning of the Constitution, are only capitation taxes, as expressed in that instrument, and taxes on real estate."[2] The stringency of the "in proportion to the Census" requirement, among other factors, has effectively ruled out any serious consideration today of implementing a federal property tax.

---

2. It is perhaps worth noting that 15 years later, the U.S. Supreme Court, affirming that a tax on real estate was a direct tax, added a tax on income from property to the list of direct taxes within the meaning of the Constitution, thus effectively voiding the recently enacted federal individual income tax. See *Pollock v. Farmers' Loan & Trust Co.*, 157 U.S. 429 (1895).

State Governments

A state government generally has the authority to levy a tax on real property, either through an enabling provision in the constitution explicitly authorizing the taxation of real property or, in the absence of such, through a provision establishing the general taxation powers of the state. Massachusetts is an example of a state in which the taxation of real property is explicitly authorized. The state constitution grants the legislative body the power "to impose and levy proportional and reasonable assessments, rates, and taxes, upon all . . . estates" (part 2, ch. 1, sec. 1, art. IV). Similarly, the New Hampshire Constitution provides that "full power and authority are hereby given and granted . . . to impose and levy proportional and reasonable . . . taxes . . . upon all estates" (part 2, art. 5). The state legislatures in states that have such explicit constitutional enabling provisions clearly have the power to levy a tax on real property, including land. This power, however, may be subject to other constitutional provisions (discussed below) that could limit the legal authority of the state to impose a land tax.

States without such explicit enabling provisions are usually empowered to tax property under the general powers of taxation granted under the state constitution—absent, of course, an explicit constitutional prohibition against property taxation. Courts recognize that the power to tax is fundamental to the power to govern and are inclined to give state legislatures extensive leeway in their power to tax, as long as it does not violate any explicit provision of the state constitution.

Some state constitutions explicitly prohibit the state government from taxing real property. The Florida Constitution, for example, states: "No tax shall be levied except in pursuance of law. *No state ad valorem taxes shall be levied upon real estate* or tangible personal property. All other forms of taxation shall be preempted to the state except as provided by general law" (art. VII, sec. 1(a); emphasis added). In effect, this provision vests the power to tax real property solely in local governments.

Local Governments

As a general rule, the taxing power of local governments is subordinate to state governmental authority. As a result, the rules governing property taxation by local governments emanate from the state legislature (subject, of course, to any constitutional requirements). As noted, the Florida Constitution prohibits the state government from levying a property tax, in effect reserving that tax solely for local governments. Still, the state constitution contains provisions that place the local taxing process under the control of the state government. For example, article VII, section 4 of the state constitution states: "By general law regulations shall be prescribed which shall secure a just valuation of all property for ad valorem taxation." Pursuant to this provision, the state has adopted statutes that dictate to local governments how property shall be valued. For example, a Florida law provides that "the cost of said property and the present replacement value of any improvements thereon" is one factor to be considered in valuing property (Fla. Stat. §193.011(5)). State statutory provisions such as this could restrict a local government's ability to enact some forms of a land tax.

LAND TAXATION AND THE GENERAL ADMINISTRATIVE FRAMEWORK OF PROPERTY TAXATION IN THE UNITED STATES

General Administrative Framework of Property Taxation

Given the current administrative framework for property taxation in the United States, several alternative legislative approaches could accomplish the objective of differentially taxing land and improvements. Although there is no single model of property tax administration in the United States, for analytical purposes one can construct a general framework of the process by which the tax liability for a specific piece of real property is determined. Five separate steps can be identified.

Classification
In many states property is classified into distinct categories, such as residential or commercial property, for purposes of property taxation. Classification plans are usually established by the legislature, although there may be constitutional limitations on the number or type of classifications, as discussed in more detail below.

Valuation
A value must be placed on the property. Fair market value is generally the valuation criterion, often considered to be constitutionally mandated.

Assessment Ratio

To ascertain taxable value (i.e., the value to which the statutory tax rate is applied to determine the amount of tax owed), assessors may apply different assessment ratios to the value of different types of property.[3] For example, a state may dictate that a 50 percent assessment ratio be applied to property classified as commercial and a 25 percent assessment ratio be applied to property classified as residential. Given these ratios, a piece of commercial property valued at $200,000 would be assigned a taxable value of $100,000, whereas a parcel of residential property of equivalent value would be assigned a taxable value of only $50,000.

Tax Rate

To determine the actual amount of property tax owed, one applies the appropriate tax rate, usually stated in mills,[4] to the taxable value of the property. Tax rates may vary according to the property's classification.

Exemptions

It is common for state constitutions to exempt certain properties from taxation. These provisions may take the form of a mandatory exemption ("shall be exempted"), an explicit permissive exemption allowing the legislature to establish an exemption for a specified type of property ("may be exempted"), or a general discretionary grant of power to the legislature to grant exemptions as it sees fit. Existing exemptions cover a wide range of factors, but in general are based either on the use of property or on some characteristic of the owner of the property. The exemption may be complete or partial. A complete exemption results in no property tax being levied against the property; a partial exemption reduces the tax owed on the property.

It should be emphasized that not every state employs each step of this general administrative framework. Some states do not have different classes of property. Many do not have the seemingly puzzling—to an economist—dis-

---

3. Although a state may specify a uniform assessment to market value fraction for all property, the concern here is with the use of *different* assessment ratios for different property classes.

4. A tax rate of 1 mill is equal to a tax of $1 on each $1,000 of taxable value.

tinction between assessment ratios and tax rates. But this framework enables one to see the alternative administrative procedures that a government may employ to enact a land tax.

A Land Tax Within the General Framework of Property Tax Administration

The fundamental objective underlying a land tax is to tax the land component of a parcel of real property at a higher rate than improvements on that parcel. There are several alternative administrative methods involving different steps in the taxation process by which this objective may be accomplished.

Differential Classification

One possibility is to classify land and improvements as different classes of property and then establish different tax rates for the different classes. Land would, of course, be assigned a higher tax rate than improvements.

Differential Valuation

A second possibility is to apply different valuation methodologies to land and improvements so that improvements are assessed at a lower value, relative to fair market value, than land. Applying the same tax rate to both would result in a lower effective tax rate on improvements.

Differential Assessment Ratios

Alternatively, one can value land and improvements using the same methodology, but apply different assessment ratios to the two values. For example, improvements could be assigned an assessment ratio of 25 percent and land an assessment ratio of 50 percent. The application of the same tax rate would then result in an effective tax rate on improvements that was one-half the effective tax rate on land.

Differential Tax Rates

One could implement a land tax by simply applying different tax rates to the value of the land and to the value of the improvements on the land. This would eliminate the need for differential classification, valuation, or assessment ratios.

Exemption of Improvements

A final alternative administrative approach to land taxation would be to exempt improvements explicitly from the tax base, either completely (a pure land tax) or partially (a split-rate tax).

Thus there exist a variety of administrative approaches to implement what is in effect a land tax.[5] Each of these approaches would face potential legal challenges, as discussed below.

GENERAL STATE CONSTITUTIONAL PRINCIPLES OF PROPERTY TAXATION: UNIFORMITY, EQUALITY, UNIVERSALITY, AND PROPORTIONALITY

Before launching into a detailed examination of specific state constitutional provisions and accompanying case law governing property taxation, we should note four interrelated constitutional principles regarding taxation that appear with regularity: uniformity, equality, universality, and proportionality. Each principle is subject to specific interpretation on a state-by-state basis, but there are general themes that underlie the interpretation of the principles across the states, and these themes may pose legal barriers for the implementation of a land tax. The presence of these principles in state constitutions is cataloged in table 7.1 (see page 159).

Uniformity is perhaps the most commonly stated constitutional principle.[6] In general, uniformity refers to the idea that tax practices should be applied in an identical—that is, uniform—manner to all taxed parties. More specifically, the rules developed in the five stages of the administrative framework outlined above must be applied in the same manner to all parties.[7] Thirty-nine states have explicit uniformity provisions in their constitutions.[8]

---

5. There are no doubt several other creative ways to implement administratively what is in effect a land tax.

6. In his authoritative treatise, Newhouse (1984, 12) says that "the constitutions of forty-two (possibly forty-four) of the fifty states contain such provisions."

7. See Newhouse (1984, 12–18) for a more detailed discussion on the meaning of uniformity clauses.

8. This number differs from that cited from Newhouse in footnote 6 because he uses a more inclusive definition of uniformity provisions; for example, he treats proportionality clauses as uniformity provisions.

Equality is closely related to uniformity. As applied to property taxation, the constitutional principle of equality means that properties of equal value should be subject to the same amount of tax. Sixteen states have equality provisions in their constitutions.

Universality is closely related to uniformity and equality. With respect to a property tax, the universality principle requires that all property be subject to taxation (in an equal and uniform manner, of course), unless specifically exempted by law. Twenty states have such provisions. The Arizona Constitution provides a clear example of this principle: "All property in the state not exempt under the laws of the United States or under this constitution or exempt by law under the provisions of this section shall be subject to taxation" (art IX, sec. 2, cl. 13).

Finally, *proportionality* is the concept that property taxes on different parcels of property should be proportional to the values of those properties. Twelve states have proportionality provisions in their constitutions.

The uniformity, equality, and universality principles are all in accord with the principle of horizontal equity expressed in the tax literature. The concept of horizontal equity embodies the idea that, as a normative principle, equals should be treated equally. In the context of property taxation, horizontal equity requires that property of equal value be assessed an equal amount of tax. If a tax is applied nonuniformly and nonuniversally, then property of equal value will not be assessed the same amount of tax, in violation of the principle of horizontal equity. The principle of horizontal equity, however, does not address the question of how we should tax persons in different (tax-related) economic circumstances. The proportionality principle, which is consistent with the notion of vertical equity, provides the answer—persons should be taxed in proportion to their economic circumstances or, in the case of a property tax, in proportion to the value of their property. Thus, under the proportionality principle, a person who owns a parcel of property valued at twice the value of a parcel of property owned by another person would pay twice as much tax.

The proportionality principle has often been linked, directly or indirectly, to the benefit principle of taxation, which states that the tax burden should be distributed in accordance with the benefits received from the governmental functions financed by the taxes. The Vermont Constitution states the principle directly: "That every member of society hath a right to be protected in the enjoyment of life, liberty, and property, and therefore is bound to contribute the member's proportion towards the expense of that protection" (ch. 1, art. 9). Similarly, the Massachusetts Constitution states: "Each individual of the society has a right to be protected by it in the enjoyment of his life, liberty and property, according to standing laws. He is obliged, consequently, to contribute his share to the expense of this protection" (part 1, article X). In *Bettigole v. Assessors of Springfield*, 178 N.E.2d 10 (Mass. 1961), the Supreme Court of Massachusetts, emphasizing the connection with the proportionality clause in the state constitution, said: "It is well settled that the words 'his share' . . . forbid the imposition upon one taxpayer of a burden relatively greater or relatively less than that imposed on other taxpayers."

With respect to property taxation, these principles are closely related and are often expressed together in provisions of the state constitution. The West Virginia Constitution serves as an excellent example, as it manages to express all four principles in one section: "Subject to the exceptions in this section contained, taxation shall be *equal* and *uniform* throughout the state, and *all* property, both real and personal, shall be taxed in *proportion* to its value to be ascertained as directed by law. No one species of property from which a tax may be collected shall be taxed higher than any other species of property of equal value" (art. 10-1; emphasis added). If the value of all property (the universality principle) is assessed according to the same procedures (the uniformity principle) and taxed at the same rate (the uniformity principle), then taxpayers owning property of equal value will pay the same amount in taxes (the equality principle), and the tax burden will be distributed in proportion to the value of property holdings (the proportionality principle).

Under a strict application of the principles of equality, uniformity, universality, and proportionality, a land tax would not pass muster. A land tax would tax equally valued properties differently, depending on the ratio of the value of improvements to the value of land. And the tax burden would not be distributed proportionally to actual property values. In other words, a land tax results in the differential treatment of equally valued property, and legal justification for such differential treatment would be required.

These issues are addressed in more detail in the next section. But one more general legal principle regarding taxation should be noted—the principle of judicial deference. As a general rule, courts have recognized the legislature's prerogative in establishing tax policy and have been reluctant to overturn legislation regarding tax matters, unless it clearly violates a constitutional provision. The U.S. Supreme Court has expressed this deference thus: "When the constituted authority of the state undertakes to exert the taxing power, and the question of the validity of its action is brought before this court, every presumption in its favor is indulged, and only clear and demonstrated usurpation of power will authorize judicial interference with legislative action" (*Walters v. City of St. Louis*, 347 U.S. 231 [1954], quoting *Green v. Frazier*, 253 U.S. 233 [1920]).

LEGAL ISSUES INVOLVED IN A LAND TAX: DIFFERENTIAL TAXATION OF LAND AND IMPROVEMENTS

The Federal Level: The Equal Protection Clause of the U.S. Constitution

A land tax would tax property owners with equally valued property in a differential manner. Would such differential treatment run afoul of the equal protection clause of the Fourteenth Amendment to the U.S. Constitution? Under the assumption that a land tax does not involve a "suspect classification,"[9] the legal test is whether the classification is rationally related to a legitimate governmental interest. In *Nordlinger v. Hahn*, 505 U.S. 1 (1992), the U.S. Supreme Court heard a challenge to California's Proposition 13, which resulted in differential property tax assessments for homeowners of (nearly) identical properties depending on the date the property was acquired. The Court said:

> The appropriate standard of review is whether the difference in treatment between newer and older owners rationally furthers a legitimate state interest. In general, the Equal Protection Clause is satisfied so long as there is a plausible policy reason for the classification, the legislative facts on which the classification is apparently based rationally may have been considered to be true by the governmental decision maker, and the relationship of the classification to its goal is not so attenuated as to render the distinction arbitrary or irrational. This standard is especially deferential in the context of classifications made by complex tax laws. "[I]n structuring internal taxation schemes 'the States have a large leeway in making classifications and drawing lines which in their judgment produce reasonable systems of taxation.'" (citations omitted)

Given the arguments that the differential taxation of land and improvements is designed to promote such legitimate governmental interests as eco-

---

9. Legislative classifications based on race, national origin, religion, and alienage have been declared "suspect classifications" and are subject to a "strict scrutiny" judicial test—is the classification necessary to achieve a compelling state interest? (This same test is applied if a fundamental right is involved, such as the right to vote.) Legislative classifications based on gender and legitimacy are considered "quasi-suspect," and will be struck down unless the classification is substantially related to an important governmental interest.

nomic development and prevention of urban sprawl, and given the Supreme Court's deference to state tax plans, it is highly unlikely that a land tax, if adopted by a state or local government, would run afoul of the equal protection clause.

The State Level

This section undertakes a detailed discussion of the state constitutional issues likely to be encountered if a state or local government attempted to implement a land tax.[10] The discussion tracks the alternative administrative strategies that a jurisdiction might adopt, as noted earlier: (1) establishing differential tax rates on land and improvements; (2) applying differential valuation methods (and assessment ratios)[11] to land and improvements; (3) classifying land and improvements as separate classes of property; or (4) exempting improvements from taxation.[12] As will become clear from the discussion below, the two most critical legal issues involve the classification and exemption strategies. If either of these administrative approaches can pass constitutional muster, other potential legal barriers to a land tax, such as the application of differential tax rates to land and improvements, become much less daunting. I take up the relatively simpler legal issues of differential taxation and differential valuation methods before turning to the more complex classification and exemption issues.

Differential Tax Rates

To an economist, the administrative implementation of a land tax would seem to be a straightforward proposition. For a given parcel of property, simply value

10. My analysis in this section benefited greatly from unpublished legal memorandums written by Rachel Carlson to Richard England in 2004 on the property taxing authority in Massachusetts, New Hampshire, Connecticut, Arizona, Virginia, and Pennsylvania.

11. The assessment ratio step is not discussed separately, but rather is subsumed under the valuation step. Many states do not use a separate assessment ratio step in administrating the property tax. Even in states that do use such a step (such as Arizona), the end result is the same as using a separate valuation methodology—differential taxable values, compared with market value, for different types of property. Youngman (2006b, ch. 7) provides a detailed legal analysis of state constitutional issues with respect to the use of differing assessment ratios.

12. It is also possible to rebate the property taxes paid on improvements, thus in effect lowering the tax rate on improvements. In *Baker v. Matheson*, 607 P.2d 233 (Utah 1979), the Utah Supreme Court upheld the constitutionality of a law that rebated to homeowners, out of general revenue funds, 27.5 percent of local property taxes. The court held that the law was an expenditure law, not a property tax law, and thus did not fall under the constitutional uniformity provisions.

the land and the improvements on the land separately, and then apply the desired tax rate separately to each component value (a zero tax rate to the value of improvements in the case of a pure land tax). This proposition appears even more straightforward when one realizes that the separate valuation of land and improvements already occurs extensively across taxing jurisdictions. In their study of property tax valuation practices in the 50 states, Brunori and Carr (2002) found that 29 states require that land and improvements be valued separately. Furthermore, in their survey of 226 local taxing authorities, they found that all but 6—including those in states that were under no legal requirement to undertake separate valuations—valued land and improvements separately. Thus, all the administrative elements appear to be in place for the relatively simple implementation of a land tax via the straightforward application of differential tax rates to land and improvements.[13]

As shown in table 7.1, the constitutions of 17 states contain an explicit provision directed at classification of property for purposes of taxation. These provisions usually take the form of either enumerating the classes that can be established or explicitly granting the legislature the power to establish classes. The enumerated classifications are generally based on different functional types of parcels and do not separate the land and improvement components of each parcel. In the absence of the legal authority to classify land and improvements as separate classes of property or to exempt improvements, the straightforward practice of applying differential tax rates to land and improvements would raise serious, most likely fatal, objections under the uniformity clauses of state constitutions. The Florida Constitution contains perhaps the clearest statement against such a practice: "All ad valorem taxation shall be at a uniform rate within each taxing unit" (art. VII, sec. 2). The Oregon Constitution states: "All taxation shall be uniform on the same class of subjects" (art. I, sec. 32), and "the Legislative Assembly shall . . . provide by law uniform rules of assessment and taxation. All taxes shall be levied and collected under general laws operating uniformly throughout the State" (art. IX, sec. 1). The courts have sensibly interpreted such constitutional provisions to require that the same tax rate be applied (by the appropriate jurisdiction) to all property in a given class. Thus, the Massachusetts Supreme

---

13. It is an open question whether the administrative elements currently in place to value land and improvements separately generate accurate values of the two components. E. Mills (1998, 144–147), for one, is highly skeptical of current practices. See also Reschovsky (1998, 225–226) in the same volume and references cited therein, as well as chapter 8 of this volume for an extended discussion of land assessment issues.

Judicial Court, upholding the constitutionality of a statute granting local governments the ability to set property tax rates, stated: "There is no reason to believe that proportionality (under the constitution) was intended to require that municipal tax rates be uniform Statewide . . . . The present statute assumes, we believe correctly, that the requirement of uniform rates (for each class of property) relates to the individual municipality, not the State" (*Opinion of the Justices to the House of Representatives*, 393 N.E.2d 306 [Mass. 1979]). These provisions make clear that tax rates may vary by class and by jurisdiction without violating constitutional uniformity provisions, but differential tax rates on the same class of property in the same jurisdiction would face a formidable constitutional challenge. It is perhaps the most fundamental requirement of state constitutional uniformity provisions that property in the same class and not subject to any exemption provision face the same statutory tax rate.

Differential Valuation Practices

In determining the separate values of land and improvements for a parcel of property, could a jurisdiction apply a different valuation methodology to each that resulted in a systematic difference between the assessed value of land relative to its market value and the assessed value of improvements relative to their market value? Such an administrative approach would run into two potential legal obstacles: (1) constitutional requirements that all property be valued at fair market value and (2) constitutional uniformity provisions.

VALUATION AT FAIR MARKET VALUE. A state constitution may contain provisions that impose requirements on the valuation methodology adopted within that state.[14] The last column of table 7.1 shows the 18 states with "just value" provisions. The Florida Constitution, for example, provides: "By general law regulations shall be prescribed which shall secure a *just valuation* of all property for ad valorem taxation" (art. VII, sec. 4; emphasis added). In *Walter v. Schuler*, 176 So. 2d 81 (Fla. 1965), a case challenging the county tax assessor's practice of systematically (i.e., uniformly) valuing property at approximately 40 percent of market value, the Supreme Court of Florida held that "'fair market value' and 'just valuation' should be declared 'legally synonymous.'" The court went on to say that fair market value "may be estab-

---

14. Property tax assessors use several different methodologies to estimate fair market value. These methodologies do not always yield the same result. For an in-depth discussion of these methodologies and the legal issues they have raised, see Youngman (2006b).

lished by the classic formula that it is the amount a 'purchaser willing but not obliged to buy, would pay to one willing but not obliged to sell.'" This valuation rule is constitutionally mandated for all types and components of property, except those classes of property explicitly exempted from such in the state constitution.[15] Thus, in *Interlachen Lakes Estates v. Snyder*, 304 So. 2d 433 (Fla. 1973), the court struck down as unconstitutional a statute that provided favorable valuation to unsold platted lots of a subdivision. In *Valencia Center v. Bystrom*, 543 So. 2d 214 (Fla. 1989), the court held unconstitutional a statute that placed an upper limit on the valuation of potential improvements on a parcel of land. (The land was subject to a lease that effectively prevented the property from being put to its highest-valued use.)

The courts in Florida have recently applied the "just valuation" holding directly to issues involving the separate valuation of land and improvements. In *Turner v. Bell Chevrolet, Inc.*, 819 So. 2d 177 (Fla. Dist. Ct. App. 2002), the taxpayer (Bell Chevrolet) challenged the property appraiser's assessment of the land component of its property. The trial court denied the tax appraiser's attempts to introduce evidence that the total assessment equaled the fair market value of the property. The trial court found that the assessment of the land component was too high and reduced the taxpayer's tax liability. The appellate court reversed, holding:

> The constitution requires assessment of all real property at market value, and an ad valorem tax assessment that is more or less than "just" or market value is unconstitutional. . . .
>
> To enforce the requirements of the constitution, [the property appraiser] must be allowed to defend the total tax assessment as correct despite a flawed internal allocation of value. While a taxpayer may be able to frame his complaint so as to challenge only a portion of his tax assessment, the trial court may not prevent the property appraiser from defending the total tax assessment as meeting the constitutional requirement of just value.

Florida is not alone in constitutionally mandating that, absent explicit constitutional exceptions, all property—including both land and improvements—be valued at fair market value. For example, the West Virginia Constitution provides that "taxation shall be equal and uniform throughout the state, and all property, both real and personal, shall be taxed in proportion to its *value*" (art. X, sec. 10-1; emphasis added). In *Killen v. Logan*

---

15. For example, article VII, section 4(a) states that agricultural land "may be . . . assessed solely on the basis of character or use."

County Commission, 295 S.E.2d 689 (W. Va. 1982), the Supreme Court of Appeals held that "the term 'value,' as used in Article 10, Section 1 of the West Virginia Constitution, means 'worth in money' of a piece of property— its market value." The court struck down the practice of explicitly assessing property at 50 percent of appraised market value. Similarly, the Massachusetts Supreme Judicial Court has ruled that it is a "foundational requirement" that all classes of property be assessed at "full and fair cash value" (*Opinion of the Justices to the House of Representatives*, 393 N.E.2d 306 [Mass. 1979]).

UNIFORMITY IN VALUATION. Constitutional requirements that property be assessed at market value would appear, then, to pose a considerable barrier to the possibility of implementing a de facto land tax via differential assessment of land and improvements. But even in the absence of a constitutional mandate that all property be valued at full market value, such differential treatment would run the risk of violating constitutional uniformity provisions. Virginia presents an interesting case. The state's constitution states explicitly: "All assessments of real estate and tangible personal property shall be at their *fair market value*" (art. X, sec. 2; emphasis added). However, this apparently has not been the practice of property appraisers in the state. In *Southern Railway Co. v. State*, 176 S.E.2d 578 (Va. 1970), the Virginia Supreme Court asserted that "this court has said that the mandate of [assessments at fair market value] has been so honored in the breach that no assessors feel called upon to apply it in practice." The Court went on to say that "the Courts, in trying to resolve this problem, while recognizing the general custom of undervaluing property and the difficulty of enforcing the standard of true value, have sought to enforce equality in the burden of taxation by insisting upon uniformity in the mode of assessment and in the rate of taxation." Thus, even in the absence of mandates that property be assessed at 100 percent of market value, differential valuations of land and improvements would face challenges based on constitutional uniformity provisions.

The courts have provided an additional interesting twist on the interplay between fair market valuation and uniform valuation, as illustrated by *Sioux City Bridge Co. v. Dakota County*, 260 U.S. 441 (1923), which reached the U.S. Supreme Court on appeal from the Nebraska Supreme Court. The taxpayer's property was valued at 100 percent of market value, whereas other property in the taxing district was valued at (approximately) 50 percent of market value. The taxpayer sued to have its valuation reduced in line with other valuations. Nebraska statutory law mandated valuation at full market value. The Nebraska Supreme Court, although noting the differential valuation, denied the taxpayer's requested remedy, arguing that the proper remedy was for the assessor to value all property at 100 percent of market value rather than reduce the value of the taxpayer's property to 50 percent. The U.S. Supreme Court reversed on equal protection grounds.

> This Court holds that the right of the taxpayer whose property alone is taxed at 100 percent of its true value is to have his assessment reduced to the percentage of that value at which others are taxed even though this is a departure from the requirement of statute. The conclusion is based on the principle that, where it is impossible to secure both the standard of true value, and the uniformity and equality required by law, the latter requirement is to be preferred as the just and ultimate purpose of the law.

CONCLUSION. Absent explicit constitutional authorization, a jurisdiction attempting to implement a land tax via an administrative practice of differential valuation of land and improvements would face significant legal barriers based on claims of nonmarket valuation and, more fundamentally, violations of constitutional uniformity provisions.

Differential Classification

Could a jurisdiction classify land and improvements as two distinct classes of property? If so, the constitutional issues surrounding uniformity in taxation would be lessened considerably, since uniformity is often interpreted, as discussed above, as requiring only that the same rules be applied within a given class of property, thus allowing for differential taxation across classes of property. What constitutional legal barriers might exist to thwart such an approach to a land tax?[16]

EXPLICIT CONSTITUTIONAL LIMITATIONS ON CLASSIFICATION PLANS. State constitutional provisions regarding the classification of real property

---

16. The distinction between classes of property for purposes of differential tax treatment and exemptions of property from the normal application of tax rules can be a fine line. A classification plan places all parcels of property into one of a limited group of broad classes, most often according to use or type of property. For example, Massachusetts has four classes of property: residential, commercial, industrial, and open space. Exemptions are generally more narrowly drawn and may be based on any number of factors, including use (e.g., religious purpose), but also such characteristics as status of owner (e.g., military veteran). Given the similarity of effect, it is not surprising that the two terms are often used interchangeably. In this regard, it is perhaps worth noting that some states have granted an exemption for open space property, which Massachusetts treats as a separate class.

for purposes of ad valorem taxation take several forms. Some state constitutions prohibit the use of classes for real property taxation. The Florida Constitution, for example, provides that "all ad valorem taxation shall be at a uniform rate within each taxing unit, except the taxes on intangible personal property may be at different rates" (art. VII, sec. 2). This requirement leaves no room for the legislature to establish different classes of real property for purposes of differential taxation.

Other constitutional provisions allow the legislature to establish different classes of property, but place explicit limitations on such a classification plan. Article CXII of the Massachusetts Constitution, for example, reads:

> Article IV of chapter 1 of Part the Second of the Constitution is hereby amended by inserting after the words "and to impose and levy proportional and reasonable assessments, rates and taxes, upon all the inhabitants of, and persons resident, and estates lying, within said Commonwealth" the words: -, except that, in addition to the powers conferred under Articles XLI and XCIX of the Amendments, the general court may classify real property *according to its use in no more than four classes* and to assess, rate and tax such property differently in the classes so established, but proportionately in the same class, and except that reasonable exemptions may be granted.[17] (emphasis added)

Limiting provisions such as this could pose substantial challenges to any attempt to classify land and improvements as separate classes of property. In Massachusetts, for example, the legislature would first have to alter its current classification plan so that it did not exceed the constitutional limit of "no more than four classes." More fundamentally, the classification plan would have to meet the constitutional requirement that the classes be based on the "use" of the property.[18]

---

17. This amendment was added by a popular vote spurred by dissatisfaction with the Supreme Judicial Court's holding in *Sudbury v. Commissioner of Corporations and Taxation*, 321 N.E.2d 641 (Mass. 1974), that it was the legal duty of tax assessors to value property at 100 percent of market value, a holding that ended the long-standing practice of assessing certain classes of property at less than 100 percent of market value.

18. In keeping with the current classification plan, one could conceive of the following four classes: land used as residential property, land used as commercial property, land used as industrial and manufacturing property, and, somewhat redundantly, land used as open space. Such a plan would satisfy the four-class limitation and arguably would be based on the use of the property. Such a plan, of course, would represent a pure land tax. It would be a more challenging proposition to devise a classification plan with only four classes based on use that could operate as a split-rate tax.

JUDICIALLY IMPOSED CONSTITUTIONAL LIMITATIONS ON CLASSIFICA-
TION PLANS.   Legislative bodies may be given broad constitutional discretion to establish classes of property. The Arizona Constitution, for example,
provides that "all taxes shall be uniform upon the same class of property
within the territorial limits of the authority levying the tax, and shall be levied and collected for public purposes only" (art. IX, sec. 1). No explicit constitutional restrictions are placed on the legislature's ability to formulate a
classification plan, except for a series of constitutionally enumerated exemptions for purposes of ad valorem taxation.

Broad legislative discretion, however, does not mean unlimited discretion,
and Arizona case law has addressed an interesting set of legal issues regarding the classification of property for purposes of ad valorem taxation. In
Apache County v. The Atchison, Topeka and Santa Fe Railway Co., 476 P.2d
657 (Ariz. 1970), a railroad challenged the legislatively enacted classification
plan as a violation of the constitutional uniformity provision. (The plan
placed railroad property in a higher assessment ratio category than other
property.) The Arizona Supreme Court, in upholding the constitutionality
of the state's classification, held that "Article IX, § 1 requires that taxes be
uniform upon the same class of property. It does not itself classify property
nor does it purport to embrace a scheme for the classification of property.
The power to classify is legislative. . . . Since only the Legislature may classify,
only the Legislature has the discretion to impose the burdens of government
on property *in proportion to use, productivity and utility*" (emphasis added).

The "use, productivity, and utility" test clearly grants considerable discretion to the state in classifying property. However, in *American West Airlines v.
Department of Revenue*, 880 P.2d 1074 (Ariz. 1994), this test was used to
strike down a legislatively enacted classification plan. American West challenged, on constitutional uniformity grounds, an Arizona statute that capped
the tax rate on airlines with a systemwide average passenger capacity below
56 seats or a systemwide average payload capacity below 18,000 pounds.
(The tax plan was intended to encourage commuter airlines in the state.)
American West did not meet these criteria, even though it had several small
planes that served commuter routes in the state. The Arizona Supreme Court
held that

> the statute penalizes American West for the number or value of its posses-
> sions (airplanes). Thus, we have an ad valorem tax graduated, not by differ-
> ences in the property or its use, but by differences in the nature of other

property belonging to the owners, a distinction that, if approved, would seemingly read the uniformity clause out of the Arizona Constitution. . . . The classification . . . violates the uniformity clause . . . insofar as it creates unequal ad valorem tax rates for property with the same physical characteristics, used in the same industry for similar purposes.

The court went on to assert that "classifications for tax purposes must be real, not fanciful, and based on the nature of the property or on some other real difference in its use, utility or productivity."[19]

The Oregon Supreme Court has also spoken on the issue of differential classification. In *Mathias v. Department of Revenue*, 817 P.2d 272 (Or. 1991), the plaintiff challenged an Oregon statute that provided a favorable valuation methodology for property "if the property consists of four or more lots within one subdivision, and the lots are held under one ownership." Although the case involved differential valuation practices, the court framed the issue as a classification question: whether the statute's creation of different classes of property, based on the ownership of a given number of lots, was a constitutionally valid classification under Oregon's uniformity clause. The court held that it was not.

Classifications, to pass state constitutional muster, must be based on inherent, qualitative, genuine, rational differences between classes of property to be accorded different treatment. . . . The amount of other property that a taxpayer owns is not a rational basis for distinguishing between otherwise identical lots for tax purposes. The classification accordingly lacks *the inherent, qualitative, genuine difference* between the subjects required under [the uniformity provision]. (emphasis added)[20]

---

19. The court also indicated some unease with rulings in previous cases, including the *Apache* case, noting, "Probably the framers [of the state constitution] would have preferred a less elastic uniformity clause, but we do not write on a clean slate. In *Apache County* and *Trico*, we expanded the limits of the uniformity clause, but, to quote the song, we have 'gone about as fer as [we] can go'" (880 P.2d 1074).

20. One of the arguments advanced by the Department of Revenue in defending the tax plan was that the legislature, in other statutory provisions, had clearly distinguished between the division of a plot of land into three or fewer lots and the division into four or more lots, by statutorily designating the former as "partitioning or parceling" and the latter as "subdividing" the plot. The court said that this language distinction did not meet the constitutional requirement of "qualitative, genuine" difference, labeling such a distinction one "without a real difference in effect (or) purpose" (817 P.2d 272).

The Pennsylvania Supreme Court has developed a similar test. In *Leonard v. Thornburgh*, 489 A.2d 1349 (Pa. 1985), a case involving differential taxes on resident and nonresident wage earners, the court said:

In cases where the validity of a classification for tax purposes is challenged, the test is whether the classification is based upon some legitimate distinction between the classes that provides a *non-arbitrary and "reasonable and just" basis* for the difference in treatment. Stated alternatively, the focus of judicial review is upon whether there can be discerned "some *concrete justification*" for treating the relevant group of taxpayers as members of distinguishable classes subject to different tax burdens. (emphasis added)

None of the cases discussed above directly addressed whether a state legislature or a local jurisdiction, absent explicit constitutional authority, could classify land and improvements as separate classes of property. But these cases provide an idea of how such a classification plan would need to be defended against a constitutional challenge that it violated the uniformity clause. Under such a classification plan, owners of equally valued parcels of property would pay different amounts of taxes if the ratio of the value of land to the value of improvements differed. Is such a distinction based on "inherent, qualitative, genuine, rational differences"? Is such a difference based on "the nature of the property" or on its "use, utility, or productivity"? Is there some "concrete justification" for treating the two groups differently?

An economist would most likely answer such questions in the affirmative. Land and improvements are two distinct inputs into the production of the goods and services (including housing services) generated by a parcel of property. These inputs derive their value from distinct sources. The value of the land (accurately valued according to its highest and best use) is essentially a function of its location.[21] The value of improvements on the land is

---

21. Interestingly, location is one factor that the Arizona Supreme Court has not spoken of favorably as a valid basis for differential classification. In *Bahr v. State*, 985 P.2d 564 (Ariz. 1999), the plaintiff challenged Arizona's classification plan, which granted favorable tax treatment (a lower assessment ratio) to property located in a foreign trade zone, arguing that such a classification violated the uniformity provision. According to the plaintiff (Bahr), the plan resulted in different tax burdens for "identical property used for the same purpose within the same industry, distinguished only *by location* in a foreign trade zone" (emphasis added). The court ruled against the plaintiff, asserting, "Contrary to Bahr's analysis, this characterization of class eight [foreign trade zone] property *does not turn on physical location*, or on politico-industrial cronyism, or *any other illegitimate criterion* unrelated to the

essentially a function of a variety of production-related characteristics, such as size, age, and structural components. Certainly the "nature" of these two types of property is different, and the differences are "inherent, qualitative, and genuine." A classification based on such differences is "rational" in that it has as a "concrete justification" the promotion of economic growth and the prevention of urban sprawl. The underlying source of the productivity of the two inputs is different, which would potentially satisfy a productivity-based requirement such as that put forth by the Arizona Supreme Court. Hence, there is a reasonably good chance that a legislatively adopted classification plan that classified land as one type of property for purposes of ad valorem taxation and improvements as another type (or types) would be deemed constitutionally valid, at least based on the rulings discussed above. However, there is at least one additional legal hurdle that might need to be addressed before the separate classification of land and improvements is accepted.

THE "SINGLE ESTATE" ISSUE. Some courts have endorsed the "single es- tate" principle of property taxation, which holds that land and improve- ments constitute one estate for purposes of property taxation. In *Town of Lenox v. Oglesby*, 41 N.E.2d 45 (Mass. 1942), the Massachusetts Supreme Ju- dicial Court said: "Land and buildings upon it are ordinarily parts of the same real estate, and they cannot be separated for the purpose of collect- ing taxes. They constitute a single estate upon which a single and indivisible tax is levied, and the separate valuation of the buildings is required merely to secure a more specific valuation of what constitutes but one item of real estate."

More recently, in *Flavorland Foods v. Washington County Assessor*, 54 P.3d 582 (Or. 2002), the Oregon Supreme Court addressed the meaning of the phrase "each unit of property in this state" contained in a tax limitation con- stitutional amendment adopted by the voters (Oregon Constitution, art. XI,

---

property's physical attributes, legal nature, use, industry of deployment, utility, productivity, or purpose" (emphasis added). The court added, "Finally, we reject Bahr's contention that the class eight [foreign trade zone] classification is *location-based*. Though [the statute] os- tensibly defines class eight [foreign trade zone] property as a function of location, the lan- guage of the statute as a whole reveals a different meaning. What brings the property within class eight is not its location, but rather its use in furthering the purposes for which [foreign trade zones] are permitted to exist." The clear implication of this language is that a classifica- tion plan that taxed similar property differently, solely on the basis of location, would run afoul of the uniformity provision.

sec. 11(1)(a)). The taxpayer argued that land and improvements constituted separate units of property within the meaning of the amendment. The taxpayer's land had increased in value by more than the amendment's limit, but the market value of the improvements had decreased, leaving the increase in the assessed value of the property—the value that the tax assessor used in calculating the property tax owed—within the constitutional limitation. The taxpayer argued that the separate increase in the value of the land should be subject to the tax limitation provision. The Supreme Court of Oregon rejected the taxpayer's argument, holding: "We conclude that the voters intended the phrase 'each unit of property in this state' to refer to all the property in a property tax account, which, in this case, includes both land and improvements."

The Oregon Supreme Court in *Flavorland Foods* interpreted as a matter of constitutional law the phrase "a unit of property" to include both land and improvements—at least within the context of the tax limitation amendment. Rulings such as *Flavorland Foods* and *Oglesby* could serve as the basis for constitutional challenges to a legislatively adopted classification plan that classified land and improvements as separate classes of property.

Exemptions

A final legislative approach to a land tax that a jurisdiction might consider is to grant an exemption to improvements. Table 7.1 shows that almost all states have some type of exemption provision. Constitutional exemption provisions can take several general forms. The constitution may contain a list of exemptions, which may be either mandatory ("shall be exempted") or permissive ("may be exempted"). Alternatively, the state constitution may leave the creation of exemptions solely to the discretion of the legislature, which may further mandate or permit local exemptions. Finally, with respect to improvements, a state constitution may explicitly allow improvements (at least to some degree) to be exempted from property taxation.

CONSTITUTIONALLY ENUMERATED EXEMPTIONS. Arizona is an example of a state that gives little discretion to state and local governments in establishing exemptions for purposes of property taxation. Article IX, section 2 of the state constitution contains 12 clauses enumerating specific exemptions. The final clause (clause 13) states: "All property in the state not exempt under the laws of the United States or under this constitution or exempt by law under provisions of this section shall be subject to taxation to be ascertained as provided by law." This provision leaves little, if any, discretion to the state legislature to enact an exemption not specifically enumerated in the constitution. In *State v. Yuma Irrigation District*, 99 P.2d 704 (Ariz. 1940), the Arizona Supreme Court, citing that clause, said: "If the legislature passes a law exempting any property in the state, its power to do so must be found in the Constitution. Most of the exemptions are specified or enumerated by the Constitution and are self-executing. In one instance only has there been delegated to the legislature the power to grant exemptions." (Here, the court cited the exemption for educational, charitable, religious, and other not-for-profit institutions.) A legislatively enacted exemption of improvements from property taxation could thus face serious constitutional challenges.

CONSTITUTIONAL DISCRETION.   On the other end of the spectrum, the Idaho Constitution provides broad discretion to the legislature to establish exemptions. The constitution provides "that the legislature may allow such exemptions from taxation from time to time as shall seem *necessary and just*" (art. VII, sec. 5; emphasis added). The Idaho Supreme Court has endorsed this grant of legislative authority. In *Simmons v. Idaho State Tax Commission*, 723 P.2d 887 (Idaho 1986), a case involving a taxpayer challenge to the validity of a partial exemption on residential improvements on owner-occupied property, the court, commenting on the debates regarding section 5 in the state's constitutional convention, stated: "These remarks regarding the version of Idaho Constitution Art. VII, §5, ultimately adopted reveal the framers' intent that the legislature have broad discretion in making property tax exemptions." The court characterized the language as "extremely broad and deferential."

Whereas the Idaho Constitution explicitly grants broad discretionary power to the legislature, the New Hampshire Constitution says little regarding exemptions from property taxation. Part 2, article 5 of the constitution empowers the legislature "to impose and levy proportional and reasonable assessments, rates, and taxes, upon all the inhabitants of, and residents within, the said state; and upon all estates within the same." The only explicit exemption called for in the constitution is contained in the same article: "For the purpose of encouraging conservation of the forest resources of the state, the general court may provide for special assessments, rates and taxes on growing wood and timber." Thus, the state constitution has a universality clause ("all estates") and one explicit exemption that has resulted in lower effective tax rates, but no provisions explicitly prohibiting or allowing the leg-

islature to enact additional exemptions. The state courts have interpreted the
constitution as affording the legislature considerable discretion to exempt
property from taxation. In *Opinion of the Justices (Municipal Tax Exemptions
for Electric Utility Personal Property)*, 144 N.H. 374 (1999), the supreme
court addressed the constitutionality, under the uniformity and proportionality clauses, of a statute authorizing municipalities to exempt from local
property taxation certain property employed in the generation and production of electric power. "Although exemptions necessarily result in a dispro-
portionate tax burden on the remaining property in the taxing district, the
legislature possesses broad discretion to select certain property for taxation
while exempting other property. Exemptions are constitutional if they are
*supported by just reasons, and thereby reasonably promote some proper object
of public welfare* or interest" (emphasis added). (The Court, in upholding the
statute, concluded that the exemption was supported by just reasons in that
it was designed to promote competition in the electric utility industry, which
was a proper object of public welfare.)

More recently, in *Appeal of Town of Bethlehem (New Hampshire Department of Environmental Services)*, 911 A.2d 1 (N.H. 2006), the court considered the constitutionality of a statute granting property tax exemptions
to a solid waste landfill. The statute did not exempt the entire landfill from
taxation; rather, it exempted certain improvements made for purposes of
pollution (runoff) control. The court upheld the exemption, finding that
the statute did not require exemption for the entire property and that the
exemption, "properly applied, would be uniform as to all property meeting
the statutory requirements both across the state and within each taxing
district or municipality. Thus, the constitutional mandate of uniformity
and equality is satisfied." Since pollution control is clearly a proper object of
public interest, the exemption was constitutional. The potential significance
of this case for a land tax is that it arguably provides support for a legislatively enacted exemption of one part of a parcel of property, such as improvements, if such an exemption could be justified as promoting the public
interest.

The constitutional test for exemptions stated by the New Hampshire Supreme Court in the *Bethlehem* case echoes language discussed earlier with
respect to both the Fourteenth Amendment's equal protection clause and the
constitutionality of state property classification plans. The various constitutional tests are similar to the equal protection clause test that differential
treatment be "reasonably related to a legitimate state interest," or alterna-

tively, "not arbitrary or capricious," and illustrate the general deference that courts show to legislative bodies on issues of taxation. When the state constitution provides few restrictions on the legislature's power to exempt property from ad valorem taxation, it is unlikely that the state courts will provide more. State legislatures operating under such loose constitutional restraints would seem to have a reasonably high probability of enacting a constitutionally valid land tax.

EXPLICIT CONSTITUTIONAL ENABLING PROVISIONS. A state constitution that explicitly allows for the exemption of improvements for purposes of ad valorem taxation provides the most favorable constitutional setting for a legislatively enacted land tax via exemptions. The Idaho Constitution, for example, states: "The legislature shall provide such revenue as may be needful, by levying a tax by valuation, so that every person or corporation shall pay a tax in proportion to the value of his, her, or its property, . . . provided, the legislature may exempt a limited amount of improvements upon land from taxation" (art. VII, sec. 2).[22] The Virginia Constitution is even more accommodating:

> The General Assembly may by general law authorize the governing body of any county, city, town, or regional government to provide for a partial exemption from local real property taxation, within such restrictions and upon such conditions as may be prescribed, (i) of real estate whose improvements, by virtue of age and use, have undergone substantial renovation, rehabilitation, or replacement or (ii) of real estate with new structures and improvements in conservation, redevelopment, or rehabilitation areas. (art. X, sec. 6(h))

The General Assembly has in fact taken advantage of this constitutional allowance and has enacted legislation allowing localities to use a land tax.[23]

Finally, a state constitution may contain a narrowly drawn enabling provision regarding the exemption of improvements, often for purposes of promoting economic development—as economic theory would suggest. For example, the Florida Constitution contains the following provision: "Any county or municipality may . . . grant community and economic develop-

---

22. Oddly, in the *Simmons* case discussed earlier, this constitutional provision was not discussed.
23. See *Code of Virginia* §§ 58.1-3220, 58.1-3221.1.

ment ad valorem tax exemptions to new businesses and expansions of existing businesses. . . . An exemption so granted shall apply to improvements to real property . . . related to the expansion of an existing business" (art. VII, sec. 3(c)).

Provisions such as this hold two lessons for land tax advocates. First, in restrictive states such as Florida, a constitutional provision was necessary to enable even this limited exemption of improvements—a considerable barrier. Second, a constitutional enabling provision to exempt improvements was indeed adopted, presumably on the basis of the efficiency rationale advanced by proponents of a land tax. Thus, the idea is not a foreign concept to legislators—the legal barrier may be considerable, but not insurmountable.

CONCLUSIONS REGARDING THE EXEMPTION OF IMPROVEMENTS. The question posed at the beginning of this section was whether a state legislature could constitutionally enact, or authorize localities to enact, a statute exempting improvements from ad valorem property taxation. The answer parallels the conclusion reached with respect to property classification plans, which is not surprising given the close similarity between classes and exemptions. The equal protection clause of the U.S. Constitution poses no barrier, under the assumption that the exemption can be linked to a legitimate state purpose. Thus, the answer to the question hinges on provisions in the state constitution. If the state constitution explicitly authorizes the legislature to grant exemptions on improvements, as do the Idaho and Virginia constitutions, then obviously there is no constitutional barrier to legislative action. If the state constitution provides only general guidelines regarding exemptions, such as Utah's "necessary and just" clause or New Hampshire's "reasonable" provision, then the state legislature very likely has the discretion to authorize the exemption of improvements. Finally, if the state constitution contains a specifically enumerated list of exemptions that the courts have held to be exhaustive, then a state constitutional amendment presumably is needed to enable the legislature to exempt improvements from taxation.

CONCLUSION

The implementation of a land tax, from an administrative perspective, would appear to be a straightforward, relatively simple proposition. Virtually all taxing jurisdictions separately value land and improvements; thus, at the very least, methodologies to value land and improvements separately have been developed. Although the accuracy of these methodologies can be improved, a version of a pure land tax could be implemented now by simply excluding the value of improvements from the tax base. To implement a split-rate version of a land tax, a jurisdiction could simply apply a lower tax rate to the separate value of improvements.

However, either approach to a land tax would most likely run into serious legal challenges in a large number of jurisdictions. The application of different tax rates to separate parts of a parcel of property is highly problematic. Absent the explicit designation of improvements either as a separate class of property or as exempt property, such a differential taxation plan would encounter serious legal obstacles as a violation of uniformity, equality, and proportionality provisions commonly found in state constitutions.

The same point stands with respect to the differential valuation of land and improvements. Could a legislature adopt a plan that applied different valuation methodologies to land and improvements, such that improvements were systematically valued at a lower percentage of market value than land? Any such plan would face difficult constitutional challenges similar to those that a differential tax rate plan would face.

Uniformity, equality, and proportionality clauses in state constitutions have generally been held to require equal, uniform, and proportional taxation within classes of property, but to allow differential taxation across classes of property. Would a legislative body face legal obstacles in classifying improvements as a separate class of property and then applying a different (lower) tax rate? The answer is a resounding "it depends." Some state constitutions do not allow the legislature to adopt a general classification plan for the purpose of differential taxation. Some state constitutions allow for a classification plan, but impose explicit conditions or restrictions on the type of plan that the legislature can implement. Whether a classification plan that defined improvements as a separate class of property was consistent with the specified constitutional conditions would no doubt be subject to legal challenge. Finally, there are states in which the courts have granted substantial discretion to the legislature to craft a classification plan, often relying on such constitutional tests as "reasonable" or "nonarbitrary." In all likelihood, the separate classification of improvements would meet such general tests to the extent that such a classification is designed to promote economic growth, prevent urban sprawl, or address other legitimate policy concerns. However, it should be noted that language in some cases provides legal fodder to argue against such a proposition—various courts have spoken of a taxable parcel of property as a unified taxable estate, not separate taxable components of land and improvements.

If classification of improvements as a separate class of property were not allowed, could the legislature use a different legal strategy and exempt improvements from property taxation? Although exemptions run afoul of the principles of uniformity, equality, universality, and proportionality, it is difficult, if not impossible, to find a state without property tax exemptions. Are improvements a legitimate candidate for legislative exemption? The answer to this question is similar to the answer to the question regarding classification plans—it depends. Some state constitutions explicitly allow, at least to some degree, the legislature to exempt improvements from property taxation. Obviously, this would be a highly favorable circumstance for a legislatively enacted land tax plan. Other state constitutions take the polar opposite approach—exemptions must be explicitly enumerated in the state constitution in order to be constitutionally valid. In that case, a constitutional amendment would be necessary in order for the legislature to exempt improvements, partially or fully, from property taxation. Finally, in some states the constitution has been interpreted as granting significant discretion to the legislature to create exemptions from property taxation, requiring only that such exemptions be "reasonable" or "necessary and just." As in the case of classification plans, there is a strong likelihood that the exemption of improvements can meet such broad constitutional tests.

It is clear that a land tax would face differing state constitutional barriers depending on the jurisdiction. The jurisdictional dependency of the constitutional validity of differential taxation of land and improvements under a uniformity clause is perhaps best illustrated by the case of Pennsylvania. As shown in table 7.1, the Pennsylvania Constitution contains a uniformity clause as well as a universality clause, both dating effectively from 1874. These provisions have had a long and convoluted history of interpretation by the Pennsylvania Supreme Court.[24] In *Madway v. Board*, 233 A.2d 273 (Pa. 1967), the Court appeared to settle on a strict interpretation of uniformity in taxation as applied to real estate, asserting, "We hold today that real estate as a subject of taxation may not validly be divided into different classes." Despite this apparent substantial constitutional hurdle, Pennsylvania is one of the very few states that have enacted a land tax, as discussed in

---

24. Newhouse (1984) devotes 234 pages to his analysis of the interpretation of the Pennsylvania uniformity clause, an entry rivaled in length only by his examination of the Illinois uniformity provision.

chapter 2.[25] In 1913 the Pennsylvania legislature statutorily authorized certain local jurisdictions to adopt a land tax, and a number of jurisdictions have done so. Despite the supreme court's apparent strict interpretation of the uniformity clause as applied to real estate, the differential taxation of land and improvements has not been seriously challenged as a violation of the state's constitution. Coughlan (1999, 262) reports that "there has been only one direct court challenge to land value taxation on Pennsylvania constitutional grounds, and that was dismissed at the trial level without a reported opinion." Thus, what in other jurisdictions would seem to be a major legal barrier to the adoption of a land tax turned out not to be the case in Pennsylvania.

In most other jurisdictions, as the law now stands, constitutional barriers to enactment of land value taxation appear to be substantial. However, even in states that currently have the most formidable legal barriers embedded in their constitutions, a state constitutional amendment granting the legislature the power to enact a land tax of whatever form is the magic elixir that cures all constitutional problems. The equal protection clause of the U.S. Constitution should pose no legal problems; thus, a state constitutional amendment would suffice. Although the adoption of a state constitutional amendment is often thought to be a more difficult hurdle than the passage of a statute,[26] it should be noted that state constitutional amendments that exempt improvements from property taxation, at least in certain situations, are not unknown. Thus, the barriers to constitutional adoption are not necessarily insurmountable. The ultimate hurdle faced by land tax proponents is whether they can convince the public of the substantive validity of their arguments in support of a land tax.

CASES

American West Airlines v. Department of Revenue, 880 P.2d 1074 (Ariz. 1994).

Apache County v. The Atchison, Topeka and Santa Fe Railway Co., 476 P.2d 657 (Ariz. 1970).

---

25. Both Hawaii and New York have had a land tax of some form. However, since neither state has a uniformity clause (or a universality clause), that constitutional barrier has been absent.

26. Given the rising popularity of adopting state constitutional amendments via referendum, this assertion is subject to question.

Apartment Operators' Association v. City of Minneapolis, 254 N.W. 443 (Minn. 1934).

Appeal of Town of Bethlehem (New Hampshire Department of Environmental Services), 911 A.2d 1 (N.H. 2006).

Bahr v. State, 985 P.2d 564 (Ariz. 1999).

Baker v. Matheson, 607 P.2d 233 (Utah 1979).

Bettigole v. Assessors of Springfield, 178 N.E.2d 10 (Mass. 1961).

Flavorland Foods v. Washington County Assessor, 54 P.3d 582 (Or. 2002).

Green v. Frazier, 253 U.S. 233 (1920).

Interlachen Lakes Estates v. Snyder, 304 So. 2d 433 (Fla. 1973).

Killen v. Logan County Commission, 295 S.E.2d 689 (W. Va. 1982).

Leonard v. Thornburgh, 489 A.2d 1349 (Pa. 1985).

Madway v. Board, 233 A.2d 273 (Pa. 1967).

Mathias v. Department of Revenue, 817 P.2d 272 (Or. 1991).

Nordlinger v. Hahn, 505 U.S. 1.

Opinion of the Justices (Municipal Tax Exemptions for Electric Utility Personal Property), 144 N.H. 374 (1999).

Opinion of the Justices to the House of Representatives, 393 N.E.2d 306 (Mass. 1979).

Pollock v. Farmers' Loan & Trust Co., 157 U.S. 429 (1895).

Simmons v. Idaho State Tax Commission, 723 P.2d 887 (Idaho 1986).

Sioux City Bridge v. Dakota County, 260 U.S. 441 (1923).

Southern Railway Co. v. State, 176 S.E.2d 578 (Va.1970).

Springer v. United States, 102 U.S. 586 (1880).

State v. Yuma Irrigation District, 99 P.2d 704 (Ariz. 1940).

Sudbury v. Commissioner of Corporations and Taxation, 321 N.E.2d 641 (Mass. 1974).

Town of Lenox v. Oglesby, 41 N.E.2d 45 (Mass. 1942).

Turner v. Bell Chevrolet, Inc., 819 So. 2d 177 (Fla. Dist. Ct. App. 2002).

Valencia Center v. Bystrom, 543 So. 2d 214 (Fla. 1989).

Walter v. Schuler, 176 So. 2d 81 (Fla. 1965).

Walters v. City of St. Louis, 347 U.S. 231 (1954).

Table 7.1 State constitutional tax provisions relevant to land value taxation

	Uniformity[a]	Equality[b]	Universality[c]	Proportionality[d]	Classification[e]	Exemptions[f]	Improvements[g]	"Just value"[h]
Alabama	Y[1]	Y[2]		Y[3]	Y[4]	Y[5]		Y[6]
Alaska[7]						Y[8]		
Arizona	Y[9]		Y[10]		Y[11]	Y[12]		
Arkansas[13]	Y[14]	Y[15]	Y[16]		N[17]	Y[18]		
California	Y[19]		Y[20]	Y[21]		Y[22]		
Colorado	Y[23]		Y[24]			Y[25]		Y[26]
Connecticut								
Delaware[27]	Y[28]					Y[29]		
Florida[30]	Y[31]					Y[32]	Y[33]	Y[34]
Georgia	Y[35]				N[36]	Y[37]		
Hawaii[38]								
Idaho	Y[39]		Y[40]	Y[41]		Y[42]	Y[43]	Y[44]
Illinois	Y[45]				Y[46]	Y[47]		
Indiana	Y[48]	Y[49]	Y[50]			Y[51]		Y[52]
Iowa	53							
Kansas	Y[54]	Y[55]			Y[56]	Y[57]	Y[58]	
Kentucky	Y[59]		Y[60]	Y[61]	Y[62]	Y[63]	Y[64]	Y[65]
Louisiana	Y[66]		Y[67]		Y[68]	Y[69]	Y[70,71]	Y[72]
Maine		Y[73]				Y[74]		Y[75]
Maryland	Y[76]				Y[77]	Y[78]	Y[79]	
Massachusetts	Y[80]		Y[81]	Y[82]	Y[83]	Y[84]		
Michigan	Y[85]					Y[86]		Y[87]
Minnesota	Y[88]					Y[89]		
Mississippi	Y[90]	Y[91]		Y[92]	Y[93]	Y[94]		Y[95]
Missouri	Y[96]		Y[97]		Y[98]	Y[99]		Y[100]
Montana						Y[101]		

(continued)

Table 7.1 *continued*

	Uniformity[a]	Equality[b]	Universality[c]	Proportionality[d]	Classification[e]	Exemptions[f]	Improvements[g]	"Just value"[h]
Nebraska	Y[102]		Y[103]	Y[104]		Y[105]		
Nevada	Y[106]	Y[107]	Y[108]			Y[109]		Y[110]
New Hampshire				Y[111]		Y[112]		
New Jersey	Y[113]					Y[114]	Y[115]	
New Mexico	Y[116]	Y[117]		Y[118]		Y[119]		
New York						Y[120]		
North Carolina	Y[121]				Y[122]	Y[123]		
North Dakota[124]	Y[125]					Y[126]	Y[127]	
Ohio	Y[128]				Y[129]	Y[130]		
Oklahoma	Y[131]		Y[132]			Y[133]		Y[134]
Oregon	Y[135]							
Pennsylvania	Y[136]		Y[137]			Y[138]	Y[139]	
Rhode Island								
South Carolina	Y[140]	Y[141]			Y[142]	Y[143]	Y[144]	Y[145]
South Dakota	Y[146]	Y[147]	Y[148]		Y[149]	Y[150]		
Tennessee	Y[151]	Y[152]	Y[153]		Y[154]	Y[155]		
Texas[156]	Y[157]	Y[158]	Y[159]	Y[160]		Y[161]		
Utah	Y[162]	Y[163]	Y[164]	Y[165]		Y[166]		Y[167]
Vermont	168							
Virginia[169]	Y[170]		Y[171]		Y[172]	Y[173]	Y[174]	Y[175]
Washington	Y[176]				N[177]	Y[178]		Y[179]
West Virginia	Y[180]	Y[181]	Y[182]	Y[183]		Y[184]		
Wisconsin	Y[185]					Y[186]		
Wyoming[187]	Y[188]	Y[189]			Y[190]	Y[191]		Y[192]

Note that the information in this table summarizes state constitutional provisions relevant to land value taxation and does not represent case law analysis. Different state courts can interpret, and have interpreted, similar constitutional language in dissimilar ways.

Explanatory notes for columns:

[a] *Uniformity* refers to constitutional provisions explicitly providing that taxation, or some aspect of taxation, is to be "uniform." The letter *Y* indicates there is such a provision. The uniformity provision is quoted in the footnote. If a constitutional provision is framed in terms that require taxes to be the "same" (in some manner), a *Y* is entered in both the uniformity and the equality columns. The uniformity column does not include general constitutional provisions requiring uniformity in the application of all general laws; nor does it include a uniformity requirement that might stem from an equal rights or equal protection clause in a state constitution. The column only references explicit language in the state constitution, and does not encompass judicial interpretations of the uniformity clause or whether state courts have read a tax uniformity provision into the state constitution.

[b] *Equality* refers to constitutional provisions that specifically refer to equality in taxation. The letter *Y* indicates that there is such a provision. The column does not include general equal protection clauses, which may be invoked in matters of taxation.

[c] *Universality* refers to constitutional provisions that provide either that "all" property is to be subject to taxation, except property explicitly exempted in the constitution, or that the legislature shall grant no exemption unless it is explicitly listed in the constitution. The letter *Y* indicates that there is such a provision.

[d] *Proportionality* refers to any constitutional provision that requires that taxes be proportional. The letter *Y* indicates there is such a provision.

[e] *Classification* refers to explicit constitutional provisions regarding the establishment of classes of real property for tax purposes. The letter *Y* indicates that there is an explicit provision establishing classes. The letter *N* indicates that there is an explicit provision prohibiting separate classes of real estate. Classification provisions are designated as *enumerated* if the constitution specifically lists the classes of real property that are to be used and *discretionary* if the constitution allows the legislature to establish classes. This column does not include states with constitutional provisions that require uniformity within classes but say no more with respect to classes.

[f] *Exemptions* refers to constitutional provisions relating to exemptions. The letter *Y* indicates there are such provisions. The letter *N* indicates there are no such provisions. Exemption provisions are classified as mandatory, permissive, or discretionary, and referenced as such in a footnote. *Mandatory* refers to constitutional provisions stating that a specific type of property may be exempted; and *discretionary* refers to explicit constitutional provisions allowing exemptions at the discretion of the legislature, with no reference to specific types of property. For purposes of this table, *exemptions* includes the favorable tax treatment of specific types of property or property owners, whether that be by favorable valuation (e.g., use value), favorable assessment ratios (other than for a general class of property), or favorable tax rates.

[g] *Improvements* refers to constitutional provisions that explicitly allow for the favorable property tax treatment of improvements relative to land.

[h] *Just value* refers to constitutional provisions providing that real property is to be valued at fair market value or the equivalent. The precise phrase is indicated in the footnote. The column does *not* include provisions relating to assessment ratios.

(continued)

Table 7.1 *continued*

Footnotes to table (Specific references are to the constitution of the given state unless otherwise indicated. Newhouse [1984] was used as a general reference throughout):

[1] Art. XI, sec. 217(b), (c): "all taxable property shall be forever taxed at the same rate." The word *uniformly* is used only to refer to laws regarding the establishment of current use value. (Note that subsection (b) applies to taxes levied by the state, and (c) applies to taxes levied by local governments.)

[2] Art. XI, sec. 217(b), (c): the "same rate" language could be considered a uniformity or an equality provision.

[3] Art. XI, sec. 211. Newhouse (1984, 57) notes that this section, in light of amended section 217, remains as an "anomaly."

[4] Art. XI, sec. 217(a): enumerated.

[5] Art. XI, sec. 217(g): discretionary; sec. 217(j), (k): mandatory. See also art. IV, sec. 91: mandatory.

[6] Art. XI, sec. 217(i),(j): "fair and reasonable market value."

[7] Alaska has a state property tax. Article X deals with differential taxation for "service areas."

[8] Art. IX, sec. 4: mandatory and discretionary.

[9] Art. IX, sec. 1: "all taxes shall be uniform upon the same class of property."

[10] Art. IX, sec. 2(13).

[11] Art. IX, sec. 1: discretionary.

[12] Art. IX, sec. 2, 2.1, 2.2: mandatory and permissible.

[13] No state property tax (amend. 47). See Newhouse (1984, 70).

[14] Art. XVI, sec. 5(a): "All real . . . property . . . shall be taxed according to its value, that value to be ascertained in such manner as the General Assembly shall direct, making the same *equal and uniform.*"

[15] Art. XVI, sec. 5(a).

[16] Art. XVI, sec. 6.

[17] Art. XVI, sec. 5(a): "No one species of property of equal value for which a tax may be collected shall be taxed higher than another species of property."

[18] Art. XVI, sec. 5(b): mandatory; sec. 15: mandatory; sec. 16: permissive.

[19] Art. XIII, sec. 1(a): "All property is taxable and shall be assessed at the same percentage of fair market value."

[20] Art. XIII, sec. 1(a).

[21] Art. XIII, sec. 1(b).

[22] Art. XIII, sec. 3: mandatory; sec. 4: permissive; sec. 8, 10: permissive.

[23] Art. X, sec. 3(1)(a): "Each property tax levy shall be uniform upon all real property."

24 Art. X, sec 3(1)(a).

25 Art. X, sec. 3(1), 3.5, 4, 5: mandatory.

26 Art. X, sec. 3(1): "just and equalized valuations," "actual value."

27 It is worth noting that article VIII, section 7 states: "In all assessments of the value of real estate for taxation, the value of land and the value of buildings and improvements thereon shall be included."

28 Art. VIII, sec. 1: "All classes shall be uniform upon the same class of subjects."

29 Art. VIII, sec. 1: discretionary (mandatory for agricultural lands).

30 State property tax forbidden (art. VII, sec. 1(a)).

31 Art. VII, sec. 2: "All ad valorem taxation shall be at a uniform rate within each taxing unit."

32 Art. VII, sec. 3, 4: mandatory and permissive.

33 Art. VII, sec. 3(c).

34 Art. VII, sec. 4: "just valuation of all property for ad valorem taxation."

35 Art. VII, sec. I, par. III(a): "all taxation shall be uniform upon the same class of subjects."

36 Art. VII, sec. I, par. III(b): no separate classes with respect to real property taxation are enumerated.

37 Art. VII, sec. I, par. III(c): mandatory; par. III(d): discretionary. Sec. II, par. II(a): permissive with strict procedures; par. III: permissive; par. IV: grandfather clause for pre-1983 statutory exemptions; par. V: mandatory.

38 The state is prohibited from taxing real property (art. VIII, sec. 3).

39 Art. VII, sec. 5: "All taxes shall be uniform upon the same class of subjects."

40 Art. VII, sec. 5.

41 Art. VII, sec. 2.

42 Art. VII, sec. 5: discretionary.

43 Art. VII, sec. 2: "the legislature may exempt a limited amount of improvements upon land from taxation."

44 Art. VII, sec. 5: "just valuation."

45 Art. IX, sec. 4(a): "taxes upon real property shall be levied uniformly by valuation."

46 Art. IX, sec. 4(b): discretionary for counties with a population of more than 200,000. (Only Cook County has elected to classify.)

(continued)

Table 7.1 continued

47 Art. IX, sec. 6: permissive.

48 Art. X, sec. 1(a): "uniform and equal rate of property assessment and taxation."

49 Art. X, sec. 1(a).

50 Art. X, sec. 1(a).

51 Art. X, sec. 1(a): permissive.

52 Art. X, sec. 1(a): "a just valuation."

53 There is no provision in the state constitution that refers specifically to uniformity in taxation. Article I, section 6 states that "all laws of a general nature shall have a uniform operation."

54 Art. XI, sec. 1(a): "uniform and equal basis of valuation and rate of taxation of all property."

55 Art. 11, sec. 1(a).

56 Art. 11, sec. 1(a): enumerated.

57 Art. 11, sec. 1(b): mandatory; sec. 12: permissive; sec. 13(d): permissive ("public purpose and promote the general welfare").

58 Article XI, section 13(a) allows for a time-limited exemption of "all or any portion" of property for economic development purposes, including land and buildings.

59 Sec. 171: "Taxes . . . shall be uniform upon all property of the same class."

60 Sec. 3, 174.

61 Sec. 174.

62 Sec. 171: discretionary.

63 Sec. 170, 172A: mandatory.

64 Sec. 172b: "moratorium" on reassessment for purpose of encouraging "repair, rehabilitation, or restoration."

65 Sec. 172: "fair cash value estimated at the price it would bring at a fair, voluntary sale."

66 Art. VII, sec. 18(A): "Property subject to ad valorem taxation shall be listed . . . at its assessed value, which . . . shall be a percentage of its fair market value. The percentage of fair market value shall be *uniform* throughout the state upon the same class of property."

67 Art. VII, sec. 21.

68 Art. VII, sec. 18(B): enumerated.

69 Art. VII, sec. 18(C), (G), 20, 21: mandatory.

[70] In article VII, section 18(B), "land" is classified as a separate class of property, distinct from "improvements for residential purposes" and "other property," which cover most business property. (There are separate classes for "electric cooperative properties, excluding land" and "public service properties, excluding land.") One might think that this would open the door constitutionally to the possibility of a split-rate land tax. However, section 18(B) also mandates the assessment ratio for each class of property. Land is to be assessed at 10 percent of fair market value, improvements for residential purposes at 10 percent, and other property at 15 percent. Thus, for residential property, there is no difference in the treatment of land and improvements. For business property, improvements are assigned a *higher* assessment ratio than land.

[71] Art. VII, sec. 21(F), (H).

[72] Art. VII, sec. 18(A), (D): "fair market value."

[73] Art. IX, sec. 8.

[74] Art. IX, sec. 8(2): permissive; sec. 5: permissive.

[75] Art. IX, sec. 8: "just value."

[76] Declaration of Rights, art. 15: "All taxes . . . shall be uniform within each class or subclass of land, improvements on land and personal property."

[77] Declaration of Rights, art. 15: discretionary ("The General Assembly shall, by uniform rules, provide for the separate assessment, classification and subclassification of land, (and) improvements on land . . . as it may deem proper.").

[78] Declaration of Rights, art. 15: see text quoted in note 77.

[79] Declaration of Rights, art. 15: see text quoted in note 77.

[80] Declaration of Rights, art. 15.

[81] Declaration of Rights, art. 15.

[82] Part 2, ch. 1, sec. 1, art. IV (as amended by art. CXII).

[83] Part 2, ch. 1, sec. 1, art. IV (as amended by art. CXII): limited discretionary.

[84] Part 2, ch. 1, sec. 1, art. IV (as amended by art. CXII): permissive, "reasonable." In addition, articles XCIX and CX grant authority to the legislature to treat agricultural and wild and recreational land differently.

[85] Art. IX, sec. 3: "The legislature shall provide for the uniform general ad valorem taxation of real . . . property."

[86] Art. IX, sec. 3: discretionary; sec. 4: mandatory (property used for nonprofit religious and educational purposes).

[87] Art. IX, sec. 3: "true cash value."

(continued)

Table 7.1 *continued*

88 Art. X, sec. 1: "Taxes shall be uniform upon the same class of subjects." Note that the uniformity clause has not prohibited the implementation of a progressive real property tax. Minnesota courts have ruled that the uniformity clause is no more restrictive than the equal protection clause. See *Apartment Operators' Association v. City of Minneapolis*, 254 N.W. 443 (Minn. 1934).

89 Art. X, sec. 1: mandatory, with some limited legislative discretion.

90 Art. IV, sec. 112: "Taxation shall be uniform and equal throughout the state."

91 Art. IV, sec. 112.

92 Art. IV, sec. 112 (in reference to assessments).

93 Art. IV, sec. 112: enumerated.

94 Art. IV, sec. 112: discretionary.

95 Art. IV, sec. 112: "true value."

96 Art. X, sec. 3: "Taxes . . . shall be uniform upon the same class or subclass of subjects."

97 Art. X, sec. 6(1).

98 Art. X, sec. 4(a), (b): enumerated.

99 Art. X, sec. 6, 7: mandatory and permissive.

100 Art. X, sec. 4(b): "true value."

101 Art. VIII, sec. 5(1): permissive and discretionary.

102 Art. VIII, sec. 1(1): "Taxes shall be levied by valuation uniformly and proportionately upon all real property."

103 Art. VIII, sec. 2(10).

104 Art. VIII, sec. 2(10).

105 Art. VIII, sec. 2: mandatory and permissive.

106 Art. X, sec. 1.1: "The Legislature shall provide . . . for a uniform and equal rate of assessment and taxation."

107 Art. X, sec. 1.1.

108 Art. X, sec. 1.1.

109 Art. X, sec. 3, 8, 10: permissive. A proposed constitutional amendment (art. X, sec. 6) allowing for discretionary exemptions that "will achieve a bona fide social and economic purpose and [whose] benefits . . . are expected to exceed any adverse effect . . . on the provision of services . . . by the State or a local government that would otherwise receive revenue from the tax" is subject to approval by popular vote in the 2008 general election.

110 Art. X, sec. 1.1: "just valuation."

111 Part II, art. 5: "proportional and reasonable."

112 Part II, art. 5: permissive for "growing wood or timber." Article 5-b permits the legislature to value "any class of real estate" at current use value.

113 Art. VIII, sec. I(1)(a): "Property shall be assessed for taxation under general laws and by uniform rules." The section goes on to say that "real property shall be taxed at the general tax rate of the taxing district."

114 Art. VIII, sec. I(1)(b), (2)–(5): mandatory, permissive, and discretionary.

115 Art. VIII, sec. I(6).

116 Art. VIII, sec. 1(A): "taxes shall be equal and uniform upon subjects of taxation of the same class."

117 Art. VIII, sec. 1(A).

118 Art. VIII, sec. 1(A).

119 Art. VIII, sec. 1(B), 3, 5, 15: mandatory.

120 Article XVI, section 1 has a discretionary exemption provision, which is modified by a prohibition against repealing the exemption for not-for-profit religious, educational, and charitable uses.

121 Art. V, sec. 2(2): "No class of property shall be taxed except by uniform rule, and every classification shall be made by general law uniformly applicable in every . . . unit of local government."

122 Art. V, sec. 2(2): discretionary.

123 Art. V, sec. 2(3): mandatory and permissive.

124 The state is prohibited from levying a tax on the assessed value of real property by article X, section 1. Sections 9 and 10 provide a limited exception to this prohibition.

125 Art. X, sec. 5: "Taxes shall be uniform upon the same class of property."

126 Art. X, sec. 5: mandatory and permissive.

127 Art. X, sec. 5: "The legislative assembly may by law exempt any or all classes of personal property from taxation and within the meaning of this section, fixtures, buildings and improvements of every character, whatsoever, upon land shall be deemed personal property."

128 Art. XII, sec. 2: "Land and improvements thereon shall be taxed by uniform rule according to value."

129 Art. XII, sec. 2a: enumerated.

(continued)

Table 7.1 continued

130 Art. XII, sec. 2: mandatory, permissive and discretionary; art. 2, sec. 36: permissive (for agricultural and forestry land).

131 Art. X, sec. 5(B): "Taxes shall be uniform upon the same class of subjects."

132 Art. V, sec. 50.

133 Art. X, sec. 6, 8: mandatory.

134 Art. X, sec. 8: "fair cash value."

135 Art. I, sec. 32: "all taxation shall be uniform upon the same class of subjects." Art. IX, sec. 1: "The Legislative Assembly shall . . . provide by law uniform rules of assessment and taxation. All taxes shall be levied and collected under general laws operating uniformly throughout the State."

136 Art. VIII, sec. 1: "All taxes shall be uniform upon the same class of subjects."

137 Art. VIII, sec. 5.

138 Art. VIII, sec. 2: permissive.

139 Included in the permissive exemptions of section 2 are (b)(iii) ("special tax provisions . . . to encourage improvement of deteriorating property or areas") and (b)(iv) ("special tax provisions on any increase in value of real estate resulting from residential construction").

140 Art. X, sec. 6: "Property tax levies shall be uniform in respect to persons and property within the jurisdiction of the body imposing such taxes." Art. X, sec. 1: "The assessment of all property shall be equal and uniform in the following classifications. . . ."

141 Art. X, sec. 1: see text quoted in note 140.

142 Art. X, sec. 1: enumerated.

143 Art. X, sec. 3: mandatory and discretionary.

144 Art. X, sec. 3(g): limited exemptions for new or expanded facilities.

145 Sec. 1 and sec. 6: "fair market value."

146 Art. VI, sec. 17: "all taxation shall be equal and uniform." Art. 11, sec. 2: "Taxes shall be uniform on all property of the same class." Art. VIII, sec. 15 (school districts): "Taxes shall be uniform on all property in the same class."

147 Art. VI, sec. 17.

148 Art. 11, sec. 7: "All laws exempting property from taxation other than enumerated in §§ 5 and 6 of this article shall be void." However, section 2 provides that the "legislature is empowered to divide all property . . . into classes and to determine what classes of property shall be subject to taxation and what property, if any, shall not be subject to taxation."

149 Art. 11, sec. 2: discretionary (see note 148).

150 Art. 11, sec. 5, 6: mandatory.

151 Art. II, sec. 28: "The ratio of assessment to value of property in each class or subclass shall be equal and uniform throughout the state. . . . Each respective taxing authority shall apply the same tax rate to all property within its jurisdiction."

152 Art. II, sec. 28.

153 Art. II, sec. 28.

154 Art. II, sec. 28: enumerated.

155 Art. II, sec. 28: permissive. Art. XI, sec. 11: mandatory (homesteads).

156 The state is constitutionally prohibited from levying a property tax (art. VIII, sec. 1-e).

157 Art. VIII, sec. 1(a): "Taxation shall be equal and uniform."

158 Art. VIII, sec. 1(a).

159 Art. VIII, sec. 1(b).

160 Art. VIII, sec. 1(b).

161 Mandatory and permissive. Several sections of article VIII provide for various exemptions. Article 11, section 9 exempts publicly owned property and "all other property devoted exclusively to the use and benefit of the public."

162 Art. XIII, sec. 2(1): "all property . . . not exempt . . . shall be: (a) assessed at a uniform and equal rate in proportion to its fair market value . . . ; and (b) taxed at a uniform and equal rate."

163 Art. XIII, sec. 2(1).

164 Art. XIII, sec. 2(1).

165 Art. XIII, sec. 2(1).

166 Art. XIII, sec. 2(3) and art. 3: mandatory and permissible.

167 Art. XIII, sec. 2(a): "fair market value."

168 Vermont has no express article in its constitution devoted to taxation and finance. The closest to a uniformity clause in the constitution is chapter 1, article 9 ("Citizens' rights and duties in the state; bearing arms, taxation"), which states: "That every member of society hath a right to be protected in the enjoyment of life, liberty, and property, and therefore is bound to contribute the member's proportion towards the expense of that protection."

169 Real estate is subject to local taxation only (art. X, sec. 4).

170 Art. X, sec. 1: "All taxes . . . shall be uniform upon the same class of subjects."

(continued)

Table 7.1 continued

171 Art. X, sec. 1.

172 Art. X, sec. 1: discretionary.

173 Art. X, sec. 2, 6: mandatory and permissive.

174 Art. X, sec. 6(h): permissive (improvements).

175 Art. X, sec. 2: "fair market value."

176 Art. VII, sec. 1: "All taxes shall be uniform upon the same class of property"; see also sec. 9.

177 Art. VII, sec. 1: "All real estate shall constitute one class."

178 Art. VII, sec. 1: discretionary; sec. 10, 11: permissive; sec. 1: mandatory (government-owned property).

179 Art. VII, sec. 2, 11: "true and fair value."

180 Art. X, sec. 10-1: "taxation shall be equal and uniform throughout the state." In addition, section 10-9 mandates uniformity in taxation by cities, towns, and villages.

181 Art. X, sec. 10-1.

182 Art. X, sec. 10-1.

183 Art. X, sec. 10-1.

184 Art. X, sec. 10-1: permissive; sec. 10-1b: mandatory. Art. VI, sec. 53; permissive.

185 Art. X, sec. 1: "The rule of taxation shall be uniform."

186 Art. X, sec. 1: permissive.

187 Art. 15, sec. 1: separate assessment of land and improvements.

188 Art. 15, sec. 11(d): "All taxation shall be equal and uniform within each class of property."

189 Art. 15, sec. 11(d).

190 Art. 15, sec. 11(b): enumerated (3 classes).

191 Art. 15, sec. 12: mandatory and discretionary.

192 Art. 15, sec. 11(a), (b): "full value"; sec. 11(d): "just valuation."

◈ 8 ◈

The Assessment Requirements for
a Separate Tax on Land

MICHAEL E. BELL, JOHN H. BOWMAN, AND
JEROME C. GERMAN

As THE AUTHORS of chapter 4 argue, there are good reasons to believe that land value taxation offers certain advantages over the sort of real property tax common in the United States and elsewhere. Before one can tax land values separately from improvement values, however, one needs to develop the appropriate concept of land value for tax purposes. Somewhat surprisingly, this fundamental matter is not settled. One view is that the value of raw land—land in its natural state—is the appropriate value for land value taxation (E. Mills 1998, 39); another is that the value of the site—including streets, sewers, lighting, and the general state of development of the area, though not the structures on the specific site—is the appropriate value (Lindholm 1969, ix). Accepting the latter view, we start with the premise that land should be valued for tax purposes at its current highest and best use, not its value in some natural state.

No matter how laudable the goals or how solid the theory underlying the discussion of land value taxation, however, implementation by ordinary tax assessors may be the defining challenge to its widespread adoption. If front-line assessors cannot routinely, accurately, and equitably split the value of individual properties into the two components of land and improvements, the promise of land value taxation will be added to the list of potentially great ideas that have gone wanting for lack of a practical implementation path.

It is an interesting historical fact that most assessment jurisdictions started out with a valuation methodology that required breaking real property value into its two main components. The earliest method of mass valuation was the *cost approach*, which estimates the market value of land and then adds the depreciated value of the replacement cost of the improvements. This inherently componentized approach has been de-emphasized over time in favor of two other valuation approaches: the market value or *sales comparison approach*, which is used almost exclusively in valuing single-family residential property, and the *income approach*, which is used in valuing income-producing commercial or industrial property. As generally applied, neither of these approaches requires or produces a separate land value; instead, each yields parcel values that combine land and improvement values.

Brunori and Carr (2002, 1023) determined—through a review of state constitutions, statutes, and appellate court rulings—that the law in 29 states requires separate values for land and improvements and that the remaining 21 states and the District of Columbia have no such legal requirement.[1] They also determined, through telephone surveys of 246 local assessing jurisdictions drawn from all 50 states and the District of Columbia, that (1) virtually all the surveyed units produce separate land and improvement values, whether or not state law requires such values, and (2) that most of the local assessing officials believe their separate values to be highly accurate, with less than 5 percent of total value misallocated. Thus, property assessment systems in the United States typically do generate separate land values, even though separate land and improvement values affect property tax liabilities in only a handful of localities, nearly all in Pennsylvania.

In this chapter we explore how land values are actually determined for tax purposes; whether different methodologies generate similar estimates of land values; and the implications of our findings for the implementation of a land value tax. In the next section, we briefly review different approaches to valuing land for tax purposes. Then we summarize several case studies on

---

1. The states requiring separate values for land and improvements are California, Colorado, Hawaii, Illinois, Iowa, Kansas, Kentucky, Maine, Maryland, Minnesota, Mississippi, Montana, Nebraska, Nevada, New Jersey, New York, North Dakota, Ohio, Oklahoma, Oregon, Pennsylvania, South Dakota, Tennessee, Texas, Utah, Virginia, West Virginia, Wisconsin, and Wyoming (Brunori and Carr 2002, 1023). The study was restricted to the sources noted and excluded administrative rules and regulations. Thus, if all 50 states and the District of Columbia were examined more fully, more than 29 might be found to have some sort of requirement for separate valuation.

how jurisdictions actually value land for tax purposes and discuss how the valuation methodologies of the case-study areas compare with a baseline valuation approach that emerges from the notion of contribution value.[2] From these studies, we conclude that analytic tools exist to estimate separate land and improvement values with reasonable accuracy. With this in mind, we then provide a closer look at how land is valued in Lucas County, Ohio. In the final section, we suggest some guidelines on how local governments might strengthen their valuation of land, separate from improvements, for tax purposes.

APPROACHES TO LAND VALUATION

For vacant land, the preferred approach to valuation is sales comparison. It is grounded in the notion that land parcels of similar utility are substitutes for one another and will yield similar prices in a competitive marketplace (Wuensch, Kelly, and Hamilton 2000, 11).[3] Market transactions for vacant land are used with appropriate adjustments for size, shape, corner influence, location, and topography (Eckert 1990, 190–195). In developed urban areas, however, there may not be enough vacant land sales to use the sales comparison approach to valuation, and alternative techniques may thus have to be used. We examine three of these approaches; all depend on the principle of substitution, but apply it in a different manner.

Abstraction: Residual Land Value

The most common approach to valuing land for tax purposes in urban areas without enough vacant land sales is the abstraction, or extraction, method. This technique starts with the market value of the entire property and subtracts the depreciated cost of replacing the improvements, attributing the residual value to land. In other words, a property's value is directly influenced

---

2. The notion of contribution value is that various individual features of land and improvements are worth what they add to the price the property can command in a market transaction; that price may be greater than, less than, or equal to the added cost. For example, if upgrading roofing from asphalt shingle to cedar shakes increases costs by $10,000 but adds $20,000 to the sales price, the contribution value is $20,000.

3. This section draws on Bell and Bowman (2006).

by the cost of acquiring a similar asset with similar utility (Eckert 1990, 195–196, 318; Wuensch, Kelly, and Hamilton 2000, 16).

This approach might work well for relatively new structures, but as time passes, economic obsolescence and depreciation occur. Adjustments for these are difficult to make, are subjective, and require informed judgments by the assessor (Eckert 1990, 196). An additional caveat is that location affects the market, or contribution, value of both land and improvements, although in percentage terms the impact on land is much greater (Gloudemans 2002). If the abstraction method—which depends on the depreciated cost of improvements to arrive at residual land values—does not make allowances for the effect of location on the value of improvements, the land value estimates may be inaccurate in many instances.[4] Finally, note that valuing land as a residual after subtracting the depreciated cost of improvements from a property's total value seems to move away from the notion of market value. The housing, or other, services provided by residential, or related, improvements may or may not be related to the cost of constructing a substitute structure.

Allocation: Typical Land Share of Value

A second land valuation approach when there are few land sales is allocation, which attributes, or allocates, a percentage of the total improved parcel value to land. The land percentage is derived from market evidence and applied to individual parcels. The approach implicitly says that if land typically accounts for 25 percent of total value, for example, then 25 percent is the likely land share of total value for a particular property. If buyers can purchase other properties providing a given level of utility for which land is 25 percent of value, why put more than that into land?

How the allocation percentage is determined is of obvious importance. In

---

4. Two types of adjustments are necessary when using the depreciated cost approach. One is to adjust for differences in the cost of materials from one area to another. For example, the cost of a two-by-four may be higher in one area than another. Using a standard cost table for all areas may miss this type of difference, so assessors may adjust the cost coefficients to reflect the market for supplies in different neighborhoods or different jurisdictions. A second type of adjustment, which is addressed by Gloudemans (2002), is needed when the contribution value of various characteristics of a house vary because the houses, although identical in structure, are located in different market areas. The market value of two houses will be different, even though they are identical structures with identical replacement costs, if one house is in a neighborhood undergoing gentrification and the other is in a neighborhood in decline.

jurisdictions with few or no sales of vacant land, finding evidence of the value of land is difficult. One approach is to derive the average land share, using the abstraction method, and then use that percentage in the allocation approach. Deriving an appropriate land allocation percentage in this way requires proper calibration to the geographic area of the construction costs and depreciation percentages used in the abstraction process. Alternatively, one might use historical sales data for the locality, from a time when there were enough land sales. This approach runs the risk of missing a change in the relative value of land over time. Still another approach is to use more contemporaneous land sales from another locality where there are enough land sales. This approach also has its risks: the other sales area will differ from the one for which an allocation percentage is being calculated, and if appropriate adjustments are not made, erroneous land value estimates will result.

Contribution Value

The market value of land can be estimated more accurately using the contribution value approach. How much does each characteristic of site and improvements contribute to the market value of the particular parcel? Market values emerge from arm's-length transactions for a number of properties that are reasonable substitutes in terms of the utility they provide—for example, in the case of residential properties, essentially the same housing services. An informed buyer might be willing to purchase any of several homes on the market at a given time. However, because no two properties are exactly alike (they will differ at least in their location, however slightly), the buyer may not be willing to pay the same amount for each property. Differences deemed important will translate into different prices that the buyer will be willing to offer. "The principle of contribution applies to the parts of a property to determine the contribution of each part to the total value. Total value may not equal total cost of the individual parts" (Eckert 1990, 88).

Some features of a property may add either more or less than their replacement costs, as evaluated by the typical buyer. An old, but still sound, barn on a site in an area no longer used for farming may add less to value than its replacement cost in the eyes of buyers looking only for a residence. Alternatively, the cost of adding a garage to a new house might be less than the amount the typical home buyer would be willing to pay to have a garage. Such considerations suggest that the abstraction method may err in its generation of land values and that the allocation method may not do any better.

The most appropriate analytical tool for addressing contribution value is a statistical model that explains the sales prices of individual properties as a function of the attributes of land and improvements. E. Mills (1998, 47) expresses strong misgivings about this approach to land valuation. We think him overly pessimistic. One must start, as Mills acknowledges, with the understanding that assessment of real property for tax purposes is not only a science but also an art. One must also acknowledge that assessments must be developed for tax purposes. The challenge is to inform the assessor's judgment as fully and as clearly as possible. The literature includes several examples of models that seem to contribute to an understanding of prices, or values.

Ashley, Plassmann, and Tideman (1999) address the question of how accurately one can assess developed commercial land in an urban center where there are limited or no sales of such land. They use sales in downtown Portland, Oregon, to develop and test a combination of simple empirical models of the value of improvements to commercial property. They conclude that even though there are relatively few sales of commercial land in downtown Portland, the available information could be used in creative ways to develop reasonable estimates of land value for developed commercial properties. Their model predicts land value for improved downtown commercial land better than the model used by assessors in the city, and they conclude that the model's performance is good enough to warrant further study.

In a related effort, Gloudemans (2000) tests the ability of modern mass appraisal techniques to develop separate estimates of land and improvement values for urban residential properties. He uses data from three North American metropolitan areas—Ada County, Idaho (Boise); Edmonton, Alberta; and Jefferson County, Colorado (suburban Denver)—to test both traditional and nontraditional regression models typical of those used by assessment authorities. Results of the nontraditional models are tested on combined sales and separately on improved and vacant land sales. On the basis of his research findings, he concludes that modern mass appraisal methods can be adapted to estimate both vacant and improved residential land values with reasonable accuracy, even when there are few or no vacant land sales in certain areas.

In a separate research project, Gloudemans, Handel, and Warwa (2002) test the efficacy of different models, using different data sets, in estimating the value of vacant land in urban areas. They are concerned that the appraisal of vacant residential land tends to be comparatively difficult and that studies of assessment performance consistently show values for vacant residential land to be far less accurate or reliable than for improved residential properties.[5] They test three different models to estimate the value of land—a land model using only vacant land sales; an improved model using only improved sales; and a combined model using both vacant and improved sales. If the combined model performs as well (or nearly as well) as the individual models in estimating land value, it should be able to perform even better in older areas with fewer vacant land sales. The authors conclude that the combined model, using both vacant and improved sales, performs as well as the individual models. Thus, a combined model lends stability to estimates of vacant land values and provides much-needed market benchmarks where vacant land sales are lacking.

We conclude that the contribution principle of value seems more consistent with the notion of market value than either the abstraction or the allocation principle. There are adequate analytical tools available to estimate with reasonable accuracy independent land and improvement values.

Sales Data for Teardowns

Another approach to valuing land in built-up areas with few vacant land sales is to consider teardowns. Dye and McMillen (2007b) investigate residential housing teardowns in Chicago and its suburbs to determine what affected the sales prices of properties for which demolition permits were sought. They include measures of location and structural variables to describe the improvements on the properties and find that structural characteristics do not significantly influence the sales prices of teardown properties. From these empirical results, they conclude that teardowns are purchased for the land underneath and that the value of that land can be estimated as the sales price of the property plus demolition costs (see also McMillen 2006).

DETERMINING LAND VALUES FOR TAX PURPOSES: CASE STUDIES OF ACTUAL PRACTICES

As noted, assessors in at least twenty-nine states are legally required to value land and improvements separately for tax purposes, and standard practice

---

5. This might be due to the greater uncertainty about prospects for vacant land, since development decisions must still be made and implemented.

usually provides separate assessments whether they are required or not.[6] To get a better understanding of how governments value land for tax purposes, Bell and Bowman (2006) conducted detailed case studies of land valuation procedures in both urban and rural areas in four of these twenty-nine states: Maryland, Ohio, Pennsylvania, and Virginia.

In all four states, property assessment is performed at the county level (or at the city level in the case of several independent cities in Virginia). In Maryland, property assessments are performed by a state agency, but the state Department of Assessments and Taxation maintains an assessment office in each county and in the city of Baltimore, pursuant to state law. Although assessment by contract appraisal firms is common in both Ohio and Virginia, the four study areas in these two states all have in-house assessment staffs. One Pennsylvania area is assessed by a private firm and the other by in-house staff. The property tax accounts for a smaller portion of local taxes in these four states—particularly Maryland—than in the nation as a whole. The case studies included older central cities, rural areas (including a vacation destination), a state capital, and two suburban counties.

The case studies reveal that four approaches are used to assess land values for tax purposes. Analysis of data from recent sales of vacant land is commonly employed in rural and suburban communities. In more developed jurisdictions, the abstraction, allocation, and contribution value approaches are used to assess land values. Within the areas that must estimate land values without the benefit of sufficient vacant land sales data, rarely is one method used to the complete exclusion of all others. In all study areas and regardless of the assessment approach emphasized, we were told that the values generated by the primary method are reviewed for reasonableness before they are put on the tax rolls. Thus, localities that rely primarily on abstraction usually consider the percentage of total parcel value represented by land (i.e., allocation), and areas that rely primarily on allocation typically consider whether the resulting land and improvement values make sense given the specific characteristics of the various parcels.

After pursuing these case studies, we are more sanguine about the ability of assessors to value land reasonably accurately for the purposes of land value taxation, even where there are not many sales of vacant land. Still, we are concerned that the choice of primary valuation method may make a difference in the final land value estimates. The biggest difference, we believe, is

---

6. This section draws on Bell and Bowman (2006).

between areas using a contribution value methodology and those using one of the other methods. Contribution value seeks to determine the effect of each of several property attributes on the market value of the entire property, and it seems to do this in a way that is likely to be more successful than one of the other methods. We explore further the relative performance of the three land valuation methods in the next section.

ESTIMATING LAND VALUES FOR TAX PURPOSES: SENSITIVITY TO METHODOLOGY

To explore the possibility of systematic differences among the three approaches, we analyze locally determined land values from three of the study areas (one for each general approach for areas lacking sufficient land sales data) in relation to baseline estimates derived in a single consistent manner:[7]

- Roanoke, Virginia, which relies primarily on the abstraction method
- Baltimore, Maryland, which relies primarily on the allocation method
- Lucas County, Ohio, which uses a set of estimation procedures that we consider a variant of the contribution value method

We do not evaluate the various approaches but seek merely to determine the extent to which different valuation methodologies result in different estimates of land values for tax purposes.

Data and Methodology

For each locality, we obtained a 2006 data file for single-family residential properties sold in a recent time period. We asked for the total assessed value of each property, as well as the separate land and improvement values. In addition, we asked for the property-record information on the attributes of those properties so that we could use this information to develop independent baseline land value estimates for each jurisdiction, using the contribution value approach. We compared these baseline estimates with the assessed land values to determine the degree to which different methodologies produce different or similar land value estimates. As already noted, although the three valuation methods are intended to arrive at estimates of market value, we believe that in practice they could well generate different assessed land

---

7. This section draws on Bell and Bowman (2008).

values.[8] Our baseline estimates were developed by a professional appraisal firm, 21st Century Appraisals.[9]

Results of Methodology Comparison

We considered several sorts of evidence on differences between the two sets of land values available to us for each of the three study areas: mean land ratios, coefficients of dispersion (CODs), price-related differentials (PRDs), and correlations between the two sets of values. The mean land ratios give the average percentage of improved residential parcel value represented by land for each set of land value estimates. The CODs provide a summary measure of the extent to which the local estimates of land value differ from the 21st Century Appraisals baseline estimates (higher values indicate greater differences). The PRDs provide a summary measure of whether the local valuation methodology produces land value estimates that, compared with the baseline, systematically favor either high- or low-value properties. Finally, the simple correlations between the two sets of land values for each locality indicate the closeness of the relationship between the two values.

Each of the four measures provides evidence that valuation results differ by valuation methodology:

- The mean land ratios are higher for the 21st Century estimates than for the local estimates in both Roanoke (abstraction method) and Lucas County (contribution value method). In Baltimore, however, the allocation approach produced a higher land ratio than the baseline estimates.
- The CODs are rather large (they range from 23 percent in Lucas

---

8. It often is argued that the income, sales comparison, and cost approaches to value should give similar results and, likewise, that in valuing land, the allocation, abstraction, and contribution approaches should give similar results. However, it seems reasonable to expect the same values to emerge from all methodologies only in cases of market equilibrium; in disequilibrium, cost and contribution approaches to the value of structures, for example, would tend to differ because contribution values of older structures would tend to be greater than replacement costs in booming markets and less than replacement costs in areas of decline. Only through the application of informed judgment for such disequilibriums, including functional and economic obsolescence, would similar results be expected.

9. This firm works in nearly one-third of the counties in Pennsylvania and has established a very good record, having been responsible for assessments in most of the Pennsylvania counties that meet or exceed International Association of Assessing Officers (IAAO) assessment standards. For more information, see Bell and Bowman (2006, 22; 2008).

County to 44 percent in Baltimore), indicating substantial differences in individual-parcel land values under the two approaches.
- The PRDs for the three areas are all greater than 1.0, indicating that the local methodologies favored high-value properties to some extent, at least compared with the baseline value estimates. Only the Roanoke PRD (1.023) is low enough to indicate a value-neutral assessment relative to the baseline under International Association of Assessing Officers (IAAO) guidelines.
- The correlations between the baseline land value estimates and the local land valuation approaches are high and positive for all three areas, ranging from 0.76 in Baltimore to 0.81 in Lucas County. They are all, however, far enough below 1.0 to indicate clear differences between the estimates.

By all four measures, the differences between the 21st Century contribution-based values and locally determined land values are greatest for Baltimore, which relies primarily on the allocation method. This seems reasonable given that the allocation method generally uses less parcel-specific information in arriving at land values than either of the other two methods. As noted, Roanoke, which relies on the abstraction method, performs best on the PRD measure. Lucas County is closest to the baseline for the other three performance measures and does nearly as well as Roanoke on the PRD. The relatively better performance of Lucas County makes sense because the comparison is between Lucas County's primary reliance on the contribution value method and 21st Century's alternative version of the contribution value method.

Implications for Policy and Further Research

Because each of the various valuation methods is intended to produce estimates of market value for individual properties, they generally are assumed to be alternative routes to the same end. Our concern that this might not be so in practice is supported by empirical results from our three study areas: different results do, indeed, flow from different valuation methods.

This is an important finding. When land value taxation is employed, it is important that land be valued as accurately as possible. If different valuation methods produce different estimates of value, the relative taxes of various property owners are influenced by a choice currently seen as simply an administrative choice, not the policy choice that it may turn out to be. Because our findings arise from an examination of just three areas, it would be useful to conduct similar research in a number of other settings to determine the robustness of our findings.

VALUING LAND FOR TAX PURPOSES: THE EXPERIENCE OF LUCAS COUNTY, OHIO

Ohio is one of the 29 states that require separate valuation of land and improvements, although an Ohio court decision holds that "the tax is on the aggregate value of land and improvements" (Brunori and Carr 2002, 1030).[10] Assessment in Ohio is performed at the county level, and we have singled out Lucas County (which includes Toledo) because of its use of different valuation methods over time and because of its use of innovative techniques for estimating land values.[11]

Before 1982, Lucas County used the cost approach. Because cost data pertain only to improvements, land values must be derived separately under this approach, even if they are not required by law. In 1982, however, Lucas County began to rely primarily on the sales comparison method. Recently, a cost approach has been developed using data and formulas from a firm that provides construction-cost estimates for appraisers and developers (Marshall & Swift), calibrated for Lucas County using market values. The sales comparison approach is used to generate appraised values for all residential properties, including condominiums but excluding apartments, and also for all industrial properties and nonresidential land. The capitalized income approach is used for improved commercial properties and apartments.

---

10. This section draws on Bell and Bowman (2006) and information obtained in a meeting with Lucas County assessment staff members Jerome C. German, Richard D. Ward, Jason Guilford, and Brian Jones.

"In Ohio, all land must be valued as vacant regardless of whether the parcel has a building on it. This represents a significant dilemma if one agrees that there is a different market and, therefore, different values for vacant and improved land" (Ward et al. 2002, 23).

11. One of the authors of this chapter, Jerome German, was formerly chief assessor in Lucas County. The other two authors of this chapter were attracted to study Lucas County by what seemed to them to be its cutting-edge efforts in estimating land values.

Computer-Assisted Assessment with Spatial Analysis

A good description of the Lucas County valuation system is provided by two articles in a professional journal for assessors (Ward, Weaver, and German 1999; Ward et al. 2002).[12] The value of land—with appropriate adjustments for size, shape, and topography—depends on location. Both papers focus on improving location variables for computer-assisted mass appraisal (CAMA) analysis. For the comparable sales approach to assessment, CAMA starts with detailed information on the structure, location, and other attributes of all properties in an assessment district. For the subset of properties that have been sold recently, CAMA models use regression analysis or other statistical methods to measure the separate contribution of each different attribute to total value. Then, for all properties, sold and unsold, the computer program can multiply each attribute value by its estimated effect, add them all up, and produce an appraisal of the total value of the property.

The neighborhood, as delineated by an expert appraiser, has been the basic building block for location analysis in assessment practice. Hence, a common method of specifying location in mass appraisal models is to use fixed-boundary neighborhoods—with a single location multiplier for all properties within each neighborhood. Ward, Weaver, and German (1999) argue that although using fixed-boundary neighborhoods improves CAMA performance, this adjustment is not sufficiently precise, because differences within neighborhoods are missed. Advances in geographic information systems (GIS) technology—computer software to manipulate spatial information—allow development of more precise location multipliers. In particular, the Lucas County researchers explored the advantages of a mathematical technique called global response surface analysis (GRSA), which relies on GIS to measure the distance to multiple sold properties.

Ward, Weaver, and German (1999) conclude that the initial surface may be estimated using either a derivative of sales price (the most common being the sales price per square foot) or building characteristics to construct the lo-

---

12. Lucas County continued to innovate its methods, so some changes have occurred since these articles were published. Also, Lucas County, like most assessment offices, uses proprietary models and valuation techniques and may not share all the details. Lucas County has provided more details than most jurisdictions in the past, and new information should be made public in professional journals over the next several years.

cation variable. They also note that this provides a better way to develop a location factor than using fixed-boundary neighborhood dummy variables, even in jurisdictions with few sales. However, they note that "the final valuation model must still be built on sales that may or may not be representative of the universe" (Ward et al. 2002, 23).

A More Detailed Look at the Determination of Location Values in Lucas County

What follows may be too detailed for some readers, but the point is this: the example of assessment practice in Lucas County shows that careful use of sales data, location, and other attributes can create more numerous and more precise measures of the value of location.

To address the need for generating land values, Lucas County assessors have developed a classification of neighborhoods (252 in the county) intended to capture different supply and demand forces. Specifically, they define four classes of neighborhoods reflecting the stage of land development: developing, mature, raw, and developing-raw (Ward et al. 2002, 23–24). They also differentiate neighborhoods according to such factors as the number of vacant parcels, the portion of the area represented by vacant parcels, the number of sales of vacant parcels, the turnover rate for vacant parcels (the number of sales relative to the number of such parcels), and the extent to which there are sales of agricultural land. Once this has been done, vacant land sales are modeled.

The analysis starts with over 900 sales of vacant residential and agricultural land, excluding parcel sales prices (or prices per square foot) above or below specified extreme values (Ward et al. 2002, 26). The Lucas County CAMA modeling team develops a model to explain sales prices using such variables as foot frontage, lot size, neighborhood stage, whether the area is unplatted (i.e., not yet laid out for residential development), land influences (e.g., golf course view, river usable, swampy, wooded, private pond), and traffic pattern (main, secondary, private road, or no outlet). Both the frontage and lot-size measures are separated into two variables to reflect the notion that increases beyond some base level add less to total value.[13] This is consistent with the notion of contribution value, as discussed above.

13. For frontage, the base value selected is 50 feet, and the excess frontage variable is simply the difference between this figure and the actual frontage of a parcel. For lot size, the base size is 20,000 square feet, and the excess size variable is the square root of the difference between this figure and the actual lot size.

The base model—with no location factor—does a poor job of explaining price differences across properties and does not meet IAAO guidelines for assessment accuracy. Adding a location variable developed from GRSA, using sales price data to estimate the response surface, greatly improves the results and does meet IAAO standards for accuracy (Ward et al. 2002, 26–30).

Ward and others (2002) then suggest subtracting the estimated land values from the sales prices for improved property to derive residual improvement values. This would reverse the usual abstraction approach. Perhaps it would overcome some of the problems associated with deriving depreciated replacement costs, but it would still fall short of implementing a contribution value approach. Ward and others suggest that the residual values be used as the variable to be explained by a statistical model. They note, "Applying both land and building models across all residential properties should produce equalized land values (for vacant and improved parcels) relative to market prices as well as equitable total values. This approach can sometimes result in negative building values," but adjustments can be made in this case, if warranted (Ward et al. 2002, 30).

In applying the sales comparison approach, it is necessary to augment sales price information in some neighborhoods where there are too few recorded sales. So, sales proxies are constructed, as needed, for land values in the county. One technique is to select representative properties in each size class in each neighborhood and then rely on the professional skills of experienced appraisers to determine the value of the land. Also, some actual sales are not representative of the overall market, and professional judgment must be used to exclude these from the analysis. Having representative land sales, or good proxies, is essential in estimating location values using the response surface method described above.

IMPROVING THE WAY LAND VALUES ARE DETERMINED FOR TAX PURPOSES

Our analysis to this point supports the conclusion that there are adequate analytical tools available to tax appraisers to estimate separate land and improvement values with reasonable accuracy. This section examines several approaches for improving the way land values are assessed for tax purposes.

Land Valuation Using CAMA Integrated with GIS

Mass appraisers have gone to great lengths in valuing land via land value maps that break down sales data for vacant lots into square-foot and front-foot rates modified with depth tables to account for varying lot dimensions. Computers have greatly assisted the linking of these value maps and tables to the detailed attributes of individual parcels. CAMA procedures for land are prime candidates for more refined manipulation and spatial analysis with GIS. The size, shape, and location of vacant land parcels that have been sold can be plotted exactly, and the sales price can be transformed into a rate per front foot or square foot. The analyst can then estimate, through an interpolation process, the appropriate land rates for other properties by street, block, or neighborhood. This is an arduous process that is most often hampered by the "feast or famine" phenomenon of having a wealth of land sales data in newly developing or suburban locations and a dearth or complete lack of vacant land sales data in urban or inner-city areas. Determining land assessments takes an artist's touch in valuing across large geographic areas with scarce or questionable sales data.

How can GIS help? The specification of location effects in CAMA models has progressed from using a single multiplier for each fixed-boundary neighborhood to quantifying the data that go into choosing and determining those areas. A neighborhood as defined in the IAAO's *Glossary for Property Appraisal and Assessment* (1997) is "(1) the environment of a subject property that has a direct and immediate effect on value" or "(2) a geographic area in which there are typically fewer than several thousand properties defined for some useful purpose, such as to ensure for later multiple regression modeling that the properties are homogeneous and share important locational characteristics." Neighborhoods have become the lingua franca of location's influence. The identification of neighborhoods is part art, part history, and part science, mixed with a heavy dose of the practical and realistic. Each property must be included within a neighborhood. However, there are often odd properties or groups of properties that do not fit well with one of their contiguous neighbors but are too few in number to constitute their own neighborhood.

Neighborhood Analysis

If you were to ask assessors where GIS could help them most, the almost universal answer would be "neighborhood analysis." Most assessing agencies spend large amounts of staff time creating and then monitoring these building blocks of location's influence. Most calculate statistics within neighbor-hoods, create profiles, and generally go to great lengths to try to identify ho-mogeneity within neighborhoods. This similarity in age, style, size, quality, and condition attempts to ensure that the inventory within a neighborhood is as alike as possible because, generally, a single locational factor or multi-plier will be assigned to all the parcels within a particular neighborhood.

Neighborhood analysis is not restricted to residential parcels; it applies to all other classes of property. There are differing commercial neighborhoods: linear strips, central business districts, and the commercial areas emanating from the central core. There are new cores or multiple nuclei such as major shopping malls or suburban central business districts with which to contend. Other government agencies designate economic development zones, urban revitalization, and neighborhood improvement areas, thereby adding to the assessor's potential list of neighborhoods.

Industrial areas or neighborhoods were once easily identifiable and lo-cated near natural resources, transportation, or workforce. Industrial areas were identified by primary industry type, such as steel, refining, and chemi-cal, or by related industrial functions, such as automotive. Modern manufac-turing practices have fractured industrial land use patterns. The proliferation of outer-belt, mixed-use industrial parks has blurred commercial and indus-trial classifications and land use and valuation. Just-in-time transportation and delivery has eliminated the need for proximity to suppliers and raw ma-terials. Inner-city industrial land is more likely to be in transition to some other use than to remain solidly in the industrial class.

Assessing agricultural land in transition is one of the assessor's more daunting tasks. Agricultural land at the urban fringe is in transition to all other classifications, including those exempt from taxation, such as parks. The assessor is charged with tracking and valuing the pure in-use agricul-tural land, the land in transition, and the land just converted. As with other classifications, there are special districts and farmland or green space exemp-tions and preferential assessment programs.

Obviously, one of the assessor's main duties is to identify the property to be appraised and taxed. GIS is becoming nearly indispensable for keeping track of all these differentially classed districts. Once the assignment of parcels to districts and neighborhoods has taken place, the task of valuation can begin.

Agricultural Land Valuation with GIS

The assessment of rural land is a multipronged issue. In most states, agricul-tural land is legally required to be assessed on the basis of its current use

(Bowman, Cordes, and Metcalf, forthcoming). The assessor often needs to differentiate between types of rural land use—such as crop, pasture, and timber—and between roads and unproductive areas as well. Also, soil type, slope, and drainage characteristics must be taken into account. In addition to the agricultural land in production, the assessor has to value the rural residential elements of a farm. The home and home site are usually segregated and valued separately. Each of these land uses and types can be displayed and analyzed separately with an integrated GIS and CAMA system.

Commercial and Industrial Land Valuation with GIS

Commercial and industrial land valuation is one of the most difficult appraisal challenges an assessment office faces. In many jurisdictions, the cost approach is the primary method used to value commercial and industrial properties, especially special-purpose, exempt, and heavy industrial property where the lack of an active market precludes the use of the sales comparison or income approaches.

The general problem of insufficient data on land sales is amplified in commercial and industrial land valuation. Simply put, the problem is that assessors are required to value too many categories of land from the current sales data inventory.

Spatial analysis through GIS can replicate, more efficiently, the manual procedures appraisers have been using for years of plotting sales on a map by class and specific land use with per-unit breakdowns. Additional complications, however, involve the subdivision of land by categories such as primary, unused, or right-of-way. These additional segmentations further exacerbate the problems of statistical reliability and data usability.

GIS can be of assistance in displaying the geographic dispersion of sales by category. A way to improve the reliability and confidence in the estimates is to add to the amount of information for the model to consider. In a procedure sometimes called *benchmarking*, pseudo or proxy sales can be added to the data.[14] In addition to assessing geographic representativeness, the modeler might also assess whether there are sufficient sales data by property size, zoning, or broad subcategories such as retail, apartment, office, restaurant, hotel-motel, warehousing, and light and heavy manufacturing. The reason for gaining both geographic and characteristic representativeness is simply

---

14. Also called *beacons* by Gloudemans (2002) and *expert appraisals* or *pseudo appraisals* by others.

to be able to better interpolate between known points (sales and benchmarks) so that unknown points (the unsold properties to be valued) can be better and more reliably estimated.

In past years commercial and industrial property appraisers have interpolated between observed (or proxy) sales points manually, by feel and by experience. Given enough experienced appraisers in a jurisdiction, this is a workable procedure. However, government budgets and staffing levels are under pressure; the most experienced appraisers are being lost to attrition; and there is a trend to require more frequent reappraisals—all of which has led the assessing profession to consider GRSA as a computer-based interpolation technique.[15]

Current State of the Art in Land Value Assessment

The current state of the art in the mass valuation of land offers four techniques that could be combined into one strategy for land valuation:

· New modeling specifications
· Data enhancement techniques
· Spatial analysis
· GIS

To our knowledge, this synthesis of the four techniques has not yet occurred.

Lucas County has demonstrated the viability of two alternative methodologies for periodic, accurate, and equitable land valuation for residential property. Over the course of four reappraisal cycles spanning twenty-four years, the county estimated a decomposed land value for each property from a unified model. Coefficients from regression models on sales prices with sufficient measures of the attributes of the dwellings and the characteristics of the locations were used to separate or decompose the component values. The model was specified to be decomposable in the main components of land, main dwelling, and other improvement features. By using data on sales of improved properties, this decomposition feature overcame the scarcity of land sales and the accompanying lack of good geographic coverage.

All things considered, this decomposition methodology worked very well. Overall, the procedure had a tendency to overvalue the land component in

---

15. The two most well-known interpolators for value across geographic space are inverse distance weighting and kriging.

the lowest-value areas and undervalue the land component in high-value areas. Vacant land sales data, where available, led to correction overrides and a smoothing of the model estimates. Economy in the time and resources required for property assessment made this scheme very attractive. The equity of total assessed values of parcels was never in question. The global market modeling met IAAO standards.

Lucas County eventually chose to abandon the technique of decomposing the land value from the total value estimate. The new strategy was to enhance the quality and quantity of the land data through benchmarking as well as to introduce GRSA along with another technique that allowed the use of divergent data sets.[16] Lucas County assessors believed that these enhancements would allow an independent land value equation to be calibrated. Then, the estimated land value could be extracted from total value to produce a residual improvement value.

Success in estimating an independent land value came only with the introduction of three key components together:

· GRSA modeling to create a more evidence-based location variable than traditional fixed-boundary neighborhood variables
· A data transformation technique to combine vacant and improved land sales data sets
· Enhancement of the quantity (and quality) of land data with benchmarking

A fourth component, not to be underestimated, was the specification and extraction of new land data variables through GIS. For example, the collection of new variables for traffic patterns and stage of development were completely automated and processed with GIS.

Valuation Prospects for Split-Rate Taxation

Various jurisdictions that are required to estimate a land value for every improved and unimproved property have demonstrated that it can be done. The accuracy of these land value estimates or their defensibility in court or in the court of public opinion has not been widely tested. In most jurisdictions, taxpayers can appeal their total assessment, but cannot question or file complaints against the separate land and improvement values on their prop-

---

16. The data combination technique is called the *z-score transformation*.

erty tax bills. Hence, land value assessments are effectively shielded from scrutiny by statute. This would not be the case with split-rate tax systems, in which each component of value (land and improvements) would be subject to the full range of examination and market value analysis to which only the total value is subject today.[17]

Greater use of split-rate taxation would also change the impact, and perhaps the substance, of the professional standards promulgated by such organizations as the IAAO. Assessors would be required to meet IAAO standards in performance statistics for both land and total values. An interesting and perhaps confounding equity confrontation might arise. The IAAO assessment standards for land and for total value estimates have changed since they were first proposed. The assessment industry has recognized the difference in degree of difficulty of appraising land versus appraising the total of land and improvements, just as they have recognized the difference in appraising commercial versus residential property. Land estimation has always had a lower standard (a higher COD is accepted) than other variously classed improved land. Will this degree of difficulty continue to be recognized as each component of value is taxed separately and differentially?

Then there is the nagging concept of the equity of valuing vacant and improved land as if they were the same. What about states that require the land component of improved parcels to be valued "as if vacant"? What about the fact that the efficiency advantage for land value taxation obtains only if land is valued in its highest and best use? Some might say that valuing improved land is entirely an exercise in speculation. Vacant, unimproved land is a reality with an entire bundle of legal and economic elements; it is free of encumbrances on its future useful potential, except for zoning or other regulatory constraints. Improved land is encumbered land. How, when, and under what circumstances it might become unencumbered is speculative. Highest and best use might be used as a valuation mantra, but most assessments are done on the basis of present use. Highest and best use is by its very nature open to differing opinions, especially in changes of use.

Perhaps the only ironclad agreement among assessors is that there should be equity between improved and vacant land. Any other scenario, even if subtly provable (a de facto value difference between the two kinds of land),

---

17. We note, however, that Pennsylvania does not allow assessment appeals on the separate land and improvement values, even where the split-rate tax is in place (Bell and Bowman 2006).

would be unworkable from a public relations standpoint. Enforcing sameness or equity is definitely desirable. Fortunately, there are no known studies that attempt to prove a difference in the values.

SUMMARY AND CONCLUSIONS

The purpose of this chapter is to explore assessment requirements for land-only or split-rate property taxation, with an emphasis on practical or applied aspects. As noted, earlier research has established that at least 29 states require separate estimates of land values and improvements values and that deriving such values is common even in states that do not require them. Less was known about how land values are derived, particularly in areas where there are few if any sales of vacant land, and even less about whether the choice of valuation approach affects resulting land values. We have provided preliminary answers to these and some other questions regarding the implementation of land value taxation, as summarized below.

HOW ARE LAND VALUES DERIVED FOR DEVELOPED LAND? We selected a variety of jurisdictions in four states to study how they were meeting the legal responsibility to value land and improvements separately. Where there are enough sales of vacant land, market sales data generally are used to arrive at land values. Otherwise, three general approaches to estimating land values for tax purposes were found: abstraction (land value is estimated as the improved parcel value less the depreciated replacement cost of improvements), allocation (land value is estimated using the typical percentage of total parcel value represented by land), and contribution value (land value is estimated using statistical analysis to determine the contribution to total parcel value made by each of various attributes of land and improvements). Each jurisdiction not relying on market sales analysis relies primarily on one of the three estimation approaches. Sole reliance on one approach is not common, however; whatever the primary approach, judgment must be used in evaluating the results, and this sometimes involves considering one or more of the other approaches.

DOES IT MATTER WHAT VALUATION APPROACH IS USED? All land valuation methodologies are intended to produce the same result—estimated market values for parcels of land. Because the three approaches differ in various respects, including the data considered and the manner in which the data are considered, it seems possible that the resulting land values might depend in part on the approach used. We selected three of our case-study areas—each relying primarily on a different estimation method to derive land values—for further study. Baseline estimates of residential land values were developed through consistent application of the contribution value approach, and these were compared to the locally determined residential land values. We found substantial and systematic differences in the two sets of land values: those based on allocation (Baltimore) differed most from the baseline estimates, followed by those based on the abstraction method (Roanoke); local values produced by a variant of the contribution approach (Lucas County) matched baseline estimates more closely, albeit not precisely. Because of the innovative work done in trying to improve land value estimation in Lucas County in recent years, we looked at that county's efforts in more detail.

From our analyses, we conclude that adequate analytical tools to estimate with reasonable accuracy separate values for land and for improvements are available. However, we also conclude that land value estimates are in part a function of the valuation methodology adopted. Additional research using data for a larger number of study areas is needed to improve the understanding of this matter.

DOES MASS VALUATION SCIENCE (CAMA) IMPOSE ANY OVERWHELMING IMPEDIMENTS TO SPLIT-RATE TAXATION? The answer is a qualified no. Mass appraisal technology across North America is quite uneven. There is no norm, and very little can be anticipated or expected from jurisdiction to jurisdiction, even in the same state or province. Some jurisdictions are better able to generate reasonable land values than others.

CAN LEADING-EDGE ASSESSMENT-RELATED TECHNOLOGY HELP IN ADMINISTERING A SPLIT-RATE TAX SYSTEM? The answer is a definitive yes. Lucas County is a prime example of innovation, research and development, and implementation of these emerging technologies. The challenge is now in their propagation. Their anticipated benefits will be realized only as the technology is moved into the mainstream of industry education and training.

IS THE ASSESSMENT WORLD READY TO SUPPORT THE FULL IMPLEMENTATION OF A SPLIT-RATE PROPERTY TAX? The tools necessary to do the job efficiently and accurately are available, but have not been broadly implemented. The assessment industry can respond when necessary. The industry has responded to calls to action when mandated. The prime examples are annual updating or annual revaluations. Frequent revaluations, once thought impossible, are now implemented regularly and efficiently in many jurisdictions. The same could be true for producing an accurate, equitable, and defensible land value for both vacant and improved parcels.

The Political Economy of
Land Value Taxation

STEVEN C. BOURASSA

As shown in chapter 4, land value taxation is appealing from an economic point of view. Rather than taxing buildings and other improvements, which are likely to be produced in smaller quantities the more they are taxed, land value taxation puts more of the tax burden on land, the supply of which is essentially fixed for the purposes of taxation. In other words, the land tax cannot be avoided or reduced by using land less productively. A tax on land therefore has the unusual characteristic of not imposing a deadweight loss on the economy. However, as attractive as land value taxation may be with respect to economic efficiency, it must also be politically and administratively feasible. Hence, this chapter pulls together various threads—many covered in previous chapters—to assess issues associated with implementing land value taxation.

In a nutshell, this chapter asks, If land value taxation is such a good idea, why haven't more jurisdictions adopted it, and why have some that have tried it later rejected it? The answers to these questions involve the following issues:

- *Taxation of unrealized capital gains:* The property tax in general is an unpopular tax, largely because it is a tax on wealth rather than current

I thank Bill Grigsby and the editors for helpful comments on earlier versions of this chapter and Shireen Deobhakta for helpful research assistance.

cash flow and therefore is not closely related to ability to pay. The land value tax can aggravate this aspect of property taxation, particularly in a volatile market.

- *Land value assessment and rate setting:* Land value taxation requires accurate land assessments, which are more challenging for tax administrators than assessments of total property value. It also requires a flexible rate-setting process designed to mitigate the undesirable impacts of property cycles on tax bills and revenue.
- *Too much development:* Land value taxation should be accompanied by appropriate land use planning and controls to avoid undesirable side effects in the form of excessively dense development or failure to preserve valuable buildings or sites. Related to this, appraisers should define highest and best use subject to planning constraints.
- *Winners and losers:* Changing from a property tax to a land value tax creates winners and losers and thus raises concerns about fairness. This issue is closely related to the question of who supports and who opposes land value taxation.
- *Lack of understanding:* Finally, and perhaps most importantly, the land value tax and its benefits are not well understood by elected officials and citizens at large.

Following a brief review of the experience with land value taxation, I discuss these five points. I then consider the question of who supports and who opposes land value taxation. The chapter concludes with an assessment of the prospects for land value taxation.

WHAT WENT WRONG AND WHAT WENT RIGHT: THE U.S. AND INTERNATIONAL EXPERIENCE

We saw in chapters 2 and 3 that land value taxation continues to be used in sixteen jurisdictions in Pennsylvania as well as in numerous places elsewhere in the world. However, the two largest jurisdictions in the United States that have employed land value taxation—Hawaii and Pittsburgh—have reverted to single-rate property taxes, as have seven smaller jurisdictions in Pennsylvania and New York. Ongoing efforts to establish land value taxation in another major U.S. city—Philadelphia—have so far been unsuccessful. Meanwhile, as we saw in chapter 3, South Africa is in the process of abolishing land value taxation, some local governments in New Zealand have been shifting from taxation of land to taxation of land and improvements, and land value taxation is under threat elsewhere in the world.

A variety of factors have led to the abolition of land value taxation. In Pittsburgh, land value taxation was the victim of the political fallout from a long overdue reassessment, the resulting increases in tax bills—particularly for homeowners in some neighborhoods—and questions about the accuracy of land valuations. In Hawaii, a high rate of development led to a perception that the tax was too effective and therefore undesirable. In some small communities in Pennsylvania, lack of demand for downtown space meant that the split-rate tax was not able to encourage renovation or redevelopment; instead, the split-rate tax was viewed as an excessive burden on current landowners. After using different forms of property taxes, including land value taxation, in different jurisdictions, South Africa has decided to standardize single-rate taxation of land and improvements throughout the country. In New Zealand, a recent government study concluded that taxation of capital values was more understandable to taxpayers and avoided valuation problems associated with taxation of only land values. In New South Wales, Australia, rapid increases in land values have raised questions about that state's land value tax.

On the other hand, policy makers in some Pennsylvania communities believe that land value taxation is encouraging development or is fairer than a single-rate system. Of the Pennsylvania jurisdictions that continue to use land value taxation, several adopted that system within the past decade and about half have increased the ratio of the land to the improvement tax rate since 2000. Advocates for land value taxation in Philadelphia and elsewhere also maintain that the economies of those places would benefit if the tax burden were shifted from improvements to land. Finally, Estonia may continue to use land-only taxation even though it initially intended to shift to taxation of both land and improvements.

ISSUES IN THE POLITICAL ECONOMY OF LAND VALUE TAXATION

Taxation of Unrealized Capital Gains

In the United States, the property tax is used primarily to fund local government, although it is a source of revenue for some state governments and for various levels of government in other countries. At the level of local government, the property tax burden is related to the range of services provided and the need for revenue to support those services. In the United States, local governments typically provide expensive services—such as education, police and fire protection, and emergency services—that may be provided by higher levels of government in other countries. Thus, the local property tax can be particularly burdensome in the United States, and citizens and state legislatures have responded by placing caps and other restrictions on the taxation of real property. Much of the antagonism to high taxes on property can be attributed to homeowners' opposition to taxation of unrealized capital gains.

Netzer (1984) dates this opposition back to the Great Depression, when local governments continued to tax properties that had been assessed on the basis of the substantial increases in values that occurred during the early decades of the twentieth century. He notes, for example, that a referendum in Florida almost succeeded in abolishing the property tax in response to this abuse. This opposition to high taxes on real property continues today, in Florida and in many other states, and for the same reasons. As Jens Peter Jensen concluded in his book *Property Taxation in the United States*, published in 1931: "If any tax could have been eliminated by adverse criticism, the general property tax should have been eliminated long ago" (p. 478).

Opposition to the tax also arose during the 1970s in the United States, when there was a rapid increase in property values, especially owner-occupied housing values. This increase produced large capital gains that were not accompanied by equal rises in incomes but did lead to a steep increase in tax bills for homeowners in particular (Netzer 1984). Voters responded negatively to the increased tax liabilities, in part because of their inability to pay, and more fundamentally because of an inherent hostility to the idea of taxing wealth and unrealized capital gains. More than 58 separate tax-limitation measures were considered by voters in numerous states between 1979 and 1984 (O'Sullivan, Sexton, and Sheffrin 1995).

The most noted tax revolt during this period took place in California and helped spur the national movement of the late 1970s and early 1980s. Inflation in California house prices and dramatic increases in assessments led to large increases in property tax bills. In 1978 California voters approved Proposition 13, a ballot initiative to amend the state constitution to (1) limit the maximum rate of taxation to 1 percent; (2) set assessments equal to market values in 1975–1976; (3) place a 2 percent ceiling on assessment increases; and (4) prohibit the state and local governments from imposing any other property taxes, sales taxes, or transaction taxes on real property

(O'Sullivan, Sexton, and Sheffrin 1995). An important consequence of Proposition 13 was a fundamental change in the definition of the property tax base from market value to the acquisition or purchase price of the property with, as noted, a maximum 2 percent adjustment for inflation (Sears and Critin 1985).[1] In 1980 Massachusetts voters followed California's precedent and approved Proposition 2½, one of the most significant tax-limitation measures passed since Proposition 13. Proposition 2½ established an aggregate levy limit for each community equal to the lesser of total current property taxes and 2.5 percent of total property values (Cutler, Elmendorf, and Zeckhauser 1999).

The real estate boom in recent years has increased property values and consequently tax liabilities in many states, leading to responses that echo the sentiments of California voters in 1978 and Massachusetts voters in 1980. According to an editorial in the *Wall Street Journal* in June 2007, household incomes in Florida increased by 37 percent between 2001 and 2007, but the average property tax bill rose by 83 percent. In response, the Florida legislature enacted a law that required localities to cap tax rates at 2006 levels and, depending on the extent to which taxes had increased in recent years, reduce tax rates (Kleindienst and Hafenbrack 2007). In early 2008, Florida voters passed a referendum that significantly expanded homestead exemptions.[2] Legislative proposals and citizen initiatives aimed at property tax relief are in various stages in at least 20 states.

The primary problem with taxation of unrealized capital gains is that those gains are not necessarily accompanied by increases in household income. More generally, highly valued properties are not necessarily owned by households with high incomes. In fact, the property tax is highly regressive with respect to owners' current cash incomes (see Bourassa and Grigsby 2000, table 3).[3] The inability to pay property taxes can and has resulted in tax foreclosures, forcing families to move out of their homes. The regressivity of

---

1. Revolts such as Proposition 13 have actually increased the inequities among homeowners because the effective tax rate varies with the gap between acquisition price and market value.

2. Homestead exemptions usually exclude a fixed dollar amount from the taxable assessed value of primary residences.

3. Most economists, however, consider the property tax to be progressive with respect to a more inclusive definition of income and after taking into account market effects that shift the economic incidence of the property tax. See Youngman (2002).

the property tax with respect to current cash income has led some states to impose homestead exemptions, as well as exemptions for senior citizens.

Netzer (1984) hypothesizes that opposition to taxation of unrealized gains is the main reason that land value taxation has not been more popular in the United States. The problems associated with taxation of unrealized capital gains are compounded by land value taxation because most of the growth in property value in a rising market is due to increases in land values rather than improvement values. Improvement values are likely to decrease or increase by small percentages each year because there are two opposing forces at work: existing improvements depreciate in value because of wear and obsolescence, but become more valuable because of inflation in construction costs for *replacement* improvements. The value of land—of location, of access to markets, of amenities, and of government services—will grow with overall increases in demand. Therefore, in order to achieve property value inflation of the magnitude experienced in the United States during the mid-2000s, land values would need to increase at a much faster rate than total property values.[4]

For example, consider a house worth $200,000 at the beginning of a property boom that lasts for four years. Of the total initial value of the property, 20 percent, or $40,000, is the value of the land and the remaining 80 percent, or $160,000, is the value of the building. If we assume that the value of the building appreciates at 1 percent per year and that land appreciates at 30 percent per year, the overall appreciation rate will be 6.8 percent in the first year, rising to 11.1 percent in the fourth year.[5] The appreciation rate increases over time because land contributes a growing proportion of total property value. If there is a single tax rate applicable to both land and improvements and the property is reassessed every year, the homeowner's tax bill will increase in proportion to the increase in the total property value. For example, if the tax rate is 10 mills (1 percent), the tax bill will increase from $2,000 at the beginning of the first year to $2,807 at the beginning of the fifth year (figure 9.1).

---

4. Bostic, Longhofer, and Redfearn (2007) point out that inflation in property prices depends on land leverage, or the proportion of total property value contributed by land (referred to as "land intensity" in chapter 5). The greater the land leverage, the greater the inflation in total property prices, all else equal.

5. According to the Office of Federal Housing Enterprise Oversight (http://www.ofheo .gov/hpi_region.aspx), the U.S. national house price index was rising at an annual rate of 6.0 percent as of the first quarter of 2000. This rate increased to a high of 12.3 percent in the second quarter of 2005. As in the example presented here, the growth rate was 6.7 percent as of the third quarter of 2000, and rose to 11.3 percent exactly four years later.

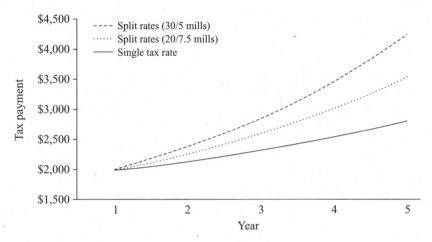

Figure 9.1. Hypothetical property tax bills with single versus split tax rates

If, instead, the tax rate is split to weigh more heavily on land, the tax bill will increase more rapidly (assuming that tax rates are not changed over the four-year period). For example, if the land tax rate is 20 mills and the improvement tax rate is 7.5 mills, the tax bill increases from $2,000 to $3,534 over the same four-year period. If the land rate is 30 mills and the improvement rate is 5 mills, the tax bill increases from $2,000 to $4,260. Note that the increase in the last case is almost three times the increase in the case assuming a single tax rate.[6]

Of course, the tax rates could be decreased during a property boom to achieve smaller increases in tax bills and total tax revenue. In practice, however, this does not always happen. Thus, the public may approve initiatives or legislatures may pass laws that place various limits on local governments' ability to tax property. Maryland and several other states have "truth in taxation" (or "full disclosure") limitations that require public notice and then a vote by the local taxing body to increase tax revenue—that is, if rates are not decreased enough to offset an increase in assessments.

Land Value Assessment and Rate Setting

There are several types of assessment issues that may complicate the administration of a land value tax. One problem is the difficulty of apportioning

---

6. Also, as previously noted, these results depend on land leverage.

total value between land and improvements. As noted in chapter 8, this is particularly difficult in a built-up urban area where there are few or no sales of vacant land that would allow for the valuation of land using a sales comparison approach. For single-family residential property in such areas, the value of the land must usually be estimated using some other technique or combination of techniques. The three alternatives are the abstraction, allocation, and contribution methods. Under the first of these methods, land value is calculated as a residual after subtracting the value of the improvements from total property value. In this case, total property value may be obtained using the sales comparison approach. The value of the improvements is calculated as their replacement cost less depreciation. Although replacement cost can be calculated fairly straightforwardly, depreciation is difficult to estimate, so there can be a wide margin of error in the valuation of improvements.

Under the allocation method, land value is assumed to be a given percentage of total property value, adjusted for characteristics of the land parcel (such as its size) and the improvements on it. This approach involves some degree of arbitrariness and, therefore, may introduce a significant amount of error into land value assessments.

The third alternative, which is advocated in chapter 8, uses statistical models to determine the relative contributions of each component of property to total value. Sophisticated use of geographic information systems may also allow for careful modeling of the impacts of location on land value. Although these techniques are available and can yield excellent results when applied by skillful assessors, they are unlikely to be implemented any time soon in many jurisdictions, particularly small ones, where budgets for assessment purposes are quite limited.

The land value assessment issue is even more problematic when it comes to commercial properties. Given the magnitude of potential tax savings, it can be particularly lucrative for owners of large commercial properties to challenge assessments. This is true under any form of property tax, but the land value tax gives property owners the additional option of challenging not only the total property assessment but also the allocation between land and improvements. Under a land value tax system, shifting assessed value from land to improvements reduces the tax bill without any need to change the total assessed value. As noted in chapter 2, one of the criticisms leveled at Pittsburgh's land value tax was that owners of downtown office buildings were taking advantage of the system by successfully challenging land assessments and shifting assessed value from land to buildings.

Another assessment issue has to do with the practice of valuing land according to its highest and best use rather than its current use. Property owners may argue that it is unfair to tax land as if it were being used for some hypothetical future use rather than its current actual use. As discussed in chapter 4, the neutrality of taxes on land depends on assessing land according to highest and best use rather than current use. Since highest and best use is a fairly standard practice for assessing land value, it can be a problem even if land and improvements are taxed at the same rate. But land value taxation tends to aggravate this issue because of the heavier tax burden on land. This affected, for example, homeowners in Connellsville, Pennsylvania, who owned side lots that were taxed as if they were used for additional houses even though the lots were used only for, say, a garden. Such owners felt that they were being taxed excessively relative to the current and likely future use of the property.[7] This example also raises the question whether assessments always reflect changing market conditions and their effects on land values. In other words, how good are assessors at defining highest and best use? Keeping on top of changing conditions may be difficult in markets with declining demand and few transactions. In such circumstances, assessors could easily be too optimistic about highest and best use.

It seems more likely, however, that assessments will be below market value (or some target percentage of market value) because of infrequent reassessments. In this case, the problem arises when reassessments do take place: the sudden increase in tax bills is amplified under a land value tax system because land valuations increase dramatically, whereas improvement valuations decrease or increase by relatively small percentages. This situation was not uncommon in the Pennsylvania and New York communities discussed in chapter 2, and this issue played a major role in the demise of the split-rate tax in Pittsburgh and elsewhere. In Pittsburgh, for example, the 2000–2001 reassessment caused land assessments to increase by an average of over 200 percent in some neighborhoods, whereas improvement assessments dropped (Belko and McNulty 2001). The mayor initially proposed retaining the approximately six-to-one ratio of the land to the improvement tax rate; the proposed tax rates would have increased city property tax revenues by at least 10 percent on average (Hughes 2006). Some property owners would have experienced much higher percentage increases in tax bills.

Reducing tax rates as property values rise is the obvious way to mitigate increases in tax bills. However, governments may be reluctant to give up the

---

7. Telephone interview with Paula Childs, Connellsville Tax Office, 28 February 2008.

windfall in revenue generated by a rising market. There may also be a need to adjust the ratio of the land to the improvement tax rate in places where land is becoming an increasing proportion of total property value. Finessing the setting of tax rates in this manner is probably more than one should expect of some of the political forums where these kinds of decisions are made. Pittsburgh is an unfortunate case in point. Tax rates were set before the full implications of the 2000–2001 reassessment were known.[8] As described in chapter 2, once the impacts on tax bills were understood more clearly and citizens started to complain, politicians blamed the valuation firm for inaccurate reassessments. At the same time, there was a dispute between the mayor, who wanted to retain the land value tax, and the president of the city council, who wanted to abolish it. In the end, the split-rate system was abruptly jettisoned in favor of a simpler flat rate. It is hard to imagine how tax rates could be fine-tuned in this kind of political environment.

Land value taxation requires a fairly sophisticated assessment and rate-setting process. Assessments need to be accurate and up to date, and rates need to be set carefully to avoid backlash from the public. In places where property tax rates are low, these issues are less pressing. In the United States, where local governments are typically responsible for expensive public services like education, property tax rates can be quite high, and both assessments and rates attract more attention. Unfortunately, assessment and rate-setting practice in the United States does not always seem to be up to the challenge, notably in the municipalities in Pennsylvania and New York where land value taxation has been implemented. This means that land value taxation has too often taken the blame for what are actually inadequacies in the assessment and rate-setting process.

Too Much Development

In the United States, land value taxation has been introduced largely as a way to encourage, or at least not discourage, economic development. But in one notable case in the United States, too much development led to the abolition of the tax. This is another example of misplaced blame. The overdevelopment of Waikiki, for example, was arguably due to poor planning and land use control rather than any flaw in Hawaii's land value tax system. Clearly, a

---

8. Property tax rates in Philadelphia are also set before the assessed values are determined (Mandel 2004).

tax system designed to encourage economic development must be accompanied by careful planning to ensure that communities are not overwhelmed by development or its side effects. In particular, communities need to take care to protect valuable buildings and sites. The definition of highest and best use for the purposes of assessment should therefore be subject to planning constraints.

Winners and Losers

In defense of land value taxation, proponents cite Henry George's argument that taxes on land are fairer than other forms of tax because land value is essentially the product of community rather than individual efforts. The value of a parcel of land reflects the value of a location, which is the result of government investment in infrastructure and provision of public services, as well as the combined activities of the other individuals and organizations in a community. Improvement values, in contrast, are the result of the efforts of particular property owners. Similarly, salaries are the result of individual effort. Consequently, it is more appropriate for government to tax land than improvements (or salaries) and to use the proceeds to benefit the community. Thus George ([1879] 1962) advocated a single tax on land. Also, the term *unearned increment* came to be applied to increases in property values due to growth in land values rather than to investment in improvements.

Although the Georgist argument about the fairness of taxing land is reasonable, it is rather abstract. It is somewhat removed from the experience of the typical property owner, who tends to think of fairness in more concrete terms. Matters such as ability to pay, whether unrealized capital gains should be taxed, whether assessments are too high, and whether owners of properties with similar values pay similar taxes are likely to be of more interest to property owners. These are the kinds of issues that have been fueling the various property tax revolts in the United States, which suggests that it might be more fruitful to focus on more traditional concepts of equity when evaluating land value taxation. That is the approach taken in chapter 5.

Since the property tax is a wealth tax whose base is the value of the property, vertical equity requires owners of more valuable properties or with higher incomes to pay higher taxes, and horizontal equity requires owners of similar properties or with similar incomes to pay similar amounts of tax. Land value taxation adds some confusion to the equity issue because it severs the relationship between total property value and tax. Instead, taxes depend on the ratio of land to improvement value, and owners of properties with similar total valuations may be levied quite different taxes. This was an issue in Pittsburgh, for example, and is related to the argument that single-rate taxes are simpler for taxpayers to understand.

Misunderstanding the Land Value Tax

One criticism of Pittsburgh's land value tax was that the split assessments were too difficult for most property owners, particularly homeowners, to understand. As noted earlier, this confusion was tied to the fact that tax bills were not related to total property value, but instead depended separately on land and improvement values.[9] The same issue was raised by the recent New Zealand government inquiry on property taxation and has been raised periodically in the ongoing debate about adopting land value taxation in Philadelphia.

Of course, one response to misunderstanding would be to try to clear up the confusion. Jurisdictions choosing land value taxation could engage in a public education program to explain why the tax was adopted, emphasizing the efficiency and equity benefits that attracted policy makers to it.

WHO SUPPORTS AND WHO OPPOSES LAND VALUE TAXATION?

The question of winners versus losers is closely related to the question of who supports and who opposes land value taxation. The latter question can be viewed from the perspective of policy makers as well as tax-paying property owners. With respect to the first group, the answer to the question appears to have to do with efficiency versus equity. Supporters of land value taxation are swayed by the argument that taxes on improvements deter investment whereas taxes on land do not. In their view, shifting the tax burden from improvements to land is good for community development. Although, as noted above, there are strong equity arguments in favor of land value taxation, those arguments seem less important to the politicians and administrators who actually implement such taxes. The practical, or efficiency, benefits of land value taxation are much more persuasive.

---

9. It would seem that the most extreme form of land value taxation, with no taxation of improvements, would be the least confusing given that it would be based solely on land value.

On the other side of the issue are those who are concerned with fairness, not in the Georgist sense, but rather in the more traditional senses of vertical and horizontal equity. Issues raised here have to do with matters such as whether homeowners can afford to pay increasing property tax bills, whether owners of properties with similar total valuations pay similar taxes, whether separate land and improvement values can be assessed accurately (and fairly), and whether owners of valuable properties can game the system by challenging land assessments. Owners of some properties may consider assessments based on highest and best use to be unfair because they are based on unrealized uses that may be unlikely to occur any time in the foreseeable future. Because highest and best use affects land valuations but not improvement valuations, land value taxation tends to amplify these kinds of concerns.

Even those who would normally be convinced by the efficiency argument will no longer find it persuasive in two different situations representing opposite ends of the spectrum of demand for real estate. At one extreme, there may be little or no demand for new or renovated improvements, meaning that lowering the tax rate on improvements relative to the rate applied to land will have little or no effect on the amount of development. In fact, it may just cause owners of land in such situations to feel that the property tax is particularly burdensome. In Connellsville, Pennsylvania, for example, this was an important factor that contributed to the abolition of that city's land value tax. If the land value tax is adopted with the unrealistic hope of developing an area that is so disfavored by the market as to be undevelopable, all the switch from a property tax to a land value tax does is redistribute tax burdens without any efficiency gains. In such circumstances, however, assessed land values and tax bills should be relatively low, assuming that assessments are accurate. At the other extreme, there may be so much demand for development that a place becomes overdeveloped in the eyes of policy makers, leading to opposition to land value taxation. This was the situation in Hawaii in the 1970s when the land value tax there was abolished. Concern about the negative externalities of dense development in Waikiki trumped the efficiency argument.

Moreover, policy makers who are convinced by the efficiency argument may decide that a more targeted approach—tax abatements for new construction and renovation—is more effective and easier to administer than a general split-rate system. In Pittsburgh, for example, officials have expanded tax abatement programs following the abolition of land value taxation. Many cities use tax abatement to encourage development and may prefer the continued use of abatements to wholesale modification of the property tax system.

From the point of view of taxpayers, owners of properties for which land value represents a relatively high percentage of total value tend to oppose the tax because they pay more than they would under a single-rate system. In Philadelphia, for example, parking-lot owners and automobile dealers have been vocal in opposing proposed land value taxes (see, e.g., Fish 1988; Gorenstein 2001). The 2000–2001 reassessment in Pittsburgh led to many appeals, but some owners of homes with relatively high ratios of land to total value (and their supporters) were particularly vocal in calling for the demise of that city's land value tax.

CONCLUSIONS AND PROSPECTS

As a somewhat confusing variant of an unpopular type of tax, land value taxation occupies a rather uncomfortable position among the range of different forms of taxation. However, the property tax is a very important source of revenue for many jurisdictions in the United States and elsewhere, and it is likely to continue in that role for the foreseeable future.[10] Consequently, it is important to make certain that the tax is implemented in the most effective way.

With this general goal in mind, recall the efficiency argument for land value taxation. Taxes on land are efficient because they are neutral with respect to development decisions. In contrast, taxes on improvements discourage investments in improvements. If a jurisdiction wishes to encourage development, then a higher tax rate on land may be preferable to a single tax rate applied to both land and improvements. For example, the leaders of Harrisburg, Pennsylvania, consider land value taxation to be a valuable tool in their ongoing efforts to revitalize a city that was once in quite dire circumstances.

However, there are some significant costs and challenges associated with a land value tax system. Land values are more volatile than total property values, and thus, unless they are administered very carefully, land value taxes

---

10. In the United States, property taxes contribute about 25 percent of all local government revenue (U.S. Census Bureau, Annual Survey of State and Local Government Finances, various years).

may be more likely to lead to the same opposition to taxes on unrealized gains that general property taxes have provoked in some parts of the United States. Also, in built-up areas, assessing land value accurately is more difficult than assessing total property value and may in many circumstances require a substantial upgrading of the assessment process. Of course, upgrading the assessment process would be a good thing to do in many instances, even if land value taxation were not under consideration. But, under a land value tax, inconsistencies in land value assessments will aggravate perceptions that the system is unfair. Moreover, fairly nimble rate-setting practices are required to respond to changes in land valuations in order to prevent sharp increases in tax bills (and, perhaps, taxpayer revolt) as well as fluctuations in tax revenue. Even if all these issues are addressed successfully, some property owners will still see inequities in or be confused by the fact that properties with similar total values are not necessarily subject to the same amount of tax, as a result of differences in the ratio of land to improvement value. Land value taxation is more complex than single-rate taxation of both land and improvements, from the points of view of both tax administrators and taxpayers.

Despite these challenges, both theory and empirical evidence suggest that, on balance, land value taxation can be an effective economic development tool. Moreover, what is clear from the experience with land value taxation is that it has often been the scapegoat for implementation problems—arguably, it was such implementation problems, rather than any inherent flaws, that led Pittsburgh and certain other jurisdictions to abolish the land value tax. Inadequate assessment and rate-setting practices, inadequate land use planning, and unnecessary confusion (sometimes sowed by opponents to the tax) have all played excessively significant roles in the history of land value taxation. Although land value taxation is more difficult to implement than the standard form of property taxation, it should be recognized that economic development itself is no easy task. The additional effort required may well be worth it.

REFERENCES

This contains only the references cited in this volume. For an extensive annotated bibliography on the topic of land value taxation, see Grote (2007).

Anderson, J. E. 1986. Property taxes and the timing of urban land development. *Regional Science and Urban Economics* 16(4):483–492.

———. 1993. Two-rate property taxes and urban development. *Intergovernmental Perspective* 19(3):19–20, 28.

———. 1999. Two-rate property tax effects on land development. *Journal of Real Estate Finance and Economics* 18(2):181–190.

Anderson, N. B. 2006. Property tax limitations: An interpretative review. *National Tax Journal* 59(3):685–694.

Arnott, R. J. 2005. Neutral property taxation. *Journal of Public Economic Theory* 7(1):27–50.

Arnott, R. J., and F. D. Lewis. 1979. The transition of land to urban use. *Journal of Political Economy* 87(1):161–170.

Arnott, R. J., and P. Petrova. 2006. The property tax as a tax on value: Deadweight loss. *International Tax and Public Finance* 13(2–3):241–266.

Ashley, R., F. Plassmann, and N. Tideman. 1999. Improving the accuracy of downtown land assessment. Working paper, Lincoln Institute of Land Policy, Cambridge, Massachusetts.

Assunção, J. 2006. Land reform and landholdings in Brazil. Research Paper 2006/137, United Nations University, World Institute for Development Economics Research, Helsinki, Finland.

Australian Bureau of Statistics. 2008. *Taxation revenue, Australia, 2005–06.* 5506.0. Canberra, Australia: Australian Bureau of Statistics (April). Also available

online at http://www.ausstats.abs.gov.au/ausstats/subscriber.nsf/0/D11E82AC
66FC6CE0CA25742B001A6487/$File/55060_2006-07.pdf.

Australian Local Government Association. Taxation arrangements: The collection
of property rates in Australia—a state by state description. http://www.alga
.asn.au/policy/finance/austax/11.propertyrates.php.

Bahl, R. W. 1998. Land vs. property taxes in developing and transition countries. In
Netzer 1998b.

———. 2002. Fiscal decentralization, revenue assignment, and the case for the
property tax. In Bell and Bowman 2002b.

Bahl, R. W., J. Martinez-Vazquez, and J. M. Youngman, eds. 2008. *Making the property tax work: Experiences in developing and transitional countries.* Cambridge,
MA: Lincoln Institute of Land Policy.

Banks, J., Z. Smith, and M. Wakefield. 2002. The distribution of financial wealth in
the UK: Evidence from 2000 BHPS data. Working paper, WP02/21, Institute
for Fiscal Studies, London.

Barker, K. 2004. *Review of housing supply: Delivering stability; Securing our Future
Housing Needs.* London: HM Treasury (March). Also available online at http://
image.guardian.co.uk/sys-files/Guardian/documents/2004/03/17/Barker.pdf.

Becker, A. P. 1969. Principles of taxing land and buildings for economic development. In *Land and building taxes: Their effect on economic development,* ed. A. P.
Becker. Madison: University of Wisconsin Press.

Belko, M., and T. McNulty. 2001. Sabre blames city for tax uproar: Reassessment
firm says its warnings were ignored. *Pittsburgh Post-Gazette,* January 16: A1.

Bell, M. E., and J. H. Bowman. 2002a. Factors influencing the choice of site value
taxation among local governments. In Bell and Bowman 2002b.

———. 2002b. *Property taxes in South Africa: Challenges in the post-apartheid era.*
Cambridge, MA: Lincoln Institute of Land Policy.

———. 2006. Methods of valuing land for real property taxation: An examination
of practices in states that require separate valuation of land and improvements.
Working paper, Lincoln Institute of Land Policy, Cambridge, Massachusetts.

———. 2008. Consistency of land values: Comparison of three general approaches to valuing land where there are few vacant land sales. Working paper,
Lincoln Institute of Land Policy, Cambridge, Massachusetts.

Bentick, B. L. 1979. The impact of taxation and valuation practices on the timing
and efficiency of land use. *Journal of Political Economy* 87(4):859–868.

Bird, R. M., and E. Slack. 2004. *International handbook of land and property taxation.* Northampton, MA: Edward Elgar.

Bostic, R. W., S. D. Longhofer, and C. L. Redfearn. 2007. Land leverage: Decomposing home price dynamics. *Real Estate Economics* 35(2):183–208.

Bourassa, S. C. 1987. Land value taxation and new housing development in Pittsburgh. *Growth and Change* 18(4):44–56.

————. 1990. Land value taxation and housing development: Effects of the property tax reform in three types of cities. *American Journal of Economics and Sociology* 49(1):101–111.

Bourassa, S. C., and W. G. Grigsby. 2000. Income tax concessions for owner-occupied housing. *Housing Policy Debate* 11(3):521–546.

Bourassa, S. C., and Y.-H. Hong, eds. 2003. *Leasing public land: Policy debates and international experiences.* Cambridge, MA: Lincoln Institute of Land Policy.

Bowman, J. H. 2006. Property tax policy responses to rapidly rising home values: District of Columbia, Maryland, and Virginia. *National Tax Journal* 59(3):717–733.

Bowman, J. H., and M. E. Bell. 2004. Implications of a split-rate real property tax: An initial look at three Virginia localities. *State Tax Notes* 32(4):261–291.

————. 2008. Distributional consequences of converting the property tax to a land value tax: Replication and extension of England and Zhao. *National Tax Journal* 61(4):forthcoming.

Bowman, W., J. J. Cordes, and L. Metcalf. Forthcoming. Preferential tax treatment of property used for "social purposes": Fiscal impacts and public policy implications. In *Erosion of the local property tax: Trends, causes and consequences,* ed. N. Y. Augustine, M. E. Bell, and D. Brunori. Cambridge, MA: Lincoln Institute of Land Policy.

Brown, H. G., H. S. Buttenheim, P. H. Cornick, and G. E. Hoover, eds. 1955. *Land-value taxation around the world.* New York: Robert Schalkenbach Foundation.

Brueckner, J. K. 1986. A modern analysis of the effects of site value taxation. *National Tax Journal* 39(1):49–58.

Brueckner, J. K., and H.-A. Kim. 2003. Urban sprawl and the property tax. *International Tax and Public Finance* 10(1):5–23.

Brunori, D., and J. Carr. 2002. Valuing land and improvements: State laws and local government practices. *State Tax Notes* 25(14):1023–1033.

Bucks, B. K., A. B. Kennickell, and K. B. Moore. 2006. Recent changes in U.S. family finances: Evidence from the 2001 and 2004 survey of consumer finances. *Federal Reserve Bulletin* (March 22):A1–A38.

Cahill, K. 2002. *Who owns Britain?* Edinburgh: Canongate Books.

Carlson, R. H. 2005. A brief history of property tax. *Fair & Equitable,* February: 3–9.

Cheshire, P., and S. Sheppard. 1998. Estimating the demand for housing, land, and neighbourhood characteristics. *Oxford Bulletin of Economics and Statistics* 60(3):357–382.

City of Harrisburg. Harrisburg, Pennsylvania—An economic profile. http://www .harrisburgpa.gov/econprofile.

Coffin, D. A., and M. A. Nelson. 1983. The economic effects of land value taxation—comment. *Growth and Change* 14(3):44–46.

Cooper, G., and G. Daws. 1985. *Land and power in Hawaii: The democratic years.* Honolulu: University of Hawaii Press.

Copes, J. M., and W. Rybeck. 2001. Jamaica and other Caribbean states. In *Land-value taxation around the world,* ed. R. V. Andelson. Malden, MA: Blackwell.

Cord, S. 1970. The role of the graded tax in urban redevelopment: A case study of Lancaster, PA. *American Journal of Economics and Sociology* 29(3):321–328.

———. 1976. The impact of a graded tax on a rural area: A case study in Indiana County, PA. *American Journal of Economics and Sociology* 35(1):71–75.

———. 1985. How much revenue would a full land value tax yield? *American Journal of Economics and Sociology* 44(3):279–293.

———. 1987. *The evidence for land value taxation.* Columbia, MD: Center for the Study of Economics.

Cordes, J. J. 1999. Horizontal equity. In *The encyclopedia of taxation and tax policy,* ed. J. J. Cordes, R. D. Ebel, and J. G. Gravelle. Washington, DC: Urban Institute Press.

Coughlan, J. A. 1999. Land value taxation and constitutional uniformity. *George Mason Law Review* 7(2):261–292.

Cutler, D. M., D. W. Elmendorf, and R. Zeckhauser. 1999. Restraining the leviathan: Property tax limitation in Massachusetts. *Journal of Public Economics* 71(3):313–334.

Davies, J. B., and A. F. Shorrocks. 2005. Wealth holdings in developing and transition countries. Paper prepared for the Luxembourg Wealth Study conference "Construction and Usage of Comparable Microdata on Wealth," Perugia, Italy.

De Cesare, C. M., L. C. P. da Silva Filho, M. Y. Une, and S. C. Wendt. 2003. Analyzing the feasibility of moving to a land value–based property tax system: A case study from Brazil. Working paper, Lincoln Institute of Land Policy, Cambridge, Massachusetts.

Deininger, K. 2003. *Land policies for growth and poverty reduction.* New York: Oxford University Press for the World Bank.

Department of Finance and Revenue, Government of the District of Columbia. 1994. *The impact of a split-rate property tax in the District of Columbia.* Washington, DC: Government of the District of Columbia (September).

DiMasi, J. A. 1987. The effects of site value taxation in an urban area: A general equilibrium computational approach. *National Tax Journal* 40(4):577–590.

Dos Santos, P., and L. Bain. 2004. *Survey of the Caribbean tax systems.* A Report of the Caribbean Organization of Tax Administrators (COTA) on behalf of the Caribbean Community Secretariat (CARICOM) (July). Also available online at http://www.cartac.com.bb/pageselect.cfm?page=11.

Dowse, G., and B. Hargreaves. 1999. Rating systems in New Zealand. In McCluskey 1999.

Dye, R. F., and D. P. McMillen. 2007a. Surprise! An unintended consequence of assessment limitations. *Land Lines* 19(3):8–13.

———. 2007b. Teardowns and land values in the Chicago metropolitan area. *Journal of Urban Economics* 61(1):45–63.

Dye, R. F., D. P. McMillen, and D. F. Merriman. 2006. Illinois' response to rising residential property values: An assessment growth cap in Cook County. *National Tax Journal* 59(3):707–716.

Eckert, J. K., ed. 1990. *Property appraisal and assessment administration*. Chicago: International Association of Assessing Officers.

Eisner, J. 1982. Bill would set two rates of property tax. *Philadelphia Inquirer*, May 19: B3.

England, R. W. 2003. State and local impacts of a revenue-neutral shift from a uniform property to a land value tax: Results of a simulation study. *Land Economics* 79(1):38–43.

———. 2004. Designing a two-rate property tax plan to reduce regressive effects and increase voter support. *State Tax Notes* 32(1):39–44.

———. 2007. Land value taxation as a method of financing municipal expenditures in U.S. cities. In *Land Policies and Their Outcomes*, ed. G. K. Ingram and Y.-H. Hong. Cambridge, MA: Lincoln Institute of Land Policy.

England, R. W., and R. D. Mohr. 2003. Land development and current use assessment: A theoretical note. *Agricultural and Resource Economics Review* 32(1):46–52.

England, R. W., and M. Ravichandran. 2007. Property taxation and density of land development: A simple model with numerical simulations. Working paper, University of New Hampshire.

England, R. W., and M. Q. Zhao. 2005. Assessing the distributive impact of a revenue-neutral shift from a uniform property tax to a two-rate property tax with a uniform credit. *National Tax Journal* 58(2):247–260.

Fish, L. 1988. How the tax "no one understands" works. *Philadelphia Inquirer*, May 15: E1.

Follain, J. R., and T. E. Miyake. 1986. Land versus capital value taxation: A general equilibrium analysis. *National Tax Journal* 39(4):451–470.

Franzsen, R. C. D. 2005a. Land value taxation in Western Australia. In McCluskey and Franzsen 2005.

———. 2005b. Property taxation in South Africa. In McCluskey and Franzsen 2005.

Franzsen, R. C. D., and W. J. McCluskey. 2005. An exploratory overview of property taxation in the Commonwealth of Nations. Working paper, Lincoln Institute of Land Policy, Cambridge, Massachusetts.

———. 2007. Implementation of the local government: Municipal Property Rates Act with reference to the Hessequa local municipality, Western Cape, South Africa. *De Jure* 40(1):69–89.

———. 2008. The feasibility of site value taxation. In Bahl, Martinez-Vazquez, and Youngman 2008.

Fullerton, D., and G. E. Metcalf. 2002. Tax incidence. In *Handbook of public economics*, ed. A. Auerbach, and M. Feldstein. Amsterdam: Elsevier.

Gaston, C. A. 1955. The Fairhope colony. In Brown et al. 1955.

Geisler, C. C. 1993. Ownership: An overview. *Rural Sociology* 58(4):532–546.

———. 1995. Land and poverty in the United States: Insights and oversights. *Land Economics* 71(1):16–34.

George, H. [1879] 1962. *Progress and poverty.* New York: Robert Schalkenbach Foundation.

Gilbert, J., S. D. Wood, and G. Sharp. 2002. Who owns the land? Agricultural land ownership by race/ethnicity. *Rural America* 17(4):55–62.

Gloudemans, R. J. 2000. Implementing a land value tax in urban residential communities. Working paper. Cambridge, MA: Lincoln Institute of Land Policy.

———. 2002. An empirical analysis of the incidence of location on land and building values. Working paper, Lincoln Institute of Land Policy, Cambridge, Massachusetts.

Gloudemans, R. J., S. Handel, and M. Warwa. 2002. An empirical evaluation of alternative land valuation models. Working paper, Lincoln Institute of Land Policy, Cambridge, Massachusetts.

Gorenstein, N. 2001. Saidel finds allies for drastic city tax overhaul. *Philadelphia Inquirer*, October 22: A1.

Grosskopf, S. 1981. The revenue potential of a site value tax: Extension and update of a general equilibrium model with recent empirical estimates of several key parameters. *American Journal of Economics and Sociology* 40(2):207–215.

Grote, K. R. 2007. Land value taxation: An annotated bibliography. Working paper, Lincoln Institute of Land Policy, Cambridge, Massachusetts.

Hargreaves, R. 1991. Is site value still an appropriate basis for property taxation? In *International Conference on Property Taxation and Its Interaction with Land Policy.* Cambridge, MA: Lincoln Institute of Land Policy.

Harriss, C. L. 1970. Transition to land value taxation: Some major problems. In Holland 1970.

Hassan, A. 2005. The local government rating system in Fiji. In McCluskey and Franzsen 2005.

Haughwout, A. F. 2004. Land taxation in New York City: A general equilibrium analysis. In *City taxes, city spending: Essays in honor of Dick Netzer*, ed. A. E. Schwartz. Northampton, MA: Edward Elgar.

Haughwout, A. F., R. Inman, S. Craig, and T. Luce. 2004. Local revenue bills: Evidence from four U.S. cities. *Review of Economics and Statistics* 86(2):570–585.

Haveman, M. 2004. Evaluating the feasibility and burden-shifting effects of a statewide land value tax on commercial and industrial property. *State Tax Notes* 34(11):745–751.

Holland, D. M., ed. 1970. *The assessment of land value.* Madison: University of Wisconsin Press.

Hornby, D. 1999. Property taxes in Australia. In McCluskey 1999.

Hughes, M. A. 2006. Why so little Georgism in America: Using the Pennsylvania case files to understand the slow, uneven progress of land value taxation. Working paper, Lincoln Institute of Land Policy, Cambridge, Massachusetts.

Hulten, J. J. 1970. Hawaii's modified property tax base law. *Proceedings of the National Tax Association 1969:*52–85.

IAAO. *See* International Association of Assessing Officers.

Ingram, G. K. 2008. Note on measuring changes in capital/land ratios related to tax changes. Working paper, Lincoln Institute of Land Policy, Cambridge, Massachusetts.

International Association of Assessing Officers (IAAO). 1997. *Glossary for property appraisal and assessment.* Chicago: IAAO.

Jäntti, M., and E. Sierminska. 2007. Survey estimates of wealth holdings in OECD countries: Evidence on the level and distribution across selected countries. Research Paper 2007/17. United Nations University, World Institute for Development Economics Research, Helsinki, Finland.

Jensen, J. P. 1931. *Property taxation in the United States.* Chicago: University of Chicago Press.

Jones, S. M., and S. C. Rhoades-Catanach. 2008. *Principles of taxation for business and investment planning.* New York: McGraw-Hill/Irwin.

Kleindienst, L., and J. Hafenbrack. 2007. Gov. Crist signs historic bill calling for $15.6 billion in tax cuts. *South Florida Sun-Sentinel,* June 22.

Lewis, J. A. 1980. *Landownership in the United States.* Agriculture Information Bulletin 435. Washington, DC: U.S. Department of Agriculture.

Li, S., and R. Zhao. 2007. Changes in the distribution of wealth in China, 1995–2002. Research Paper 2007/03, United Nations University, World Institute for Development Economics Research, Helsinki, Finland.

Lindholm, R. W., ed. 1969. *Property taxation, USA.* Madison: University of Wisconsin Press.

Liu, B.-C. 1985. Mathis and Zech's "empirical test" of land value taxation: A critique of a commendable but unsuccessful effort to measure the effects of a basic levy. *American Journal of Economics and Sociology* 44(2):137–143.

Local Government Rates Inquiry Panel. 2007. *Funding local government.* Wellington, New Zealand: Local Government Rates Inquiry (August). Also available online at http://www.ratesinquiry.govt.nz/Pubforms.nsf/URL/Rates InquiryFullReport.pdf/$file/RatesInquiryFullReport.pdf.

Lubowski, R. N., M. Vesterby, S. Bucholtz, A. Baez, and M. J. Roberts. 2006. *Major uses of land in the United States.* Economic Information Bulletin 14. Washington, DC: U.S. Department of Agriculture.

Lusht, K. 1992. The site value tax and residential development. Working paper, Lincoln Institute of Land Policy, Cambridge, Massachusetts.

Lyons, S., and W. J. McCluskey. 1999. Unimproved land value taxation in Jamaica. In McCluskey 1999.

MacGee, J. C. 2006. Land titles, credit markets and wealth distributions. Research Paper 2006/150, United Nations University, World Institute for Development Economics Research, Helsinki, Finland.

Mandel, B. 2004. *No city limits: The story of tax reform in Philadelphia.* Philadelphia: Philadelphia Forward.

Mathis, E. J., and C. E. Zech. 1982. An empirical test: The economic effects of land value taxation. *Growth and Change* 13(4):2–5.

———. 1983. An empirical test: The economic effects of land value taxation: Reply. *Growth and Change* 14(3):47–48.

McCluskey, W. J., ed. 1999. *Property tax: An international comparative review.* Aldershot, England: Ashgate.

———. 2005a. Land taxation: The case of Jamaica. In McCluskey and Franzsen 2005.

———. 2005b. Property tax systems and rating in New Zealand. In McCluskey and Franzsen 2005.

———. 2005c. Site value taxation in Queensland. In McCluskey and Franzsen 2005.

McCluskey, W. J., and R. C. D. Franzsen. 2004. The basis of the property tax: A case study analysis of New Zealand and South Africa. Working paper, Lincoln Institute of Land Policy, Cambridge, Massachusetts.

———, eds. 2005. *Land value taxation: An applied analysis.* Aldershot, England: Ashgate.

McCluskey, W. J., A. Grimes, A. Aitken, S. Kerr, and J. Timmins. 2006. Rating systems in New Zealand: An empirical investigation into local choice. *Journal of Real Estate Literature* 14(3):381–397.

McCluskey, W. J., and B. Williams. 1999. Introduction: A comparative evaluation. In McCluskey 1999.

McMillen, D. P. 2006. Teardowns: Costs, benefits, and public policy. *Land Lines* 18(3):2–7.

Mikesell, J. L., and C. K. Zorn. 2008. Data challenges in implementing a market value property tax: Market and market-informed valuation in Russia, Ukraine, and the Baltic States. In Bahl, Martinez-Vazquez, and Youngman 2008.

Mills, D. E. 1981a. The non-neutrality of land value taxation. *National Tax Journal* 34(1):125–129.

———. 1981b. Urban residential development timing. *Regional Science and Urban Economics* 11(2):239–254.

———. 1983. The timing of urban residential land development. In *Research in urban economics,* ed. J. V. Henderson. London: JAI Press.

Mills, E. S. 1998. The economic consequences of a land tax. In Netzer 1998b.

Muellbauer, J. 2007. Housing and personal wealth in a global context. Research Paper 2007/27, United Nations University, World Institute for Development Economics Research, Helsinki, Finland.

Musgrave, R. A. 1990. Horizontal equity, once more. *National Tax Journal* 53(2):113–123.

Nechyba, T. J. 1998. Replacing capital taxes with land taxes: Efficiency and distributional implications with an application to the United States economy. In Netzer 1998b.

Netzer, D. 1984. On modernizing local public finance: Why aren't property taxes in urban areas being reformed into land value taxes? *American Journal of Economics and Sociology* 43(4):497–501.

———. 1998a. Introduction to Netzer 1998b.

———. 1998b. *Land value taxation: Can it and will it work today?* Cambridge, MA: Lincoln Institute of Land Policy.

———. 1998c. The relevance and feasibility of land value taxation in the rich countries. In Netzer 1998b.

———. 2001. What do we need to know about land value taxation? *American Journal of Economics and Sociology* 60(5):97–118.

Newhouse, W. J. 1984. *Constitutional uniformity and equality in state taxation.* Buffalo, NY: William S. Hein & Co.

Oates, W. E., and R. M. Schwab. 1997. The impact of urban land taxation: The Pittsburgh experience. *National Tax Journal* 50(1):1–21.

O'Sullivan, A., T. A. Sexton, and S. M. Sheffrin. 1995. *Property taxes and tax revolts: The legacy of Proposition 13.* New York: Cambridge University Press.

Pennsylvania Department of Community and Economic Development. 2003. *Home rule in Pennsylvania.* Harrisburg, PA: Pennsylvania Department of Community and Economic Development (March). Also available online at http://www.newpa.com/download.aspx?id=43.

Philadelphia Tax Reform Commission. 2003. *Final report*, vol. 1. Philadelphia: Philadelphia Tax Reform Commission (November). Also available online at http://www.philadelphiataxreform.org/Volume_One_Final.pdf.

Plassmann, F., and T. N. Tideman. 2000. A Markov chain Monte Carlo analysis of the effect of two-rate property taxes on construction. *Journal of Urban Economics* 47(2):216–247.

Pollakowski, H. O. 1982. Adjustment effects of a tax on land: The Pittsburgh case. Working paper, Lincoln Institute of Land Policy, Cambridge, Massachusetts.

Pollock, R., and D. Shoup. 1977. The effect of shifting the property tax base from improvement value to land value: An empirical estimate. *Land Economics* 53(1):67–77.

Pro-Housing Property Tax Coalition. 1991. Real property tax rates for tax year

1992. Testimony presented to the Committee of the Whole, Council of the District of Columbia, June 21. (As reported in Schwab and Harris [1997].)

Pullen, J. 2003. Henry George's lecture tour of Australia in 1890. University of Tasmania. Paper presented at the 16th HETSA [History of Economic Thought Society of Australia] Conference, Australian Catholic University.

Ralston, J. H. 1945. *Confronting the land question.* Bayside, NY: American Association for Scientific Taxation.

Reeb, D. J. 1998. The adoption and repeal of the two-rate property tax in Amsterdam, New York. Working paper, Lincoln Institute of Land Policy, Cambridge, Massachusetts.

Reinhardt, S., and L. Steel. 2006. A brief history of Australia's tax system. Paper presented at the 22nd APEC Finance Minister's Technical Working Group meeting, Khanh Hoa, Vietnam. Available online at http://www.treasury.gov.au/documents/1156/PDF/01_Brief_History.pdf.

Reschovsky, A. 1998. Can the land value tax play an important role in the financing of state and local governments in the United States? In Netzer 1998b.

Rose, L. A. 1973. The development value tax. *Urban Studies* 10(2):271–275.

Saidel, J. A. 2001. *Tax structure analysis report.* Philadelphia: Office of the City Controller.

Schwab, R. M., and A. R. Harris. 1997. An analysis of the graded property tax. In *Taxing simply, taxing fairly.* Washington, DC: District of Columbia Tax Revision Commission.

Sears, D. O., and J. Critin. 1985. *Tax revolt: Something for nothing in California.* Cambridge, MA: Harvard University Press.

Shoup, D. C. 1970. The optimal timing of urban land development. *Regional Science Association Papers and Proceedings* 25:33–44.

Sjoquist, D. L. 2004. The land value tax in Jamaica: An analysis and options for reform. Working paper, Andrew Young School of Policy Studies, Georgia State University.

———. 2007. How should land be taxed? Analyzing the Jamaican land value tax. *Public Finance Review* 35(1):127–149.

Skaburskis, A., and R. Tomalty. 1997. Land value taxation and development activity: The reaction of Toronto and Ottawa developers, planners, and municipal finance officials. *Canadian Journal of Regional Science* 20(3):401–417.

Skouras, A. 1978. The non-neutrality of land value taxation. *Public Finance* 33(1–2):113–134.

Smith, J. P. 2000. Land value taxation: A critique of "Tax reform, a rational solution." Discussion Paper 417, Centre for Economic Policy Research, Australian National University. Available online at http://econrsss.anu.edu.au/pdf/DP417.pdf.

Smith, S. 2005. *Land tax: An update.* NSW Parliamentary Library Briefing Paper 5/

05. New South Wales, New Zealand: NSW Parliamentary Library Research Service (April). Also available online at http://www.parliament.nsw.gov.au/prod/ parlment/publications.nsf/0/7c1c209e3f8342edca256ff100023cbb/$FILE/FINAL %20VERSION%20Land%20Tax.pdf.

South Africa National Treasury. 2007. *Local government budgets and expenditure review: 2001/02–2007/08*. Pretoria, South Africa: South Africa National Treasury.

Stephens, D. 1955. The three Ardens. In Brown et al. 1955.

Subramanian, S., and D. Jayaraj. 2006. The distribution of household wealth in India. Research Paper 2006/116, United Nations University, World Institute for Development Economics Research, Helsinki, Finland.

Thorsnes, P. 2000. Internalizing neighborhood externalities: The effect of subdivision size and zoning on residential lot prices. *Journal of Urban Economics* 48(3):397–418.

Tideman, T. N. 1982. A tax on land value is neutral. *National Tax Journal* 35(1):109–111.

Tideman, T. N. and C. Johnson. 1995. *A statistical analysis of graded property taxes in Pennsylvania*. Cambridge, MA: Lincoln Institute of Land Policy.

Tideman, T. N., and F. Plassmann. 1995. The impact of two-rate property taxes on construction in Pennsylvania. Unpublished research paper.

Tiits, T. 2008. Land taxation reform in Estonia. In Bahl, Martinez-Vazquez, and Youngman 2008.

Tiits, T., and A. Tomson. 1999. Land value taxation in Estonia. In McCluskey 1999.

U.S. Census Bureau. Various years. Annual survey of state and local government finances. http://www.census.gov/govs/www/estimate.html.

Van Ryneveld, P., R. Hunter, R. C. D. Franzsen, and Y. Abrams. 2006. Shift of tax incidence resulting from the implementation of the Property Rates Act in four metropolitan municipalities. Unpublished report for the National Treasury, South Africa.

Vickrey, W. 1970. Defining land value for taxation purposes. In Holland 1970.

———. 1999. Simplification, progression, and a level playing field. In *Land-value taxation: The equitable and efficient source of public finance*, ed. K. C. Wenzer. Armonk, NY: M.E. Sharp.

Wall Street Journal. 2007. Florida tax revolt. Editorial, June 30: A6.

Ward, R. D., J. Guilford, B. Jones, D. Pratt, and J. C. German. 2002. Piecing together location: Three studies by the Lucas County research and development staff. *Assessment Journal* 9(September/October):15–48.

Ward, R. D., J. R. Weaver, and J. C. German. 1999. Improving CAMA models using geographic information systems/response surface analysis location factors. *Assessment Journal* 6(January/February):30–38.

Wildasin, D. 1982. More on the neutrality of land taxation. *National Tax Journal* 35(1):105–108.

Williams, V. 1988. Goode's 2-level approach to taxing property is not without precedent. *Philadelphia Inquirer*, May 6: B8.

Wolff, E. N. 1998. Distributional consequences of a national land value tax on real property in the United States. In Netzer 1998b.

Wuensch, J., F. Kelly, and T. Hamilton. 2000. Land value taxation views, concepts, and methods: A primer. Working paper, Lincoln Institute of Land Policy, Cambridge, Massachusetts.

Youngman, J. M. 2002. Enlarging the property tax debate—regressivity and fairness. *State Tax Notes* 26(1):45–52.

———. 2006a. Core module outline: Alternative perspectives on property taxation. Outline available in the Lincoln Institute of Land Policy Property Valuation and Taxation Library. http://www.lincolninst.edu/subcenters/pvtl/.

———. 2006b. *Legal issues in property valuation and taxation: Cases and material.* Cambridge, MA: Lincoln Institute of Land Policy.

———. 2008. The property tax in development and transition. In Bahl, Martinez-Vazquez, and Youngman 2008.

Youngman, J. M., and J. H. Malme. 1994. *An international survey of taxes on land and buildings.* Boston: Kluwer.

Zodrow, G. R. 2001. The property tax as a capital tax: A room with three views. *National Tax Journal* 54(1):139–156.

———. 2007. The property tax as a capital tax: A room with three views. Working paper, James A. Baker III Institute for Public Policy, Rice University.

CONTRIBUTORS

Editors

RICHARD F. DYE
Visiting Fellow
Lincoln Institute of Land Policy; and
Professor
Institute of Government and Public
Affairs
University of Illinois at Chicago

RICHARD W. ENGLAND
Visiting Fellow
Lincoln Institute of Land Policy; and
Professor
Department of Economics
University of New Hampshire

Authors

JOHN E. ANDERSON
Associate Dean and
Baird Family Professor of Economics
College of Business Administration
University of Nebraska

MICHAEL E. BELL
Research Professor
The George Washington University

STEVEN C. BOURASSA
KHC Real Estate Research Professor
and
Director
School of Urban and Public Affairs
University of Louisville; and
Research Fellow
CEREBEM, BEM Management School
Bordeaux, France

JOHN H. BOWMAN
Emeritus Professor
Virginia Commonwealth University

RICHARD D. COE
Associate Professor of Economics
New College of Florida

RIËL C. D. FRANZSEN
Professor and Director
African Tax Institute
Department of Economics
University of Pretoria, South Africa

JEROME C. GERMAN, ASA, IFAS
Lucas Assessment Research LLC
Toledo, Ohio

WALLACE E. OATES
Professor
Department of Economics
University of Maryland

ELIZABETH PLUMMER
Associate Professor of Accounting
Neeley School of Business
Texas Christian University

ROBERT M. SCHWAB
Associate Dean
College of Behavioral and Social
Sciences
University of Maryland

INDEX

ability-to-pay principle, 7, 73
administration issues: in international experience, 27; of land value tax, 209; of property tax, 132–135, 133nn3–4, 135n5, 154–155
Africa, 28 (table). *See also specific countries*
Alabama, 12, 12n3
Aliquippa, 14, 15 (table), 22, 22n19
Allegheny County, 13, 16, 21
Altoona, 14n5, 15 (table), 22, 22n18
American West Airlines v. Department of Revenue, 146–147, 147n19
Amsterdam, 12, 14, 15 (table), 20–21
Anderson, J. E., 107, 108, 122–126 (table)
Anderson, N. B., 3
annual rental value system: in Australia, 30, 31, 32, 33 (table), 35; economic theory and, 52–55, 52n2, 54n3, 61n7; international experience and, 27–28, 28n2; New Zealand and, 30, 36–37, 38 (table)
Apache County v. The Atchison, Topeka and Santa Fe Railway Co., 146, 147n19
Appeal of Town of Bethlehem, 152
Arden, 12, 12n3
Arnott, R. J., 63, 107, 108, 109, 122–126 (table)
Ashley, R., 176
Asia, 28 (table), 93, 93nn14–15, 98
assessment issues: abstraction method for residual land value and, 173–174, 174n4;

agricultural land valuation with GIS and, 187–188; allocation approach for typical land share of value and, 174–175; analytical tools and, 4, 173, 177, 183–190, 188n14, 193; approaches to land valuation and, 8–9, 171, 173–177, 177n5, 192–193; baseline valuation approach and, 173, 173n2; CAMA and, 183–184, 186; case studies on valuation approaches and, 172, 177–179; commercial and industrial land valuation with GIS and, 188–189, 188n14; contribution value approach and, 173, 173n2, 175–177, 177n5; estimating land values, and methodology for, 179–182, 180nn8–9, 192; GIS and, 183, 186, 187–189, 188n14; GRSA and, 183, 185, 189, 190; history of, 172, 194; improving determination of land values and, 185–189, 209; leading-edge technologies and, 189–190, 193; Lucas County experience and, 9, 182–185, 182–184nn10–13; neighborhood analysis and, 186–187; sales data for teardown approach and, 177; separate values of land and improvement issues and, 172, 172n1; split-rate tax valuation and, 190–192, 191n17, 193–194; state legal requirements and, 172, 192
Assunção, J., 92
Australia: annual rental value system in, 30,

ABOUT THE LINCOLN INSTITUTE OF LAND POLICY

The Lincoln Institute of Land Policy is a private operating foundation whose mission is to improve the quality of public debate and decisions in the areas of land policy and land-related taxation in the United States and around the world. The Institute's goals are to integrate theory and practice to better shape land policy and to provide a nonpartisan forum for discussion of the multidisciplinary forces that influence public policy. This focus on land derives from the Institute's founding objective—to address the links between land policy and social and economic progress—that was identified and analyzed by political economist and author Henry George.

The work of the Institute is organized in four departments: Valuation and Taxation, Planning and Urban Form, Economic and Community Development, and International Studies. We seek to inform decision making through education, research, demonstration projects, and the dissemination of information through publications, our Web site, and other media. Our programs bring together scholars, practitioners, public officials, policy advisers, and involved citizens in a collegial learning environment. The Institute does not take a particular point of view, but rather serves as a catalyst to facilitate analysis and discussion of land use and taxation issues—to make a difference today and to help policy makers plan for tomorrow.

The Lincoln Institute of Land Policy is an equal opportunity institution.

L LINCOLN INSTITUTE
OF LAND POLICY
CAMBRIDGE, MASSACHUSETTS

113 Brattle Street
Cambridge, MA 02138-3400 USA

Phone: 1-617-661-3016 x127 or 1-800-LAND-USE (800-526-3873)
Fax: 1-617-661-7235 or 1-800-LAND-944 (800-526-3944)
E-mail: help@lincolninst.edu
Web: www.lincolninst.edu